The Last Things

Herman Bavinck (1854–1921)
Graphite sketch by Erik G. Lubbers

The Last Things
Hope for This World and the Next

Herman Bavinck
Edited by John Bolt
Translated by John Vriend

paternoster

Baker Books

A Division of Baker Book House Co
Grand Rapids, Michigan 49516

© 1996 by the Dutch Reformed Translation Society, P.O. Box 7083, Grand Rapids, MI 49510

Published by Baker Books
a division of Baker Book House Company
P.O. Box 6287, Grand Rapids, MI 49516-6287

and

Paternoster Press
P.O. Box 300, Carlisle, Cumbria CA3 0QS
United Kingdom

Printed in the United States of America

Library of Congress Cataloging-in-Publication Data is on file at the Library of Congress, Washington, D.C. British Library of Congress Cataloguing-in-Publication Data is on file at the British Library.

U.S. ISBN: 0-8010-2088-3
U.K. ISBN: 0-85364-761-5

Sketch of Herman Bavinck ©1996 by Erik G. Lubbers.

Contents

Preface   7
Editor's Introduction   9

Part 1 The Intermediate State

1   The Question of Immortality   21
2   After Death, Then What?   39
3   Between Death and Resurrection   59

Part 2 The Return of Christ

4   Visions of the End   79
5   Israel, the Millennium, and Christ's Return   99

Part 3 The Consummation

6   The Day of the Lord   131
7   The Renewal of Creation   155

Appendix   171
Bibliography   173
Notes   189
Select Scripture Index   205

Dutch Reformed Translation Society
Board of Directors

Preface

The financing for the translation and editing of *The Last Things* was provided by the Dutch Reformed Translation Society. The DRTS was formed in 1994 by a group of businesspeople and professionals, pastors, and seminary professors, representing five different Reformed denominations, to sponsor the translation and facilitate the publication in English of classic Reformed theological and religious literature published in the Dutch language. It is incorporated as a nonprofit corporation in the State of Michigan and governed by a board of directors.

Believing that the Dutch Reformed tradition has many valuable works that deserve wider distribution than the limited accessibility of the Dutch language allows, Society members seek to spread and strengthen the Reformed faith. The DRTS's first project is the definitive translation of Herman Bavinck's complete four-volume *Gereformeerde Dogmatiek (Reformed Dogmatics)*. This volume on eschatology is the first installment of that project. The Society invites those who share its commitment to and vision for spreading the Reformed faith to write for additional information.

Editor's Introduction

As we approach the third millennium of the Christian era, interest in the "last things" (eschatology) is intensifying. In the evangelical Christian world, sermons, articles, and books on biblical prophecy, Armageddon, the millennium, the rapture, our Lord's return, and the final judgment proliferate. At the same time, the popular culture of Western society, overwhelmed by a darkening sense of civilizational decline, seems obsessed with death, near-death experiences, and questions about life after death. Apocalyptic fever grows as we approach the year 2000 *anno domini*. One longs for a sane, biblical voice to guide the Christian church through the shoals of eschatological confusion. It is in such a context and to address this specific need that the Dutch Reformed Translation Society chose to publish the "last things" section of Herman Bavinck's *Reformed Dogmatics* as the first installment of its initial project—the complete English translation from Dutch of Bavinck's classic four-volume work. Who was Herman Bavinck, and why is this work of theology so important?

Herman Bavinck's *Reformed Dogmatics* (*Gereformeerde Dogmatiek*), first published one hundred years ago, represents the concluding high point of some four centuries of remarkably productive Dutch Reformed theological reflection. From Bavinck's numerous citations of key Dutch Reformed theologians such as Voetius, De Moor, Vitringa, van Mastricht, Witsius, and Walaeus as well as the important Leiden *Synopsis purioris theologiae*,[1] it is clear he knew that tradition well and claimed it as his own. At the same time it also needs to be noted that Bavinck was not simply a chronicler of that tradition. He seriously engaged other theological traditions, notably the Roman Catholic and the modern liberal Protestant ones, effectively mined the Church Fathers and great medieval thinkers, and placed his own distinct neo-Calvinist stamp on the *Reformed Dogmatics*.

Kampen and Leiden

To understand the distinct Bavinck flavor a brief historical orientation is necessary.

9

Herman Bavinck was born on December 13, 1854. His father was an influential minister in the Dutch Christian Reformed Church (*Christelijke Gereformeerde Kerk*) that had seceded from the National Reformed Church in the Netherlands twenty years earlier.[2] The secession of 1834 was in the first place a protest against the state control of the Dutch Reformed Church; it also tapped into a long and rich tradition of ecclesiastical dissent on matters of doctrine, liturgy, and spirituality as well as polity. In particular, mention needs to be made here of the Dutch equivalent to English Puritanism, the so-called Second Reformation[3] (*Nadere Reformatie*), the influential seventeenth- and early-eighteenth-century movement of experiential Reformed theology and spirituality,[4] as well as an early-nineteenth-century international, aristocratic, evangelical revival movement known as the *Réveil*.[5] Bavinck's church, his family, and his own spirituality were thus definitively shaped by strong patterns of deep pietistic Reformed spirituality. It is also important to note that though the earlier phases of Dutch pietism affirmed orthodox Reformed theology and were also nonseparatist in their ecclesiology, by the mid-nineteenth century the Seceder group had become significantly separatist and sectarian in outlook.[6]

The second major influence on Bavinck's thought comes from the period of his theological training at the University of Leiden. The Christian Reformed Church had its own theological seminary, the Kampen *Theologische School*, established in 1854. Bavinck, after studying at Kampen for one year (1873–74), indicated his desire to study with the University of Leiden's theological faculty, a faculty renowned for its aggressively modernist, "scientific" approach to theology.[7] His church community, including his parents, was stunned by this decision, which Bavinck explained as a desire "to become acquainted with the modern theology firsthand" and to receive "a more scientific training than the Theological School is presently able to provide."[8] The Leiden experience gave rise to what Bavinck perceived as the tension in his life between his commitment to orthodox theology and spirituality and his desire to understand and appreciate what he could about the modern world, including its worldview and culture. A telling and poignant entry in his personal journal at the beginning of his study period at Leiden (September 23, 1874) indicates his concern about being faithful to the faith he had publicly professed in the Christian Reformed church of Zwolle in March of that same year: "Will I remain standing [in the faith]? God grant it."[9] Upon completion of his doctoral work at Leiden in 1880 Bavinck candidly acknowledged the spiritual impoverishment that Leiden had cost him: "Leiden has benefited me in many ways: I hope always to acknowledge that gratefully. But it has also greatly impoverished me, robbed me, not only of much ballast (for which I am happy), but also of much that I recently, especially when I preach, recognize as vital for my own spiritual life."[10]

It is thus not unfair to characterize Bavinck as a man between two worlds. One of his contemporaries once described Bavinck as "a Secession preacher and a representative of modern culture," concluding: "That was a striking characteristic. In that duality is found Bavinck's significance. That duality is also a reflection of the tension—at times crisis—in Bavinck's life. In many respects it is a simple matter to be a preacher in the Secession Church, and, in a certain sense, it is also not that difficult to be a modern person. But in no way is it a simple matter to be the one as well as the other."[11] However, it is not necessary to rely only on the testimony of others. Bavinck summarizes this tension in his own thought clearly in an essay on the great nineteenth-century liberal Protestant theologian Albrecht Ritschl:

> Therefore, whereas salvation in Christ was formerly considered primarily a means to separate man from sin and the world, to prepare him for heavenly blessedness and to cause him to enjoy undisturbed fellowship with God there, Ritschl posits the very opposite relationship: the purpose of salvation is precisely to enable a person, once he is freed from the oppressive feeling of sin and lives in the awareness of being a child of God, to exercise his earthly vocation and fulfill his moral purpose in this world. The antithesis, therefore, is fairly sharp: on the one side, a Christian life that considers the highest goal, now and hereafter, to be the contemplation of God and fellowship with him, and for that reason (always being more or less hostile to the riches of an earthly life) is in danger of falling into monasticism and asceticism, pietism and mysticism; but on the side of Ritschl, a Christian life that considers its highest goal to be the kingdom of God, that is, the moral obligation of mankind, and for that reason (always being more or less adverse to the withdrawal into solitude and quiet communion with God), is in danger of degenerating into a cold Pelagianism and an unfeeling moralism. *Personally, I do not yet see any way of combining the two points of view, but I do know that there is much that is excellent in both, and that both contain undeniable truth.*[12]

It is interesting to observe that in Bavinck's mature expression of his theology, the *Reformed Dogmatics*, he still appreciates Ritschl's emphasis though, in his view, it suffers from onesidedness. In the seventh chapter of this eschatology volume, on the "new creation," Bavinck refers to Ritschl and his followers "onesidedly [stressing] the present-world orientation of people," but insists that Ritschlian this-worldliness "stands for an important truth" over against the "abstract supernaturalism [and subsequent asceticism] of the Greek Orthodox and Roman Catholic Church."[13]

Grace and Nature

Yet it is too simple merely to characterize Bavinck as a man trapped between two apparently incommensurate tugs at his soul, that of other-worldly pietism and this-worldly modernism. His heart and mind sought a synthesis of Christianity and culture, a Christian world-view that incorporated what was best and true in both pietism and modernism, while above all honoring the theological and confessional richness of the Reformed tradition dating from Calvin. After commenting on the breakdown of the great medieval synthesis and the need for contemporary Christians to acquiesce in that breakdown, Bavinck expressed his hope for a new and better synthesis: "In this situation, the hope is not unfounded that a synthesis is possible between Christianity and culture, however antagonistic they may presently stand over against each other. If God has truly come to us in Christ, and is, in this age too, the Preserver and Ruler of all things, such a synthesis is not only possible but also necessary and shall surely be effected in its own time."[14] Bavinck found the vehicle for such an attempted synthesis in the trinitarian worldview of Dutch neo-Calvinism and became, along with neo-Calvinism's visionary pioneer Abraham Kuyper,[15] one of its chief and most respected spokesmen as well as its premier theologian.

Unlike Bavinck, Abraham Kuyper grew up in the National Reformed Church of the Netherlands in a congenially moderate-modernist context. Kuyper's student years, also at Leiden, confirmed him in his modernist orientation until a series of experiences, especially during his years as a parish minister, brought about a dramatic conversion to Reformed, Calvinist orthodoxy.[16] From that time Kuyper became a vigorous opponent of the modern spirit in church and society[17]—which he characterized by the siren call of the French Revolution, *"Ni Dieu! Ni maitre!"*[18]—seeking every avenue to oppose it with an alternative worldview, or as he called it, the "life-system" of Calvinism:

> From the first, therefore, I have always said to myself,—"if the battle is to be fought with honor and with a hope of victory, then *principle* must be arrayed against *principle*; then it must be felt that in Modernism the vast energy of an all-embracing *life-system* assails us, then also it must be understood that we have to take our stand in a life-system of equally comprehensive and far-reaching power. . . . When thus taken, I found and confessed and I still hold, that this manifestation of the Christian principle is given us in *Calvinism*. In Calvinism my heart has found rest. From Calvinism have I drawn the inspiration firmly and resolutely to take my stand in the thick of this great conflict of principles.["][19]

Kuyper's aggressive, this-worldly form of Calvinism was rooted in a trinitarian theological vision. The "dominating principle" of Calvinism, he contended, "was not soteriologically, justification by faith, but in the widest sense cosmologically, *the Sovereignty of the Triune God over the whole Cosmos,* in all its spheres and kingdoms, visible and invisible."[20]

For Kuyper, this fundamental principle of divine sovereignty led to four important derivatory and related doctrines or principles: common grace, antithesis, sphere sovereignty, and the distinction between the church as institute and the church as organism. The doctrine of common grace[21] is based on the conviction that prior to and, to a certain extent, independent of the *particular* sovereignty of divine grace in redemption, there is a *universal* divine sovereignty in creation and providence, restraining the effects of sin and bestowing general gifts on all people, thus making human society and culture possible even among the unredeemed. Cultural life is rooted in creation and common grace and thus has a life of its own apart from the church.

This same insight is expressed more directly via the notion of sphere sovereignty. Kuyper was opposed to all Anabaptist and ascetic Christian versions of world-flight but was also equally opposed to the medieval Roman Catholic synthesis of culture and church. The various spheres of human activity—family, education, business, science, art— do not derive their raison d'être and the shape of their life from redemption or from the church, but from the law of God the Creator. They are thus relatively autonomous—also from the interference of the state— and are directly responsible to God.[22] In this regard Kuyper clearly distinguished two different understandings of the church—the church as institute gathered around the Word and sacraments and the church as organism diversely spread out in the manifold vocations of life. It is not explicitly as members of the institutional church but as members of the body of Christ, organized in *Christian communal* activity (schools, political parties, labor unions, institutions of mercy) that believers live out their earthly vocations. Though aggressively this-worldly, Kuyper was an avowed and articulate opponent of the *volkskerk* tradition, which tended to merge national sociocultural identity with that of a theocratic church ideal.[23]

To state this differently: Kuyper's emphasis on common grace, used polemically to motivate pious, orthodox Dutch Reformed Christians to Christian social, political, and cultural activity, must never be seen in isolation from his equally strong emphasis on the spiritual *antithesis.* The regenerating work of the Holy Spirit breaks humanity in two and creates, according to Kuyper, "two kinds of consciousness, that of the regenerate and the unregenerate; and these two cannot be identical." Furthermore, these "two kinds of people" will develop "two kinds of science." The conflict in the scientific enterprise is not between science and faith but between *"two scientific systems . . . each having its own faith."*[24]

It is here in this trinitarian, world-affirming, but nonetheless resolutely antithetical Calvinism that Bavinck found the resources to bring some unity to his thought.[25] "The thoughtful person," he notes, "places the doctrine of the Trinity in the very center of the full-orbed life of nature and mankind. . . . The mind of the Christian is not satisfied until every form of existence has been referred to the triune God and until the confession of the Trinity has received the place of prominence in all our life and thought."[26] Repeatedly in his writings Bavinck defines the essence of the Christian religion in a trinitarian, creation-affirming way. A typical formulation: "The essence of the Christian religion consists in this, that the creation of the Father, devastated by sin, is restored in the death of the Son of God, and re-created by the Holy Spirit into a kingdom of God."[27] Put more simply, the fundamental theme that shapes Bavinck's entire theology is the trinitarian idea that *grace restores nature.*[28]

The evidence for "grace restores nature" being the fundamental defining and shaping theme of Bavinck's theology is not hard to find. In an important address on common grace, given in 1888 at the Kampen Theological School, Bavinck sought to impress on his Christian Reformed audience the importance of Christian sociocultural activity. He appealed to the doctrine of creation, insisting that its diversity is not removed by redemption but cleansed. "Grace does not remain outside or above or beside nature but rather permeates and wholly renews it. And thus nature, reborn by grace, will be brought to its highest revelation. That situation will again return in which we serve God freely and happily, without compulsion or fear, simply out of love, and in harmony with our true nature. That is the genuine *religio naturalis*." In other words: "Christianity does not introduce a single substantial foreign element into the creation. It creates no new cosmos but rather makes the cosmos new. It restores what was corrupted by sin. It atones the guilty and cures what is sick; the wounded it heals."[29]

The Last Things

This volume, the eschatology section in the *Reformed Dogmatics*, clearly displays these distinctive characteristics of Bavinck's thought. The fundamental theme that grace does not undo nature but restores and heals it is hinted at in numerous places and shapes the entire last chapter on the new creation. At the same time Bavinck clearly repudiates the potential tendency toward universalism implied in this theme, displaying another key characteristic of his thought: scriptural reserve. The spiritual antithesis between life in the service of sin and life in the service of the Lord is firmly maintained. There is thus no explicit or implicit triumphalism here; from the givens of Scripture and his own cultural sensitivity Bavinck was attuned to the real possibility of apostasy and growing public hostility to the Christian religion in the West. While strong in his affirmation of the earthly, life-affirming, bodily character of Christian hope, he is also true to his pietist roots when he insists that a this-worldly hope alone is inadequate. The goal is eternal fellowship with God. Bavinck carefully and judiciously engages Roman Catholic as well as millennialist/chiliast thought, each time using scriptural argumentation. In fact, Bavinck's salvation-historical approach to biblical prophecy in chapter 4 is a model of Reformed hermeneutics that remains valuable to this day. His treatment of the "signs of the times" remains thoroughly relevant in the apocalyptic context of this last decade before the third millennium. There is hardly a better resource for providing a solid Reformed, biblical critique of claims made by contemporary dispensational premillenarians on topics such as Israel and the millennium. Also, Bavinck's biblically circumspect conclusions about hypothetical universalism and conditional immortality need to be thoughtfully considered by contemporary evangelicals flirting with both views.

It is thus clear from this volume that Bavinck's work is not simply a repristination of older Reformed dogmatic systems. Throughout he engages not only modern theological and philosophical scholarship but the modern scientific enterprise more broadly as in his discussion of entropy and evolution in chapter 4. Bavinck's thoughtful appreciation for what is good in the modern world can be seen in his comments about its more humane treatment of criminals and the mentally ill (pp. 147f.). Here, too, he demonstrates his biblically and confessionally informed balance. Greater humanitarianism divorced from a biblical view of man, he observes in a telling aphorism, is potentially no less evil than the earlier cruelty: "[W]hereas before the mentally ill were treated as criminals, now criminals are regarded as mentally ill." And then follows this penetrating insight into the collapse of normative morality in a therapeutic culture: "Before that time every abnormality was viewed in terms of sin and guilt; now all ideas of guilt, crime, responsibility, culpability, and the like, are robbed of their reality" (148). This means, he adds, that all notions of right and wrong, justice and injustice, are no longer found in God and his law but in swayable human opinion with the result that "certainty and safety is lost" and justice is sacrificed to power. How prophetic a description of the condition of our great and lawless cities today! And could anyone have written anything more prescient about the mass horrors of the twentieth century than Bavinck, when he observed: "The voice of the people (*vox populi*), which is often wrongly revered as the voice of God (*vox dei*), recoils from no horrors whatever" (148)?

Bavinck, it should also be noted, was fully cognizant not only of other Christian traditions but also of the world's non-Christian religions and their eschatologies. Above all, his work remains useful because of its pastoral quality. His discussion of the final judgment (ch. 6) as well as the destiny of those who have never heard the gospel and children who die in infancy (ch. 7) clearly show Bavinck's pastoral heart. He is profoundly interested in Christian hope as consolation to believers and about the believer's struggle to be a disciple of Jesus Christ in the modern world. Bavinck's own earthly pilgrimage ended on July 12, 1921, in the comfort of the hope so eloquently summarized in these pages.

In sum, *Reformed Dogmatics*, of which this volume is a truly representative sample, is biblically and confessionally faithful, pastorally sensitive, challenging, and still relevant. Bavinck's life and thought reflect a serious effort to be pious, orthodox, and thoroughly contemporary. To pietists fearful of the modern world on the one hand and to critics of orthodoxy skeptical about its continuing relevance on the other, Bavinck's example suggests a model answer: an engaging trinitarian vision of Christian discipleship in God's world.

In conclusion, a few words about the editing decisions that govern this volume that is based on the second, expanded edition of the *Gereformeerde Dogmatiek*.[30] Bavinck's threefold division of the eschatology chapter in *Gereformeerde Dogmatiek*[31] has been retained in the three major sections of the translation but the material has been further divided into seven chapters with additional subheadings in each chapter. The chapter divisions, titles, and subtitles, as well as the chapter synopses, are not in the original but have been supplied by the editor. Bavinck's original footnotes have all been retained and brought up to contemporary bibliographic standards. Additional notes added by the editor are clearly marked. All works from the nineteenth century to the present are noted with full bibliographic information given in the first note of each chapter and with subsequent references abbreviated. Classic works produced prior to the nineteenth century (the Church Fathers, Aquinas's *Summa*, Calvin's *Institutes*, post-Reformation Protestant and Catholic works) for which there are often numerous editions are cited only by author, title, and standard notation of sections. More complete information of an accessible edition for each is given in the bibliography appended at the end of this volume. Where English translations of foreign titles were available and could be consulted they have been used rather than the original. Unless indicated in the note by direct reference to a specific translation, translations of Latin, Greek, German, and French material are those of the translator taken directly from Bavinck's original text. References in the notes that are incomplete or could not be confirmed are marked with an asterisk (*). Internal page references to other volumes of the *Gereformeerde Dogmatiek* are to the fourth edition of 1928.

The editor here gratefully acknowledges the significant contribution of Dr. M. Eugene Osterhaven, emeritus Albertus C. Van Raalte Professor of Systematic Theology at Western Theological Seminary, Holland, Michigan, for his careful reading of the manuscript and his many helpful translation and stylistic suggestions as well as critical corrections.

John Bolt

Part 1
The Intermediate State

The Question of Immortality   1

The desire to know what happens to us after death is a universal human desire. The world's religions testify to the longing to overcome the finality of death. Classic philosophy developed sophisticated arguments for the immortality of the human soul though materialistic modern philosophy after Kant has abandoned them. While Christian theology may find some of the traditional arguments for the immortality of the soul useful at points, Scripture itself is more restrained. In the face of death the immortality of the soul is no real comfort. While death is not the end, the shadowy afterlife of Sheol is seen as a diminished existence. The Bible affirms and celebrates God's gift of life as a blessing; death is punishment for sin. The victory of Christ over sin and death means that believers enjoy the firstfruits of Christ's kingly reign now and immediately after death a provisional bliss with Christ in heaven while unbelievers enter a state of torment.

The end of things, like their origin and essence, is unknown to us. To the question of their destiny science no more furnishes a satisfying answer than to that of their origin. Still, religion has an urgent need to know something of the destiny of the individual, of humanity, and of the world. All the peoples of the world, accordingly, have some idea of it and all religions include some kind of eschatology. Admittedly, there are still some scholars who say that originally belief in the immortality of the soul was certainly not typical of all people and is to this day still lacking, for example, among the Weddas in Ceylon [Sri Lanka], the Seelongs in India, and others.[1]

True: from an evolutionary viewpoint, belief in God, the independent existence of the soul, and its immortality cannot have been an original part of human nature but must, as a consequence of a variety of circumstances, have arisen and evolved gradually and accidentally. Ancestor worship, affection for deceased relatives, the love of life and the desire for its continuation, a hope for better living conditions on the other side of the grave, the fear of punishment, and the hope of reward are then the factors that promoted the gradual rise of belief in immortality.

Over against this view, however, the most respected historians of religion tell us that belief in the immortality of the soul occurs among all peoples and is a component even of the most primitive religions. It is found everywhere and at every stage of human development, wherever it has not as yet been undermined by philosophical doubts or thrust into the background by other causes; and in every case it is bound up with religion.[2] One can even say that originally this belief was a very natural thing. Like the author of the Garden of Eden narrative in Genesis, says Tiele, all peoples take for granted that humans are by nature immortal and that it is death, not immortality, which requires explanation. It is death that seems an unnatural thing. Something must have happened to bring something so illogical into the world. The sagas of many different peoples, differing in origin and development, express the same idea: there was a time when neither sickness nor death was known on earth. Earlier humans in their natural state cannot even believe in death when they see it before their eyes. They call it "sleep," a state of unconsciousness; the spirit has taken leave of the body but may still return. And so they wait several days to see if this will happen. And if the dead man's spirit does not return, why, then he has only disappeared in order to enter into another body or to join the superterrestrial spirits.[3]

The forms in which the afterlife of the soul were presented were very diverse and often variously combined. Sometimes it was thought that souls after death lived on near their grave, and for their continued existence needed the ongoing care of their blood relatives, or led a gloomy shade-like existence in Hades, far removed from the gods and living humans. Then again it was believed that the souls of the deceased, who before their indwelling in a human body had sometimes undergone a series of metamorphoses, after their departure from the human body still had to spend a period of time in other bodies, animal or human, to be purified or to attain perfection and be absorbed into the Deity or into an unconscious Nirvana. There was also a doctrine saying that immediately after death the souls entered into divine judgment. If they had done good, they would pass over a dangerous bridge-of-the-dead into the land of the blessed, where they lived in communion with the gods. If they had done evil, they were plunged into a place of everlasting darkness and torment.

Philosophy

This teaching of personal immortality passed from religion into philosophy. Following the example of Pythagoras, Heraclitus, and Empedocles, especially Plato (in his *Phaedo*) sought to undergird his religious belief in immortality by philosophical argumentation. Essentially his proofs come down to the view that the soul, which draws its knowledge of ideas from memory, existed already before dwelling in a body and will therefore continue to exist after leaving it. Furthermore, by its contemplation of the eternal ideas, the soul is akin to the divine being and as an independent and simple entity, by its control over the body and its desires, is on a level far above that of the body. Above all, Plato argues that the soul—the principle of vitality and thus identical with life itself—cannot be conceived as nonliving and transient. With this theory of the immortality of the soul Plato then combined a variety of notions about the preexistence, fall, union with the body, judgment, and transmigration of the soul that in large part bear a mythical character and are certainly not all intended, even by Plato himself, in a purely scientific sense. Although other philosophers such as Democritus, Epicurus, and Lucretius opposed the doctrine of the immortality of the soul or, like Aristotle, were not positive in their statements about it, Plato's doctrine exerted immense influence in both theology and philosophy. The mythical components of preexistence, metempsychosis, and the like, often found acceptance in sectarian circles. And under Plato's influence theology devoted much more attention to the immortality of the soul than Holy Scripture does. The doctrine of the natural immortality of the soul became an *articulus mixtus,* whose truth was argued more on the basis of reason than revelation.[4]

Still, some awareness of the difference between the two persisted. People never completely lost the sense that aside from a physical meaning Scripture also consistently attaches a religious-ethical meaning to life and death. In Scripture life is never merely ongoing existence and death is never extinction; on the contrary, life includes communion with God and death means the loss of his grace and blessing. That is the reason the Church Fathers keep saying that Christ came to *give* us immortality *(athanasia),* and sometimes it seems they deny the natural immortality of the soul. Also, on the grounds that God alone was in himself immortal and that the soul could only be immortal by his will, they were bound to oppose Plato's theory of preexistence, that is, of the noncreatedness of the soul, and for that reason sometimes objected to calling the soul by nature immortal.[5] This is something to be borne in mind in researching the question whether among the Church Fathers there were also advocates of conditional immortality. For although the odd theologian like Arnobius taught the annihilation of evil souls, and though Tatian believed that at death the soul died along with the body in order to rise again on the Last Day, there was nevertheless a general belief that the soul was immortal in virtue of its God-given nature.[6]

In philosophy as well Plato's doctrine of immortality retained an important place. Descartes conceived spirit and matter, soul and body, as two separate substances, each with its own attribute, thought, and extension, each capable of existing by itself and therefore capable only of being united mechanically. Spinoza adopted the same two attributes but viewed them as manifestations of one eternal and infinite substance, as two sides of the same thing, which cannot exist separately but are always joined as subject and object, image and contrasting image, idea and thing. In his system there was no room for immortality, nor did he need it, for "even if we did not know that our mind is eternal, we should still consider as of primary importance piety and religion, and absolutely everything which in the Fourth Part we have shown to be related to strength of mind and generosity."[7] The philosophy of the eighteenth century, however, was not well disposed toward Spinoza; it bore a deistic character and was content with the trilogy of God, virtue, and immortality, and of the three it most esteemed the third. In the wake of Leibniz, Wolf, Mendelsohn and others, its truth was argued by means of a wide assortment of metaphysical, theological, cosmic, moral, and historical proofs and urged on readers by means of sentimental observations on the blissful recognition and reunions of souls on the other side of the grave.[8] According to Strauss, the statement by the poet of Psalm 73:25 ["there is nothing on earth that I desire other than you"] was converted into the sentiment that "as long as I am sure of myself, God and the world are not important to me." Kant, however, put an end to this certainty of the self by demonstrating the inadequacy of all proofs advanced for the immortality of the soul and regarded this theory as acceptable only as a postulate of practical reason. Over against the self-centered wishes of rationalism Schleiermacher made the statement "whosoever has learned to be more than himself knows that he loses little when he loses himself" and knew no other and higher immortality than "in the midst of finitude to be one with the Infinite and in every moment to be eternal in the immortality of religion."[9]

Similarly, the idealistic philosophy of Fichte, Schelling, and Hegel left no room at all for the immortality of the soul, even though it was reluctant to express its convictions candidly on this issue. However, Richter's book on the doctrine of the last things[10] brought to light the implications of Hegel's system and, despite much criticism, paved the way to the materialism that had already been loudly advocated by Feuerbach and was later supported by Vogt, Moleschott, Büchner, Haeckel, and others with arguments said to be derived from the natural sciences. These arguments so strongly impressed many people that they have totally abandoned the immortality of the soul[11] or at most assert its possibility and merely speak of a hope of immortality.[12] Theologians, too, often attach little or no value to the proofs for the immortality of the soul.[13] But in contrast to them there are still numerous men of repute who regard all or some or at least one or two of the proofs strong enough for them to build on them a firm faith in the immortality of the soul.[14]

History and Reason

The arguments for the immortality of the soul derived from history and reason, though they fail to furnish adequate certainty, are nevertheless not without value. In the first place, it is significant that belief in immortality occurs among all peoples at every stage of their development. The consensus of the nations *(consensus gentium)* is as strong at this point as in the case of belief in God.[15] Though various considerations from which people have inferred belief in immortality (such as the fear of death and thirst for life, the experiences of dreams and ecstasy, the riddle of death and the impossibility of imagining an absolute annihilation of the cognitive essence of humans, the fear of punishment and the hope of reward)[16] may a posteriori support and confirm belief in immortality, they do not furnish a satisfying explanation of its origin. Even in places where such considerations are absent or are considered worthless, belief in immortality still occurs. Often, in the case of numerous people, the desire for continued existence is weaker than the desire that death might end their lives. The hope of reward does not explain the belief in the case of those who have died to all self-seeking and have found the highest bliss in communion with God. The notion of retribution is alien to representations of the afterlife as a shadowy existence in a spirit world. The riddle of death does not, except in rare instances, elicit conclusions about the immortality of animals and plants. And experiences of dreams and ecstasy do not extinguish the awareness of the real distinction existing between these phenomena and the phenomenon of death.

In the case of the belief in the immortality of the soul, as in that of the existence of God, we are dealing rather with a conviction that was not gained by reflection and reasoning but precedes all reflection and springs spontaneously from human nature as such. It is self-evident and natural, and is found wherever no philosophical doubts have undermined it. Along with the consciousness of having an independent individual existence of one's own, there also arises an awareness of the continuation of the self after death. Genuine self-consciousness—not the abstract self-consciousness with which psychology occupies itself— the self-consciousness of humans as personal, independent, rational, moral, religious beings always and everywhere includes belief in immortality. Accordingly, it is not a mere wish or desire, nor an inference drawn from premises, but a mighty, ineradicable witness that arises from human nature itself and maintains itself in the face of all contrary argumentation and opposition. And the so-called arguments for immortality amount to nothing more than an assortment of rational attempts this belief undertakes to give some account of itself, without ever really depending on them. Therein lies their power and at the same time their weakness; they are witnesses *of*, not grounds *for*, the belief in immortality. The "knowing" lags far behind the "believing."

The *ontological* argument, which deduces the reality of immortality from the idea of it, no more succeeds in bridging the gap that separates thought from being than the ontological argument does for the existence of God. It only gives verbal form to the sense that belief in immortality is not arbitrary or accidental but a fact of human nature and morally necessary to human beings. A person does not derive the idea of immortality from the world about him—the message the world conveys to him is exclusively one of decay and death; rather, the idea is forced on him by his own nature. Just as God does not leave himself without a witness but speaks to us from all the works of his hands, so the conviction that a person does not perish like the beasts of the field is thrust upon him from within his own being. And this is what the ontological argument aims to show; it does not cross from the realm of thought to that of being but gives expression to the universality, the necessity, and the apriority of the belief in immortality.

The *metaphysical* argument, which deduces the soul's immortality from its very nature, goes a step further. It is able to do this and does this, however, in various ways. One can point to the idea that as vital principle and as identical with life itself, the soul is inviolable by death. Or that, in virtue of the unity of the consciousness of the self, the soul is a simple indivisible entity devoid of composition, and is therefore not capable of decomposition. Or that the soul, beneath all the material and physical changes that take place, consistently remains identical with itself—as appears again from the consciousness of the self—and therefore must possess a life and an existence independent of the body. And by these various routes one can then attempt to get to the conclusion that the soul is immortal.

But this argument is subject to certain very serious objections. Even though the soul is an active vital principle, it is nevertheless never identical with life itself. God alone is life itself; he alone is immortal (1 Tim. 6:16). If the soul continues to exist this can only occur in virtue of God's omnipresent and omnipotent power. The soul is a created entity and therefore limited, finite, relative, never exempt from all passivity and composition, from change and variation. We can, for that matter, see before our own eyes that it changes, increases or decreases in knowledge and vitality, is dependent on the body and subject to various influences. And the subjective unity and identity of the ego by no means proves the objective unity and simplicity of the soul; if this were the case, it would also prove the immortality of plants or at least of animals, as this has been consistently held by Leibniz, Bonnet, and Bilderdijk,[17] among others. Contradicting these objections again is the undeniable fact that life cannot be explained in terms of a mechanical metabolic process but points to a principle of its own. "Every living thing arises from something living" (*omne vivum ex vivo*) is to this day the last word of science. And something that is true of life in general is even more compelling when applied to conscious life: even the most primitive perception is unalterably separated from any neural vibration. By means of it we enter a totally new and higher world that differs essentially from that of sensible, tangible, and measurable things. The fact that life and by implication conscious life is most intimately bound up with the world of the senses has been known for a long time and can certainly not be called a recent scientific discovery. But the idea that it is generated by a cause in the world of the senses, though often asserted, has so far not been proven by anyone. The metaphysical argument retains its value to the degree that from *sui generis* psychic phenomena it concludes to an autonomous spiritual principle that is distinct from matter.

Still, this leaves untouched the objection that one can pursue the same line of reasoning in the case of plants or at least animals, and still not make their immortality plausible. For that reason we need to supplement the metaphysical argument with the *anthropological* argument which, starting from the uniqueness of the psychic life of human beings, comes to the conclusion that there is a spiritual existence distinct from animals and plants. The soul of an animal, although simple and independent of the animal's metabolism, is oriented to the sensible; it is restricted to the finite; it lives in the present; it is so restricted to the body that it cannot exist apart from it. Humans not only possess perception and observation but also intellect and reason. By the thinking process a person transcends the sensible, material, finite world. He lifts himself up toward the ideal, the logical, the true, the good, and the beautiful that eye has not seen and cannot be touched with hands. He seeks a lasting, an *ever*lasting, happiness, a highest good that this world cannot give him, and as a result of all this is a citizen and inhabitant of another, a higher, kingdom than that of nature. The rational, moral, religious consciousness of humans points to a psychic existence that reaches beyond the visible world. That which by virtue of its nature seeks the eternal must be destined for eternity.

To this must be added the *moral* argument and the argument of *retribution,* which demonstrates the disharmony existing between morality *(ethos)* and nature *(phusis)* and infers from it another kind of existence in which the two are reconciled. Let no one object to this by saying that this argument is based on human egoism and that virtue is its own reward, just as sin brings with it its own punishment.[18] But this the devout of all ages knew very well; they were profoundly aware that God must be served for his own sake and not for the sake of any reward.[19] At the same time they maintained that if for this life only they had hoped in Christ they would be of all people most to be pitied (1 Cor. 15:17, 19, 30, 32). At issue here is absolutely not the satisfaction of a selfish desire but nothing less than the rule and triumph of justice. The question underlying the moral argument is this: In the end, is it good or evil, God or Satan, Christ or the Antichrist who will win? History itself fails to furnish an adequate answer.

From the viewpoint of the present world *(Diesseits)* no satisfying explanation of the world is possible; on this position there is all too much reason for the despair of pessimism. And our sense of justice, which a righteous God has himself implanted deep in the human heart, therefore demands that at the end of time the balance of justice be redressed. It demands harmony between virtue and happiness, between sin and punishment, and truth eternally overcoming the lie and light the darkness. Although it has been rightly said that "nothingness always was the horizon of bad consciences," even those who have no reason to expect any good from a life after this life are persuaded by their sense of justice that such restoration of justice is necessary. If justice does not prevail in the end there is no justice. And if in the end God does not prove to be the conqueror of Satan, life is not worth living. What comes to expression in the moral argument is not an egoistic desire but a profound sense of justice, the thirst for harmony, a yearning for the total glorification of God in whom holiness and bliss are one. Even art, when it exhibits ideal reality visibly before our eyes, prophesies such a future. All these arguments or proofs, and especially those derived from human perfectibility, from the moral personality of humans, from the numerous uninhabited stars, from spiritistic experiences, and so on, are not proofs in the sense that they silence all contradiction. Rather, they are witnesses and indications that belief in immortality arises with complete naturalness and spontaneity from human nature itself. Whoever denies and combats it violates his own nature. "The idea of immortality is already the first act of immortality."[20]

However valuable these indications may be that nature and history offer us in support of belief in the immortality of the soul, Scripture takes a position with respect to this doctrine that at first blush can only seem strange to us. While the immortality of the soul may seem to be of the greatest importance for religion and life, Scripture never explicitly mentions it. Scripture never announces it as a divine revelation, nor does it highlight it anywhere; still less does it ever make an attempt to argue its truth or to uphold it against those who oppose it. That is the reason why at various times many scholars have asserted that the doctrine of the immortality of the soul does not occur at all in the Old Testament, at least not in the oldest books, and was first imported into Israel from the outside.[21] But little by little they backed away from this position and presently there is a general recognition that, like all other peoples, Israel in fact did believe in the soul's continued existence after death. In recent years many authors have even argued that in ancient times in Israel, as in other nations, the dead were venerated and were therefore undoubtedly assumed to exist. Arguments for this view were derived from the rituals followed in case of bereavement, such as ripping up one's garments and wearing mourning attire, covering one's face and head, removing ornaments, special hairstyles and self-mutilation, throwing up dust and ashes, refraining from washing and anointing oneself, fasting and eating, singing lament songs, and bringing sacrifices. All these customs are said to be explicable only from the veneration of the dead practiced earlier.[22] But Schwally himself has to admit that "at the time Israel emerged in history animistic nature religion had already been basically overcome."[23] And others have advanced such serious objections to his inferring bereavement practices from an original animism that the hypothesis of an original cult of the dead in Israel can only be made plausible by fresh evidence. Still it is clear that in Israel there was a great difference between the popular religion that encompassed an assortment of superstitious and idolatrous components and the service of Yahweh championed by Moses and his followers. Yahwism on the one hand opposed, prohibited, and eradicated that popular religion but, on the other, quietly tolerated or adopted and sanctioned various religious notions and customs that in themselves were not wrong.[24]

The Old Testament

In revealing himself to Israel God accommodated himself to the historical circumstances under which it lived; grace did not undo nature but renewed and consecrated it. This is also what happened with the popular belief in the afterlife. The custom of burial and the great importance attached to it was as such already proof for that belief. Cremation was not indigenous in Israel; it occurred only after an execution (Gen. 38:24; Lev. 20:14; 21:9; Josh. 7:15). From 1 Samuel 31:12 and Amos 6:10 we cannot draw any conclusions because the text is perhaps corrupt or else contains a report of isolated cases while 2 Chronicles 16:14, 21:19, and Jeremiah 34:5 only deal with burning aromatic spices at the time of burial. Burial, however, was highly valued and is therefore mentioned repeatedly in the Old Testament as something special. To remain unburied was a terrible disgrace (1 Sam. 17:44, 46; 1 Kings 14:11, 13; 16:4; 2 Kings 9:10; Ps. 79:3; Eccl. 6:3; Isa. 14:19, 20; Jer. 7:33; 8:1, 2; 9:22; 16:6; 25:33; Ezek. 29:5). A dead person no longer belongs in the land of the living; his unburied body arouses loathing. Shed blood calls for vengeance (Gen. 4:10; 37:26; Job 16:18; Isa. 26:21; Ezek. 24:7) because blood is the basis of the soul (Lev. 17:11) and the deceased must therefore be covered, concealed, withdrawn from view.

Through death all souls enter the abode of the dead, Sheol *(šĕ'ôl)*. The etymology of the word is uncertain but according to some, derives from *š'l*, to inquire, require, or to claim, bring to decision; according to others, from *š'l*, *šwl*, to be feeble, hang down, sink.[25] Sheol is located in the depths of the earth so that one goes down into it (Num. 16:30; Pss. 30:3, 9; 55:15; Isa. 38:18); it belongs to the lowest places of the earth (Ps. 63:9; Ezek. 26:20; 31:14; 32:18), lying even below the waters and the foundations of the mountains (Deut. 32:22; Job 26:5; Isa. 14:15), and is therefore repeatedly reinforced by the adjective "lowest" *(taḥtît)* in such passages as Deuteronomy 32:22 and Psalms 86:13; 88:6. For that reason Sheol is linked closely with the grave *(qeber)* or the pit *(bôr)*. However, the two are not identical, for the dead who have not been buried are nevertheless in Sheol (Gen. 37:35; Num. 16:32f.). Yet, just as soul and body together form one human and are thought to be in some kind of reciprocal relation also after death, so the grave and Sheol cannot be pictured in isolation from each other. The two belong to the lowest places of the earth, are both represented as the dwelling of the dead, and are repeatedly exchanged for each other. Sheol is the one great grave that encompasses all the graves of the dead; it is the realm of the dead, the underworld, and accordingly often mistakenly translated in the King James Version[26] by *hell*. Sheol, after all, is the place where all the dead without exception congregate (1 Kings 2:2; Job 3:13f.; 30:23; Ps. 89:48; Isa. 14:9ff.; Ezek. 32:18; Hab. 2:5), and from which no one returns except by a miracle (1 Kings 17:22; 2 Kings 4:34; 13:21). The realm of the dead is as it were a city, furnished with barred gates (Job 17:16 ["Will it [my hope] go down to the bars of Sheol?"]; 38:17; Pss. 9:14; 107:18; Isa. 38:10; Matt. 16:18) and which by its power (Pss. 49:15; 89:48; Hos. 13:14) holds all people captive as in a prison (Isa. 24:22). Sheol is the eternal home (Eccl. 12:5). Israel's enemies who have been plunged into it will never rise up again (Isa. 26:14); those who go down to Sheol do not come up again (Job 7:9, 10; 14:7–12; 16:22). This realm of the dead is therefore squarely opposed to the land of the living (Prov. 15:24; Ezek. 26:20; 32:23ff.).

True, the dead are thought of as existing and living: they are often pictured and described in the way they showed themselves here on earth, and are also recognized by each other and are moved by this encounter (1 Sam. 28:14; Isa. 14:9ff.; Ezek. 32:18f.). There is also mention of the innermost chambers of Sheol (Prov. 7:27; Ezek. 32:23). Among the dead there is distinction inasmuch as each is gathered to his fathers (Gen. 15:15; Judg. 2:10) or to his people (Gen. 25:8, 17; 35:29; 49:29), and the uncircumcised are all laid out together (Ezek. 32:19). But otherwise Sheol is always described in terms of its negative aspects, by contrast with the earth as the land of the living. It is the region of darkness and the shadow of death (Job 10:21, 22; Pss. 88:12; 143:3), the place of corruption—indeed as corruption itself (*Abaddon*, Job 26:6; 28:22; 31:12; Ps. 88:11; Prov. 27:20)—without "ordinances" (i.e., firm contours and clear distinctions [Job 10:22]), a land of rest, silence, and forgetfulness (Job 3:13, 17, 18; Ps. 115:17), where neither God nor humans are visible anymore (Isa. 38:11), God is no longer praised or thanked (Pss. 6:5; 115:17), his virtues are no longer proclaimed (Ps. 88:5, 11, 12; Isa. 38:18, 19), and his wonders are no longer being witnessed (Ps. 88:10, 12). It is the place where the dead know nothing, no longer work, no longer calculate their chances, no longer possess wisdom and knowledge, and have no share whatever in all that happens under the sun (Eccl. 9:5, 6, 10). The dead are *rĕpā'îm* from the adjective *rāpăh*, feeble (Job 26:5; Prov. 2:18; 9:18; 21:6; Ps. 88:10; Isa. 14:9), weak (Isa. 14:10), without strength (Ps. 88:4; cf. KJV).

This entire representation of Sheol is formed from the perspective of this earthly existence and is valid only by contrast with the riches of life enjoyed by people on earth. In that framework death indeed means a breaking off of all ties, being dead to the rich life lived on earth, being at rest, being asleep, being silent, nonbeing in relation to things on this side of the grave. The state of Sheol, though not an annihilation of one's existence, is still a dreadful diminution of life, a deprivation of everything in this life that makes for its enjoyment.

In the Old Testament there is no room for a view that permits only the body to die and comforts itself with the immortality of the soul. The whole person dies when at death the spirit or "breath" (Ps. 146:4; Eccl. 12:7) or the soul (Gen. 35:18; 2 Sam. 1:9; 1 Kings 17:21; Jonah 4:3) departs from him. Not only his body but also his soul is in a state of death and belongs to the underworld; this is the reason there is mention of the death of the soul (Gen. 37:21; Num. 23:10; Deut. 22:20f.; Judg. 16:30; Job 36:14; Ps. 78:50) and of defilement by contact with the soul of a dead person (i.e., a corpse, Lev. 19:28; 21:11; 22:4; Num. 5:2; 6:6, 7, 10;

Deut. 14:1; Hag. 2:13). Just as the whole person was destined for life in the way of obedience, so the whole person also by his transgression succumbs body-and-soul to death (Gen. 2:17). This idea had to be deeply impressed upon the consciousness of mankind; and in antiquity it was also realized by all peoples that death is a punishment, that it is something unnatural, something inimical to the essence and destiny of human beings. The revelation God gave to Israel is therefore bound up with this realization. In the same way that this revelation took over so many customs and ceremonies (sacrifice, priesthood, circumcision, etc.) while purging them of impure accretions like self-mutilation (Lev. 19:28; 21:5; Deut. 14:1) or consulting the dead (Lev. 19:31; 20:6, 27; Deut. 18:10, 11), so the idea of the unnaturalness of death was also allowed to continue and take over.

But revelation does something else and more as well. It not only maintains and reinforces the antithesis existing between life and death but introduces into this life an even sharper contrast. This life, after all, is not the true life, inasmuch as it is a sinful, impure life plagued by suffering and destined for death. It only becomes real life and only achieves real content through the service of Yahweh and in fellowship with God. Entirely in keeping with the then-prevailing dispensation of the covenant of grace and with the election of Israel as the people of God, the Old Testament conceives the connection between godliness and life in a way that regards the former as receiving its benefits and reward in a long life on earth (Exod. 20:12; Deut. 5:16, 29; 6:2; 11:9; 22:7; 30:16; 32:47, etc.). Into the fabric of the universally known natural antithesis between life and death, there is also woven a moral and spiritual contrast—that between a life in the service of sin and a life in the fear of the Lord. Death is bound up with evil; life is bound up with good (Deut. 30:15). Those who are bent on finding the philosophical theory of the immortality of the soul in the Old Testament have not understood the revelation of God to Israel and have read Western ideas into the religion of an Eastern people. Pfleiderer, striking a much truer note, says: "What people have often considered a weakness of Israel's prophetic Yahweh religion [namely, that the Beyond has so little place in it] was in reality its characteristic strength. The living God who reveals himself in historical deeds has nothing in common with the shadows of Sheol."[27] The God of Israel is not a God of the dead but of the living.

For that reason the eschatological hope of Israel's pious was almost exclusively directed toward the earthly future of the nation, the realization of the kingdom of God. The question concerning the future of individuals in Sheol remained totally in the background. God, nation, and land were inseparably bound up with each other, and individuals were incorporated in that "covenant" and viewed accordingly. Only after the exile, when Israel became a religious community and religion was individualized, did the question of each person's future fate force itself into the foreground; the spiritual contrast that revelation had woven into the natural then made itself felt; increasingly the distinction between the righteous and the ungodly replaced that between Israel and the nations and extended itself on the other side of the grave as well.

The basic elements for this development were already present, for that matter, in the revelation of the past. The person who serves God continues to live (Gen. 2:17); life is bound up with the keeping of his commandments (Lev. 18:5; Deut. 30:20); his word is life (Deut. 8:3; 32:47). Though in Proverbs life is frequently understood as length of days (2:18, 19; 3:16; 10:30), it is nevertheless remarkable that as a rule this book only associates death and Sheol with the wicked (2:18; 5:5; 7:27; 9:18) and, by contrast, attributes life almost exclusively to the righteous. Wisdom, righteousness, the fear of the Lord is the way to life (8:35, 36; 11:19; 12:28; 13:14; 14:27; 19:23). The wicked is thrust down when misfortune strikes, but the righteous maintains confidence and consolation even in death (14:32, KJV). He is blessed whose God is Yahweh (Deut. 33:29; Pss. 1:1; 2:11; 32:1, 2; 33:12; 34:8, etc.), even in the most dreadful adversities (Ps. 73:25–28; Hab. 3:17–19). The wicked, on the other hand, perish and come to an end no matter how much they prosper for a time (Ps. 73:18–20).

From within this perspective the pious not only expect deliverance from oppression and adversity in time, but by looking at things through the eyes of faith frequently penetrate the world beyond the grave and anticipate a blessed life in fellowship with God as well. The passages usually adduced to support this viewpoint (Gen. 49:18; Job 14:13–15; 16:16–21; 19:25–27; Pss. 16:9–11; 17:15; 49:15; 73:23–26; 139:18) can be variously interpreted and, according to many commentators, apply only to a temporary salvation from death. But even if this were the case, the whole Old Testament still teaches that God is the Creator of heaven and earth, that there are no limits to his power, and that he is also absolutely sovereign over life and death. He is God, the Lord, who has given life to humanity (Gen. 1:26; 2:7) and still creates and upholds every human being and all that exists (Job 32:8; 33:4; 34:14; Ps. 104:29; Eccl. 12:7). He sovereignly binds life to [the keeping of] his law and decrees death upon its violation (Gen. 2:17; Lev. 18:5; Deut. 30:20, 32:47). Though heaven is his dwelling, he is also present with his Spirit in Sheol (Ps. 139:7, 8). Sheol and Abaddon lie open before the Lord, as do the hearts of the children of mankind (Job 26:6; 38:17; Prov. 15:11). The Lord kills, keeps alive and makes alive, brings down to Sheol, and raises up from there again (Deut. 32:39; 1 Sam. 2:6; 2 Kings 5:7). He provides escape from death, can deliver when death threatens (Ps. 68:22; Isa.

38:5; Jer. 15:20; Dan. 3:26, etc.), take Enoch and Elijah to himself apart
from death (Gen. 5:24; 2 Kings 2:11), and cause the dead to return to
life (1 Kings 17:22; 2 Kings 4:34; 13:21). He can annihilate death and by
raising the dead completely triumph over its power (Job 14:13–15;
19:25–27; Isa. 25:8; 26:19; Ezek. 37:11, 12; Dan. 12:2; Hos. 6:2; 13:14).

Intertestamentary Judaism

This teaching of the Old Testament, though not entirely absent from
later Jewish literature, was nevertheless modified and expanded by various nonindigenous elements. In general the writings of this period
agree in that they have a more individualistic view of religion. Also,
under the influence of the idea of retribution, they teach a provisional
separation immediately at death between the righteous and the wicked,
and offer a more elaborate account of the different places they inhabit.
Still, they can be clearly divided into two groups, a Palestinian and an
Alexandrian one. The first, to which especially the apocryphal writings
of the Maccabees, Baruch, 4 Ezra [in Vulgate Appendix; 2 Esdras in
NRSV], Enoch, the Testament of the Twelve Patriarchs, and so on belong,
attributes only a provisional character to the intermediate state. Admittedly they, too, already include foreign elements and teach a certain division between the righteous and the wicked immediately at death. The
Apocalypse of Enoch, for example, locates Sheol in the West, describes
it as being transected and surrounded by streams of water, and distinguishes four sections in it, two for the good and two for the wicked
(17:5, 6; 22:2f.). It further assumes the existence of a Paradise that was
situated high above and at the ends of the earth and became the abode
of Enoch and Elijah at the moment of their death (12:1; 87:3; 89:52),
and will be the abode for all who walk in their ways (71:16, 17). But in
the case of all the authors of this group the point of gravity lies in their
universal eschatology, in the coming of the Messiah, and in the establishment of the kingdom of God at the end of time. Until then the souls
of the dead are kept in Hades—be it in different sections and a provi-
sionally distinct state—as in a storehouse, *tamieia, promptuaria anima-
rum* (a repository of souls) (Apoc. Baruch 21:23; 4 Ezra 4:35; 5:37).
Resting and sleeping, they await the final judgment (4 Ezra 7:32–35;
Apoc. Baruch 21:24; 23:4; 30:2).

But the writings of the second group, such as the Wisdom of Jesus
Sirach, the Book of Wisdom, Philo, Josephus, and so on, particularly
stress individual eschatology, allowing the coming of the Messiah, the
resurrection, final judgment, and the kingdom of God on earth to either
recede totally into the background or to be kept completely out of the
picture. The principal dogma is that of the immortality of the soul

which, according to Philo, was preexistent. On account of its fall it was temporarily locked up in the prisonhouse of the body and, depending on its conduct, moves into other bodies after death or, in any case, receives the definite settlement of its fate immediately after death (Sir. 1:12; 7:17; 18:24; 41:12; Wisdom 1:8, 9; 3:1–10). In the end it goes either to a holy heaven or to a dark Hades.[28]

At the time of Christ, accordingly, a wide range of sometimes overlapping eschatological images whirled about the people of Israel. The Pharisees believed in a continued existence and a provisional retribution after death, but alongside of these held to the expectation of the Messiah, of the resurrection of the dead—if not of all people, then certainly of the righteous—and of the establishment of God's kingdom on earth. The Sadducees denied the resurrection (Matt. 22:23; Mark 12:18; Luke 20:27; Acts 23:8) and, according to Josephus,[29] retribution after death and immortality as well. The Essenes believed that the body was mortal but that the soul was immortal. Originally the souls dwelt in the finest ether but, being caught up in sensual lust, were placed in bodies from which they are again liberated by death. Good souls were given a blessed life on the other side of the ocean in a place untouched by either rain, snow, or heat, but the bad must suffer everlasting pains in a place of darkness and cold.[30]

The New Testament

In line with the Law and the Prophets, the New Testament devotes much more attention to universal than to particular eschatology. Still it is incorrect to contend, as do Episcopius and others,[31] that Scripture says virtually nothing about the intermediate state or at least contains no teaching that is valid for us. Similarly, the opinion of Kliefoth[32] that the New Testament probably says everything that can be said about it is incorrect. Scripture is not lacking in statements that spread as much light as we need in and for this life. The New Testament brings out—even more forcefully than the Old—that death is a consequence of, and punishment for, sin (Rom. 5:12; 6:23; 8:10; 1 Cor. 15:21) and that death extends to all people (1 Cor. 15:22; Heb. 9:27). Only a rare individual, like Enoch, is taken so that he would not see death (Heb. 11:5). And also those who experience the parousia of Christ are changed in a twinkling of an eye without the intervention of death (1 Cor. 15:51; 1 Thess. 4:14–17; cf. John 21:22, 23), so that Christ will not only judge the dead but also the living (Acts 10:42; 2 Tim. 4:1; 1 Peter 4:5). But death is not the end of a person; the soul cannot be killed (Matt. 10:28), the body will one day be raised (John 5:28, 29; Acts 23:6; Rev. 20:12, 13), and believers even take part in an eternal life that cannot be destroyed (John 3:36; 11:25).

All the dead, according to the New Testament, will be in Hades, the realm of the dead, until the resurrection. In Matthew 11:23 and Luke 10:15 the expression "be brought down to Hades" *(eōs tou adou katabēsē)* signifies that haughty Capernaum will be profoundly humbled. In Matthew 16:18 Jesus promises his church that "the gates of Hades" *(pylai adou)* will have no power over it, that death will not triumph over it. According to Luke 16:23, the wretched Lazarus will be carried by angels to Abraham's bosom and the rich man, upon his death and burial, immediately arrives in Hades, where Hades is not yet the same as a place of torment since this is indicated only by the addition "being in torment" *(hyparchōn en basanois)*. Jesus, too, as long as he was in the state of death, dwelt in Hades, even though it could not hold him there (Acts 2:27, 31). He, after all, descended to the "lower parts of the earth" *(eis ta katōtera merē tēs gēs)* (Eph. 4:9). And so all the dead are "under the earth" *(katachthonioi)* (Phil. 2:10). Not only the wicked but also believers find themselves in Hades after death. They are the dead in Christ (1 Thess. 4:16; cf. 1 Cor. 15:18, 23). At the time of the resurrection the sea, Death, and Hades give up all the dead that were in them, in order that they may be judged by their works (Rev. 20:13). Hades follows with and after Death, so that Death always brings about a relocation [of souls] into Hades (Rev. 6:8). This view—from death until the resurrection believers, too, according to Scripture, are in Hades—is reinforced by the expression "raised from the dead" *(ek nekrōn anastēnai; ek nekeōn egerthē)* (Matt. 17:9; Mark 6:14; Luke 16:30; John 20:9; Eph. 5:14 etc.), which means, not "from death," but "from the dead," that is, from the realm of the dead.

However, this common situatedness in the state of death does not exclude the fact that the lot of believers and unbelievers in it is very diverse. The Old Testament, too, already expressed this idea but it is much more striking in the New Testament. According to the parable in Luke 16, the wretched Lazarus is carried by the angels to Abraham's bosom, which conveys the truth that in heaven, where the angels live, Lazarus enjoys blessedness in proximity to and in fellowship with Abraham (Matt. 8:11). Jesus promises one of the men crucified alongside him that "today you will be with me in Paradise" (Luke 23:43). The word "Paradise" is of Persian origin and in general refers to a garden (for pleasure) (Neh. 2:8; Eccl. 2:5; Song of Sol. 4:12). The Septuagint used it as the word for the Garden of Eden in Genesis 2:8–15 and the Jews used the word to describe the place where God grants his fellowship to the righteous after their death.[33]

Undoubtedly, according to the New Testament as well, Paradise, like Abraham's bosom, is to be thought in heaven. Shortly after Jesus had promised the murderer that "today" he would be with him in Paradise, he commended his spirit into the hands of his Father (Luke 23:46); in 2 Corinthians 12:2, 4, "Paradise" is used interchangeably with "the third heaven"; in Revelation 2:7, 22:2 it refers to the place where in the future God will dwell among his people. In keeping with this, the Gospel of John teaches that believers who here on earth already possess the beginning of eternal life and have escaped the judgment of God (3:15–21; 5:24) share in a communion with Christ that is broken neither by his going away (12:32; 14:23) nor by death (11:25, 26), and which will someday be completed in being together with him eternally (6:39; 14:3, 19; 16:16; 17:24). Stephen at the time of his death prayed that the Lord Jesus would take his spirit to him in heaven (Acts 7:59). Paul knew that the believer shares in a life that is far superior to death (Rom. 8:10) and that nothing, not even death, could separate him from the love of God in Christ (8:38; 14:8; 1 Thess. 5:10). Although he must for a time still remain in the flesh for the sake of the churches, he nevertheless desires to depart and to be with Christ (2 Cor. 5:8; Phil. 1:23). According to Revelation 6:9, 7:9, the souls of the martyrs are with Christ beneath the altar that stands before the throne of God in the temple of heaven (cf. 2:7, 10, 17, 26; 3:4, 5, 12, 21; 8:3; 9:13; 14:13; 15:2; 16:17; see also Heb. 11:10, 16; 12:23).

And just as immediately after death believers enjoy a provisional state of bliss with Christ in heaven, so unbelievers from the moment of their death enter a place of torment. The rich man was in torment when he opened his eyes in Hades (Luke 16:23). Unbelievers who reject Christ remain under the wrath of God and are condemned already on earth (John 3:18, 36) and must—along with all others—expect judgment immediately after death (Heb. 9:27). Still, this place of torment is not yet identical with Gehennah or the lake of fire *(limēn tou pyros)* for Gehennah is the place of inextinguishable and eternal fire prepared for the devil and his messengers (Matt. 18:8; 25:41, 46; Mark 9:43, 47, 48) and the pool of fire is not the present but the future place of punishment of the kingdom of the world and the false prophet (Rev. 19:20), Satan (Rev. 20:10), and all the wicked (Rev. 21:8; cf. 2 Peter 2:17; Jude 13). The case is rather that now they are all kept in a prison *(phylakē)* (1 Peter 3:19) or in the abyss *(abyssos)* (Luke 8:31; cf. Matt. 8:29; Rom. 10:7; Rev. 9:1, 2, 11; 11:7; 17:8; 20:1, 3). This difference in the intermediate state between the good and the evil does not conflict with the fact that they are all together in Hades, for all the dead are as such *katachthonioi* (inhabitants of the lower regions); before the resurrection they belong to the realm of the dead and are only completely liberated in soul and body by that resurrection from the rule of death (1 Cor. 15:52–55; Rev. 20:13).

After Death, Then What? 2

Early Christian theology honored the scriptural reserve concerning the intermediate state. The delay of the parousia and challenges to Christian eschatology forced the church's theologians to seek greater clarity. The initial understanding of a more-or-less neutral abode of all the dead became increasingly differentiated into immediate bliss for believers and punishment for unbelievers. The notion of purification by fire and purgatory was developed to further discriminate among levels of merit and perfection in believers. The intercession of the church was believed to help hasten the process. The Reformation repudiated the idea of purgatory and again pictured entry into the intermediate state as entry into immediate bliss or judgment. However, other ideas, including soul sleep, annihilation, reincarnation, and varieties of universalism also sprang up after the Reformation. This preoccupation with the intermediate state is not scriptural. The Bible gives the notion of the soul's immortality after death a decidedly subordinate value. Death breaks the varied and wonderful bonds of life-relations in this world. In comparison with life on this side of the grave, death results in nonbeing, the disturbing negation of the rich and joyful experience of life on earth. Death is the fruit of sin; sin is death. Christ's death and resurrection is thus the restoration of life. For those who are in Christ, death is no longer the end but a passage into eternal life. This rich biblical perspective rules out other attempts to reduce the sting of death such as belief in soul sleep, intermediate corporeality, and contact between the dead and the living, including veneration of saints.

In the early period Christian theology limited itself to the simple givens of Holy Scripture. The Apostolic Fathers still had no doctrine concerning the intermediate state and in general believed that at death the devout immediately experience the blessedness of heaven and the wicked the punishment of hell. Burnet and others who followed him, such as Blondel, Ernesti, and Baumgarten-Crusius, attempted to show that the most ancient Christian writers had the real blessedness of believers begin only after the judgment of the world, but they have not been able to advance adequate proofs for that position.[1] Only when the parousia of Christ did not come as soon as almost all believers initially expected, and various heretical thinkers distorted or opposed the doctrine of the last things, did the church's thinkers begin to reflect more intentionally on the intermediate state. Ebionitism tried to hold onto the national privileges of Israel at the expense of Christian universalism and was therefore generally disposed to millenarianism. Gnosticism, by virtue of its basic dualism, rejected Christian eschatology altogether and held to no other expectation than that of the liberation of the spirit from matter and its assumption into the divine pleroma immediately after death. As a result, Christian theology was compelled to seek a clearer understanding of the character of the intermediate state and of its connections both with this life and with the final state following the last judgment.

Justin already stated that after death the souls of the devout were in a better place and the souls of the unrighteous in a worse one as they awaited the time of judgment. He condemned as un-Christian the teaching that there is no resurrection of the dead and that souls are taken up into heaven immediately at the time of death. According to Irenaeus, the souls of the devout at death do not immediately enter heaven, Paradise, or the city of God—which following the last judgment will be three distinct dwellingplaces of the righteous—but an invisible place determined by God, where they await the resurrection and the subsequent vision of God. His reason was that Christ, too, first spent three days in the place of the dead, the lower places of the earth, to save the holy dead from it and, having thus fulfilled "the law of the dead" *(lex mortuorum)*, was raised and taken up into heaven. There, in the shadow of death, in Hades, every human receives a fitting habitation even before the judgment, the pious probably in Abraham's bosom, which is, accordingly, a division of Hades.

We encounter the same view of the various "receptacles" in Hades, where the dead await the last day, in Hippolytus, Tertullian, Novation, Commodian, Victorinus, Hilary, Ambrose, Cyril, and also still in Augustine.[2] But to the degree that the parousia of Christ receded into the distance it became increasingly harder to maintain the old representation of Hades and to regard the stay in it as a brief, provisional, more or less neutral experience. Already at an early date an exception was made for the martyrs. These, said Irenaeus, Tertullian, and others, had entered heaven immediately after their death and were immediately admitted to the vision of God. In this connection Christ's descent into Hades was interpreted to mean that by it believers who had died before Christ's sacrifice were released from the limbo of the fathers *(limbus patrum)* and transferred to heaven. And the teaching of the necessity and meritoriousness of good works, which made increasing inroads in the church, automatically led to the idea that those who had in a special way devoted their entire lives to God were now also, immediately at the time of their death, worthy of heavenly bliss. Thus Hades was gradually depopulated. Admittedly unbelievers still remained, but this led precisely to the effect that Hades was increasingly viewed as a place of punishment and equated with Tartarus or Gehennah. Only those Christians who up until then had not made enough progress in sanctification to be able, immediately at death, to enter the glory of heaven would have to spend time in Hades.

The Move toward Purgatory

Gradually linked with this development was the idea of purification by fire, first uttered by Origen. According to him, all punishments were medicines *(pharmaka)*, and all of Hades, Gehennah included, a place of purification. Sins were specifically consumed and people cleansed by purifying fire *(pyr katharsion)*, which at the end of this dispensation would set the world aflame.[3] Following Origen, Greek theologians later adopted the idea that the souls of many of the dead would have to suffer sorrows and could only be released from them by the intercessions and sacrifices of the living; they nevertheless objected to a special fire of purification, as the Western church taught it.[4] Not until the Council of Florence (1439) did the Greeks make any concessions on this point.[5] In the West, on the other hand, the fire of purification of which Origen spoke was moved from the last judgment to the intermediate state. Augustine occasionally said that following the general resurrection or at the last judgment certain additional purgatorial pains would be imposed.[6] Still, he usually has the development of the city of God end with the last judgment and therefore does not regard it as impossible that "some of the faithful are saved by a sort of purgatorial fire, and this sooner or later according as they have loved more or less the goods that perish."[7] Caesar of Arles and Gregory the Great, working this out, developed the idea that specifically venial sins could be expiated here or in the hereafter. And when this teaching was combined with the church practice, already reported by Tertullian,[8] of making intercessions and sacrifices for the dead, the dogma of purgatory was complete.

The Scholastics[9] developed the dogma of doctrine of purgatory extensively; the councils of Florence (1439) and Trent (1545–63)[10] made it a church doctrine; and later theology attached to it ever-increasing importance for the life of religion and the church. According to Catholic doctrine, the souls of the damned immediately enter hell (Gehenna, the abyss, the inferno), where they, along with the unclean spirits, are tormented in everlasting and inextinguishable fire. The souls of those who after receiving baptism are not again tainted by sin or purified from it here or hereafter, are immediately taken up into heaven. There they behold the face of God, be it in various degrees of perfection depending on their merits.[11] By Christ's descent into hell also the souls of the saints who died before that time are transferred from the limbo of the fathers (Abraham's bosom) to heaven. Infants who die before being baptized— about whose lot the Church Fathers in some cases judged more gently, in others more severely—were consigned to the lower regions, where, however, the punishments are extremely unequal. On the most common view they go to a special division *(limbus infantum)* where they only suffer an "eternal punishment of condemnation" *(aeterna poena damni)* but no "physical punishment" *(poena sensa).*[12] But those who, after having received sanctifying grace in baptism or the sacrament of penance, commit venial sins and have not been able to "pay" the appropriate temporal punishments in this life, are not pure enough to be immediately admitted to the beatific vision of God in heaven. They go to a place in between heaven and hell, not to acquire new virtues and merits, but to clear up the hindrances that stand in the way of their entry into heaven.

To that end, at the first moment after death, they are delivered from the guilt of venial sins by an act of repentance (payment made for a pardonable sin) and subsequently still have to bear the temporal punishments that remain the set penalty for those sins even after forgiveness. Purgatory,[13] accordingly, is not a place of repentance, of trial, or of sanctification, but of punishment, where fire—usually thought of as a material agent—serves, ideally, that is, by the representation of great pain, to have a purifying impact on "poor souls." In addition, by virtue of the communion of saints, the church can come to the aid of these suffering souls for the purpose of softening and shortening their punishment by intercessions, sacrifices of the Mass, good works, and indulgences. It is true that nobody knows for certain which souls have to go to purgatory, how long they must stay there, and under what conditions on their part the prayers and sacrifices of the living are to their benefit; but this uncertainty is in no way detrimental to the cult of the dead. For increasingly the rule is that, barring a few exceptions, such as martyrs or particular saints, the great majority of believers first go to purgatory. In any case they are far ahead of the living, who must go to heaven by way of purgatory as well. Though on the one hand they are "poor souls," viewed from another angle they are "blessed" souls who along with the angels and those in a state of beatitude are invoked for help by the living in distress.[14]

Reformation and Deformation

The Reformation saw in this notion of purgatory a limitation on the
merits of Christ and taught—in virtue of its principle of justification by
faith alone—that a human, immediately after a particular judgment undergone in the death struggle, entered into the blessedness of heaven or
the perdition of hell. Luther himself frequently pictured the intermediate state of the pious as a sleep in which they quietly and calmly awaited
the future of the Lord.[15] Later Lutheran theologians, however, almost
completely wiped out the distinction between the intermediate state
and the final state, and said that immediately after death the souls of
the faithful enjoyed a full and essential beatitude and the ungodly immediately received a full and consummate condemnation.[16] In the
main, we have to say, that was also the opinion of the Reformed.[17] But
they usually showed more clearly than the Lutherans the difference
that existed in the state of the dead before and after the Last Day. In his
writing on "the sleep of the soul" Calvin states that "Abraham's bosom"
only means that after death the souls of the faithful will enjoy full peace,
but that up until the day of resurrection something will still be lacking,
namely, the full and perfect glory of God to which they always aspire,
and that therefore our salvation always remains in progress until that
day that concludes and terminates all progress.[18] Others went even further, adopting a specific kind of intermediate state. L. Capellus said that
after death the souls of the pious entered a state which, though it can
be called blessed by comparison with that which exists on earth, is very
different from the blessedness that begins after the resurrection. The
intermediate state, after all, consisted almost entirely "in the hope and
expectation of a future glory, not indeed in the enjoyment of that glory."
And in the same way the souls of the wicked arrived after death in a
state in which they awaited in dread and fear the future punishment determined for them but did not yet suffer that punishment itself, for "the
expectation of punishment is not the punishment itself." So, in the
main, also William Sherlock, Thomas Burnet, and numerous other English theologians believed, and among the Lutherans, Calixtus, Hor-
neius, Zeltner, and others.[19]

   In Protestant theology, following the eighteenth century, all the ideas
expressed earlier by pagans and Christians, philosophers and theologians returned. The Catholic doctrine of purgatory was again taken up
by many mystics and pietists like Böhme, Antoinette Bourignon, Poiret,
Dippel, Petersen, Arnold, and Schermer, and further by Leibniz, Lessing, J. F. von Meyer, and many others.[20] The Socinians, following certain ancient Christian writers, taught that just as bodies returned to
earth, so souls returned to God and there, until the resurrection, led an

existence without perception or thought, pleasure or discomfort.[21] Closely connected with this view was the doctrine of soul sleep, which had earlier already been advocated by certain heretics, later by the Anabaptists, and found acceptance again in the eighteenth century in the work of Artobe, Heyn, Sulzer,[22] and further in that of Fries, Ulrici, and the Irvingians. Others again modified this psychopannychism by saying that though the soul retained a kind of internal consciousness it was cut off from contact with the external world.[23] Still others avoided this theory of the soul sleep by assuming that upon laying aside the material shell the soul retained the basic organic form of the body or that after death it received a new body made up of the finest, most delicate material, which enabled it to stay in contact with the external world.[24] Not a few thinkers have even returned to the ancient doctrine of the transmigration of souls or metempsychosis, commending a form of it that says that by a process of repeated passages from one human body into another souls may eventually arrive at perfection.[25] Nowadays the idea of development is so strong that it is being applied even to the state after death. The doctrine of the limbo of the fathers *(limbus patrum)* has again been taken over by Martensen, Delitzsch, Vilmar, and the like,[26] and the view that in the intermediate state there will still be gospel preaching and the possibility of conversion is a favorite notion of the new theology.[27] Many even view the whole of the Beyond *(Jenseits)* as an ongoing purgation. The result of this is that some may be lost forever (hypothetical universalism), or that those who persist in the wrong will be annihilated (conditional immortality), or that in the end all will be saved *(apokatastasis)*.[28]

The Need for Scriptural Reserve

The history of the doctrine of the intermediate state shows that it is hard for theologians and people in general to stay within the limits of Scripture and not to be wiser than they ought to be. The scriptural data about the intermediate state are sufficient for our needs in this life but leave unanswered many questions that may arise in the inquisitive mind. If one nevertheless insists on solving them one can only take the course of conjecture and run the risk of negating the divine witness by the inventions of human wisdom. This becomes immediately evident when we speak about death and immortality. Philosophy deals with this subject in a way that is very different from Scripture. Philosophy views death as something natural and thinks that the idea of immortality, that is, the continued existence of the soul, is enough for it. But the judgment of Scripture is vastly different. Death is not natural but arises from the violation of the divine commandment (Gen. 2:17); from the devil insofar as he by his seduction caused man to fall and die (John 8:44); from sin itself inasmuch as it has a disintegrating impact on the whole of human life and, as it were, produces death from within itself (James 1:15); from the judgment of God since he pays the wages of sin in the currency of death (Rom. 6:23). And in Scripture this death is never identical with annihilation, with nonbeing, but always consists in the destruction of harmony, in being cut off from the various life-settings in which a creature has been placed in keeping with its nature, in returning to the elementary chaotic existence which, at least logically, underlies the entire cosmos.

According to Herbert Spencer, life consists in continual adaptation to internal and external relations. Although this definition by no means explains the essence of life, it is nevertheless true that life is all the richer to the degree that the relations in which it stands to its surroundings are greater in number and healthier in nature. The highest creature, therefore, is the human being. In virtue of their creation, humans are linked with nature and the human world, visible and invisible things, heaven and earth, God and angels. And they live if and to the degree they stand in the right, that is, the God-willed, relation to the whole of their surroundings. Accordingly, in its essence and entire scope death is disturbance, the breakup of all these relations in which humans stood originally and still ought to stand now.[29] Death's cause, therefore, is and can be none other than the sin that disturbs the right relation to and breaks up life-embracing fellowship with God. In this sense sin not only results in death but coincides with it; sin is death, death in a spiritual sense. Those who sin, by that token and at the same moment, put themselves in an adversarial relationship to God, are dead to God and the things of God, have no pleasure in the knowledge of his ways, and in hostility and hatred turn away from him. And since this relation to God, this being created in his image and likeness, is not something extraneous and additional, a *donum superadditum*, but belongs to the essence of being human and bears a central character, the disturbance of this relationship will inevitably have a devastating impact on all the other relationships in which human beings stand to themselves, to their fellow humans, to nature, to the angels, to the whole creation. Actually, in terms of its nature, at the very moment it was committed, sin should have resulted in a full across-the-board death (Gen. 2:17), a return of the entire cosmos to its primeval chaotic condition.

But God intervened: he broke the power of sin and death. True, as Schelling remarked, underlying all that exists there is an irrational remainder. Everything that is left to itself disintegrates. Nature, when it is not cultivated, becomes wild; persons who are not brought up prop-

erly degenerate; a people who fall outside the circle of civilization will
become corrupt. By nature all that is in and outside humanity is torn
up into mutually hostile segments, but God in his mercy has intervened.
He intervened first with his common grace to curb the power of sin and
death, then with his special grace to break down and conquer that
power. Not only is physical death postponed, and not only did God by
various measures make human existence and development possible;
but Christ, by his cross, fundamentally achieved a victory over sin and
death and brought life and immortality to light (Rom. 5:12ff.; 1 Cor.
15:45; 2 Tim. 1:10; Heb. 2:14; Rev. 1:18; 20:14), so that everyone who
believes in him has eternal life and will never die (John 3:36; 5:24; 8:51,
52; 11:25). Now it is this life and this immortality that in Holy Scripture
stands in the foreground.

Immortality in a philosophical sense—the continuation of the soul
after death—is of subordinate value in the Bible; Scripture does not
deny its reality but neither does it deliberately set out to teach it. Least
of all has Scripture been given, as deism thought, to make this immortality known to us as one of the weightiest truths of religion. This truth,
after all, is sufficiently well known to humans. What Scripture had to
teach us was that naked existence, mere unenhanced being, is not yet
life as it befits and behooves human beings; this is the case on this side
of the grave and even more on the other side. On earth human life, also
the life of one who has no fellowship with God, still stands in a web of
varied relations and from it receives a measure of content and value.
But when all this falls away and all these connections are broken, life
sinks back into a poor, vacuous, and shadowy existence devoid of content. The Old Testament usually views the Beyond from this side of the
grave. Death, then, is an exit from this life, the breaking of *all* bonds
with *this* world. By comparison with life on this side death is nonbeing,
a rest or sleep; in a word, it is being completely dead to the entire range
of the rich and joyful experience of life on earth. Never again will the
dead have any share in all that happens under the sun (Eccl. 9:6).

In the foreground, in the concept of Sheol, stands the negation of our
earthly life and work and if this negation is not its only component, it is
certainly its most important one. The question whether in Sheol this
completely broken-down earthly life yields to another reality in which
the deceased enter into new relations in another direction is touched
upon only a few times in the Old Testament when the eyes of faith of
the pious pierce the shadows of death and catch a glimpse of eternal life
in fellowship with God. From the viewpoint of Old Testament revelation it was enough to plant in the human consciousness the great idea
that true life can be found only in fellowship with God. To the believers
of the old dispensation the horror of hell remained as nebulous as the

joy of heaven. Only when Christ died and rose again did imperishable life come to light. Christ did not gain or disclose immortality in the philosophical sense, the sense of the continued existence of souls after death. On the contrary, both here and hereafter he again filled the life of humans, exhausted and emptied by sin, with the positive content of God's fellowship, with peace and joy and blessedness. For those who are in Christ Jesus death is no longer death but a passage into eternal life and the grave a place of sanctified rest until the day of resurrection.

Those who lose sight of this scriptural teaching on immortality fall into various errors. It is simply a fact that we cannot picture a pure [disembodied] spirit—its existence, life, and activity. About God, who is pure Spirit, we can only speak in an anthropomorphic manner, a procedure modeled to us by Scripture itself. Angels are spiritual beings but are presented in human form; when they appear on earth they often assume human bodies. And though human persons are not merely physical beings, all their activities are bound to the body and dependent on it, not just the vegetative and animal functions but also the intellectual ones of thinking and willing. Although our brains are not the cause of our higher faculties of knowing and desiring, they are nevertheless the bearer and organ of these faculties. Every malfunction in the brain results in the abnormal functioning of the rational mind. Inasmuch as the body is not the prisonhouse of the soul but belongs integrally to the essence of our humanity, we cannot form any mental picture of the life and activity of a soul that is separated from the body and are therefore readily inclined to conjectures and guessing. Accordingly, in the main three hypotheses have been conceived to make the existence of souls after death somewhat intelligible: soul sleep, intermediate corporeality, and some form of contact between the living and the dead.

Soul Sleep?

Many pagan thinkers and also some Christians have believed that souls, after being separated from the body, are capable only of leading a dormant life. The change that begins at death is indeed of extraordinary significance. The entire content of our psychic life is derived after all from the external world; all knowledge begins with sense perception; the entire form of our thought is material; we even speak of spiritual things in words that originally had a sensorial meaning. If then, as Scripture teaches, death is a sudden, violent, total, and absolute break with the present world, there is ostensibly no other possibility than that the soul is completely closed to the external world, loses all its content, and sinks back as it were into itself. In sleep as well the soul withdraws from the outside world and breaks off its interaction with it. But in sleep it does this only in a relative sense, since it continues to be united with the body and retains the rich life it has acquired from the world. In dreaming it even continues to occupy itself with that world, albeit in a confused fashion. Still, what enormous change mere sleep brings about in human life: the faculties of knowing and desiring cease their activity; the consciousness stands still; all perception and observation stop; only the vegetative life continues its regular rhythms. But if this is the case in sleep, how much more will all the activity of the soul come to a halt when death enters in and totally tears up the ties that unite it with this world! Everything, therefore, seems to argue for the position that after death souls are in a dormant, unconscious state. And as would appear from a superficial reading, Scripture is so far removed from condemning the doctrine of soul sleep that it rather commends and favors it. After all, not only the Old but also the New Testament repeatedly refers to death as a sleep (Deut. 31:16 KJV; Jer. 51:39, 57; Dan. 12:2; Matt. 9:24; John 11:11; 1 Cor. 7:39; 11:30; 15:6, 18, 20, 51; 1 Thess. 4:13–15; 2 Peter 3:4, etc.). Sheol is a land of silence, rest, and forgetfulness where nothing ever shares in anything that happens under the sun. Jesus speaks of the night of death in which no one can work (John 9:4), and Scripture nowhere makes mention of anything that those who like Lazarus and others returned to life from the dead reported concerning what they saw or heard in the intermediate state.

Still, all these arguments are not sufficient to prove the theory of psychopannychism. For, in the first place, it is clear that the soul's dependence on the body does not necessarily exclude its independence. The external world may prompt the awakening of our self-consciousness and be the initial source of our knowledge; thinking may be bound to our brains and have its seat and organ there; it has not been and cannot be proven that the psychic life of humanity has its source and origin in physical phenomena. Thinking and knowing are activities of the soul; it is not the ear that hears and the eye that sees but the psychic "I" of a human being that hears through the ear and sees through the eye. The body is the instrument of mind or spirit. For that reason there is nothing preposterous in thinking that if necessary the soul can continue its activities without the body. Also, those who would deny conscious life to spirit as such would logically have to assume that consciousness and will are also impossible in the case of God and the angels. For though we speak of God in human fashion and often picture angels as corporeal, they are in themselves spirit and nevertheless possess consciousness and will.

In the second place, Scripture teaches with the greatest possible clarity that death is a total break with all of this earthly life and to that extent a sleeping, resting, or being silent. The state of death is a sleep; the deceased person sleeps because interaction with the present world has ended. But Scripture nowhere says that the soul of the deceased sleeps. On the contrary, it always represents it after death as being more or less conscious. As revelation progresses it becomes increasingly clear that, whereas in death all the soul's relations with this world are cut off, they are immediately replaced by other relations to another world. The great scriptural idea that life is bound up with service to the Lord and death with its rejection also casts its light on the other side of the grave. Whereas immediately after his death the rich man is in torment, the wretched Lazarus is carried to Abraham's bosom (Luke 16:23). And all believers who on earth already participated in eternal life, so far from losing it by dying (John 11:25, 26), after death enjoy it all the more intensely and blessedly in fellowship with Christ (Luke 23:43; Acts 7:59; 2 Cor. 5:8; Phil. 1:23; Rev. 6:9; 7:9, 10). Being at home in the body is being away from the Lord; therefore, to die is the way to a closer, more intimate fellowship with Christ.

In the third place, it need not surprise us that those who rose again and returned to this life tell us nothing of what they saw and heard on the other side. For aside from the possibility that they have reported some things not recorded in Scripture, it is most likely that they have not been permitted or are unable to convey their experiences on the other side of the grave. Moses and the prophets are enough for us (Luke 16:29). After being caught up in the third heaven Paul could only say that he had heard things that are not to be told and that no mortal is permitted to repeat (2 Cor. 12:4).[30]

Intermediate Corporeality?

Others believe that after death souls receive a new corporeality and are on that account able again to enter into contact with the external world. They base this opinion on the fact that we cannot visualize the life and activity of the soul aside from the body and, further, on those passages in Scripture that seem to accord a kind of corporeality to the souls of the dead. The denizens of the realm of the dead are described precisely as they appeared on earth. Samuel is pictured as an old man clothed with a mantle (1 Sam. 28:14); the kings of the nations sit on thrones and go out to meet the king of Babel (Isa. 14:9); the Gentiles lie down to rest with the uncircumcised (Ezek. 31:18; 32:19ff.). In speaking of the dead Jesus still refers to their eyes, fingers, and tongues (Luke 16:23, 24). Paul expects that if the earthly tent is destroyed he will have a building from God and not be unclothed but further clothed (2 Cor. 5:1–4). And John saw a great multitude, standing before the throne and the Lamb, robed in white, with palm branches in their hands (Rev. 6:11; 7:9).

But, in the first place, from this mode of speech in Scripture one cannot infer anything about the corporeality of souls after death. Scripture can only speak of God and angels, of the souls in Sheol, of joy in heaven and torment in hell in human language, in imagery derived from earthly conditions and relations. But alongside of this it states clearly and decisively that God is spirit and that the angels are spirits and, by saying this, gives us a standard by which all these anthropomorphic expressions need to be understood. And it does the same with respect to the dead. It can only speak of them as people of flesh and blood but states additionally that while their body rests in the grave they are souls or spirits (Eccl. 12:7; Ezek. 37:5; Luke 23:46; Acts 7:59; Heb. 12:23; 1 Peter 3:19; Rev. 6:9; 20:4). We have to hold to these clear pronouncements. Those who nevertheless attribute to souls a kind of body must, to be consistent, follow through and, along with theosophists, represent God and the angels as in some sense physical as well.

Second, the strongest passage speaking for a kind of "intermediate corporeality" *(Zwischenleiblichkeit)* of souls is 2 Corinthians 5:1–4. But also this text, when properly exegeted, loses all its evidential value. There is no difference of opinion, after all, about the main point Paul is making here. The apostle knows that when his earthly body is "dissolved" he has "a building from God." Still he groans and feels burdened in this body, being anxious about death, and would therefore wish not to be "unclothed" from this body, but to be clothed instantaneously, in both soul and body, with a heavenly dwelling, so that what is mortal is swallowed up by life. However, though this may be his dearest wish, he knows that after the destruction of this earthly body, even if it be that he has his body "taken off,"[31] he will still not be found naked but be at home with the Lord (vv. 1, 3, 8). But if this is the main idea, we cannot construe the dwelling from God as the resurrection body and, still less, as an intermediate body. For the thing Paul particularly longs for is to be clothed with that dwelling from God, without dying, while keeping his earthly body. Now the resurrection body is not one existing alongside the earthly body and is not put on over it but under the impact of God's word of power arises from it or, in the case of those who are still alive, results from a transformation (1 Cor. 15:42, 51, 52). And an intermediate body is all the more inconceivable because in that scenario Paul would know of no fewer than three bodies, each consecutively put on over the other. Holtzmann therefore correctly remarks that "it is best no longer to speak of any 'intermediate' body at all. Paul knows two, not three *sōmata,*"[32] bodies which, accordingly, cannot be put dualistically after and alongside of each other. For this reason the "building from God" cannot be anything other than a place and, simultaneously, the heavenly glory thought of as a garment, the eternal light that God himself inhabits (1 Tim. 6:16). It is something from God, not made with hands, from and in heaven, into which at death or at the resurrection believers are transposed (cf. John 14:2; 17:24; Col. 1:12).

Finally, the corporeality ascribed to souls after death is a concept without any specifiable content; for this very reason, opinions on it tend to be very diverse. Frans Delitzsch, with his trichotomistic viewpoint, assumes that the soul performs the function of the intermediate body for the spirit. In his writings the soul stands between the spirit and matter; it is the principle of bodily life derived from the spirit, the external corporeal clothing of the spirit and still at the same time the immaterial internal side of the body.[33] Güder teaches the theory that the power that organized our earthly body is preserved and, on the other side of the grave, forms a new body from the elements present there. Splittgerber says that the basic organic form of the body accompanies the soul and in the intermediate state gives it an imperfect provisional corporeality. Rinck believes that the "neural body" *(Nervenleib)*, a fine and delicate internal body that is the bearer of the life of the soul, accompanies the soul after death and is clothed in the case of regenerates by the Spirit of God and formed into an intermediate body by the irradiation of the glorified body of Christ, while in the case of the ungodly it is increasingly pervaded by sin and darkness. But no matter how it is presented, it does not become any clearer. We know only of spirit and matter. An "immaterial corporeality" is a contradiction that was inauspiciously taken from theosophy into Christian theology and seeks in vain to reconcile the false dualism of spirit and matter, of thesis and antithesis.

Contact with the Living?

In the third place, there are many who believe that souls after death still maintain some kind of relations with life on earth. Prevalent among many peoples is the idea that souls after death remain near the gravesite. The Jews, too, believed that for a time following death the soul hovered about the corpse, and used this circumstance to explain how the witch of Endor could still call up the spirit of Samuel.[34] There was the widespread practice of providing the deceased in their grave with food, weapons, possessions, sometimes even wives and slaves. Usually this veneration of the dead was not restricted to the day of the burial or the time of mourning but continued afterward as well and was incorporated into ordinary private or public cultic practice. Not only the dead in general were venerated but also deceased blood relatives, parents and ancestors, the fathers and heads of the tribe, the heroes of the people, the princes and kings of the country, sometimes even when they were still living; in Buddhism and Islam the saints were venerated as well. This veneration consisted in maintaining their graves, taking care of their bodies (sometimes by embalming), from time to time placing flowers and foods on their graves, paying respect to their images and relics, holding meals and conducting games in their honor, sending up prayers and making sacrifices to them. Though in this connection people frequently made a distinction—as they did in Persia, India, and Greece—between venerating these deceased persons and honoring the gods, still the cult of the dead was a prominent part of the religion. The purpose of this veneration by the people was in part to come to the aid of the dead but especially to avert the evil the dead could do and to ensure themselves, whether in ordinary or extraordinary ways, by oracles and miracles, of their blessing and assistance.[35]

From as early as the second century all these elements penetrated Christian worship as well. Just as monks in Buddhism and mystics in Islam, so the martyrs in the Christian church soon became the object of religious veneration. Altars, chapels, and churches were built at sites where they had died or their relics were interred. Especially on the death dates of the martyrs, believers assembled at these sites to commemorate them by vigils and the singing of psalms, reading the acts of the martyrs, listening to sermons in their honor, and especially by celebrating the Holy Eucharist. And after the fourth century this veneration of the virgin Mary, angels, patriarchs, prophets, and martyrs was extended to include bishops, monks, hermits, confessors, and virgins, as well as a variety of saints, their relics, and their images.[36] Despite resistance to this cult of the dead both in and outside the Catholic Church, it is still, in an alarming way, consistently and increasingly forcing the worship of the one true God and of Jesus Christ into the background.

In this cult the Catholic Church in a practical way celebrates the communion of the saints. The one Christian church has three divisions: the triumphant church *(ecclesia triumphans)* in heaven, the suffering church *(ecclesia patiens)* in purgatory, and the militant church *(ecclesia militans)* on earth. The share that the suffering church has in this communion consists in three things: (1) the blessed souls in heaven by their intercessions come to the aid of the poor souls in purgatory; (2) the church on earth, by its prayers, alms, good works, indulgences, and especially the offering of the Mass, seeks to soften and shorten the punishment of the souls in purgatory; (3) and, finally, the souls in purgatory, who in any case are far ahead of the majority of the members of the militant church and may for that reason be invoked, by their intercessions help and strengthen believers on earth. This latter element, while it already plays a growing role in the communion with the suffering church, nevertheless constitutes the main constituent of the communion of the militant church with the triumphant church. The blessed in heaven, like the angels, share in perfect supernatural holiness, and are for that reason the objects of adoration and veneration. In that holiness they do not all participate in the same degree; like the angels they form a spiritual hierarchy—at the top stands Mary and after her follow the patriarchs, prophets, apostles, martyrs, confessors, and so on. It is a descending series but in all of them something of the divine attributes shines forth. Participating in this sanctity, further, is everything that has in some way been connected with the saints—their body, parts of their body, clothes, dwellings, portraits, and the like. And in the measure in which a thing is closer to God and has a greater share in his holiness, to that extent it is the object of religious veneration.

In this veneration, therefore, there are also various differences. Adoration *(latria)* is due only to God. The human nature of Christ and all its parts (e.g., his holy heart) is in itself *(in se)*, not by itself and on account of itself *(per se* and *propter se)* object of *latria*. Mary is entitled to *hyperdulia*, the saints to *dulia* (veneration), their relics to relative religious devotion, and so on; there are as many kinds of adoration as there are kinds of excellence; adoration is varied according to the diversity of excellence.[37] In general, the veneration of saints consists in prayers, fastings, vigils, feast days, gifts, pilgrimages, processions, and the like; the purpose of it is, by their intercessions, to gain the favor of God and to obtain some kind of benefit from him.

This veneration and intercession, however, is not only general but also particular. There are specific saints for specific peoples, families, and persons; and there are special saints for distinct forms of distress and needs. St. George is the patron saint of England, St. James of Spain, St. Stephen of Hungary. Painters venerate St. Luke, carpenters St. Joseph, shoemakers St. Crispin. St. Sebastian is especially helpful in times of the plague; St. Ottilia in case of eye trouble; St. Anthony for recovering lost objects. Even animals have their patron saints: geese receive protection especially from St. Gall, sheep from St. Wendelin, and so forth.[38]

Many of these notions returned from time to time in Protestant theology. Lutherans acknowledged that angels as well as the saints pray for the universal church generally.[39] Just as earlier Hugo Grotius in his *Votum pro Pace* defended the invocation of saints, so Leibniz later gave his approval to this practice and even to the veneration of images and relics.[40] Ritualism in England moved in the same direction.[41] Numerous theologians assumed that after death there continues to be a certain connection between the soul and the body, that souls maintain some kind of relations with the earth, know about the most important events, pray for us, look down upon us, and bless us.[42] Many eighteenth-century thinkers, like Swedenborg, Jung-Stilling, and Oberlin, believed they were in direct contact with the spirits of the dead.[43] The possibility of such apparitions was acknowledged as well by men like Kant, Lessing, Jung-Stilling, J. H. Fichte, and others; and spiritism, which arose after 1848, seeks intentionally to put itself in touch with the spirit-world and believes it can by this route receive all kinds of revelations.[44]

To start with this latter issue, we need to note that superstitious practices occur among all peoples, also those with whom Israel came in contact, like the Egyptians (Gen. 41:8; Exod. 7:11), the Canaanites (Deut. 18:9, 14), the Babylonians (Dan. 1:20; 2:2), and so on. These practices penetrated Israel as well and often flourished there (1 Sam. 28:9; 2 Kings 21:6; Isa. 2:6). Among these practices was that of consulting the dead; those who practiced it were called ʾōbôt or yidʿōnîm (mediums or wizards). The word ʾwb refers first of all to the familiar spirit indwelling a person (Lev. 20:27), whom someone possesses (1 Sam. 28:7, 8), who is consulted by someone (1 Sam. 28:8), by whom someone can bring up a dead person (1 Sam. 28:9), and who, as the dead were imagined doing, announces oracles in a mysterious, whispering tone (Isa. 8:19; 19:3; 29:4). In the second place, it refers to the medium himself (1 Sam. 28:5, 9; 2 Kings 21:6; 2 Chron. 33:6; LXX *engastromythos*, ventriloquist). The other word yidʿōnîm, the knowers or wizards, further describes the ʾōbôt and refers, first, to the mediums and, second, to the familiar spirit that was in them (Lev. 19:31; 20:6, 27; Isa. 19:3). Soothsaying might occur in many different ways, among others by consulting the dead (Deut. 18:11).[45] But the Law and the Prophets were firmly opposed to the practice and called the people back to the Lord, his revelation, and his testimony (Exod. 22:18; Lev. 19:26, 31; 20:6, 27; Deut. 18:11; 1 Sam. 28:9; Isa. 8:19; 47:9–15; Jer. 27:9; 29:8; Mic. 3:7; 5:12; Nah. 3:4; Mal. 3:5); the New Testament puts its seal on this witness (Luke 16:29; Acts 8:9ff.; 19:13–20; Gal. 5:20; Eph. 5:11; Rev. 9:21; 21:8; 22:15).

One cannot even prove that Holy Scripture accepts the possibility of calling up the dead and having them appear. Admittedly, by God's miraculous power the dead have sometimes been raised, and Scripture acknowledges the demonic powers and workings that surpass the capacity of humans (Deut. 13:1, 2; Matt. 24:24; 2 Thess. 2:9; Rev. 13:13–15). But nowhere does it teach the possibility or reality of the dead appearing. The only passage that can be cited for this view is 1 Samuel 28, where Saul seeks out the medium at Endor. (The appearance of Moses and Elijah with Christ on the Mount of Transfiguration [Matt. 17; Luke 9] was effected by God alone without any human mediation.) But though we must reject the rationalistic explanation that only sees in this story the account of an intentional deception by the woman, neither can we accept the idea of a real, objective appearance of Samuel. The fact is Saul does not actually see Samuel (v. 14); the woman does see him but is in an hypnotic state (v. 12), and she sees him as he looked during his lifetime, as an old man wrapped in a prophet's mantle (v. 14). The woman's horror (v. 12) is not inspired by the fact that, contrary to what she expected, she really saw Samuel, but by the fact that, being in a hypnotic state and seeing Samuel, she also immediately recognized King Saul and was in dread of him. After Saul has been given the impression that a subterranean spiritual being *(ᵓlhym)* has come up from the earth and that Samuel himself had appeared, the latter speaks to Saul from within and through the woman and announces his judgment. There is nothing in 1 Samuel 28 that goes beyond the familiar phenomena of hypnotism and somnambulism and cannot be explained in the same way.

There are many people, however, who believe that precisely from these phenomena of hypnotism, somnambulism, spiritism, and the like, they must deduce the operation of spirits. But as yet this hypothesis seems completely unwarranted. Aside from the many hoaxes that have been perpetrated in this domain, the things that have been said of the appearance and operation of spirits are so puerile and insignificant that we certainly do not have to assume the involvement of the spirit world to explain them. This is not to deny that a wide range of phenomena occur that have not yet been explained; but these are all of such a nature (as, e.g., the sudden onset of the ability to understand and speak foreign languages, clairvoyance, hypnosis, suggestion, second sight, premonition, synchronic telecognition, telepathy, etc.) that they are by no means made any clearer by the hypothesis of spirit apparitions. If in addition we consider that in their perceptions human beings are bound and restricted to a specific number of etheric vibrations so that any modification in that number would show them a totally different image of the world; and that they themselves possess a rich and profound psychic life that is only partially manifest in self-consciousness, then there is, even on this side of the "other" world *(Diesseits)*, still so much room for occultism that for the time being we need not resort to the [hypothesis of] uncanny influences of the world of spirits.[46]

Further, the whole of Scripture proceeds from the idea that death is a total break with life on this side of the grave. True: the dead continue to remember the things that happened to them on earth. Both the rich man and Lazarus know who and what they were on earth and under what conditions they lived (Luke 16). In the final judgment people know what they have done on earth (Matt. 7:22). Their deeds follow those who died in the Lord (Rev. 14:13). The things we have done on earth become our moral possession and accompany us in death. There is no doubt either that the dead recognize those whom they have known on earth. The denizens of the underworld mockingly salute the king of

Babylon (Isa. 14). Out of the midst of Sheol the mighty chiefs address Egypt's king and people (Ezek. 32:21). The rich man knows Lazarus (Luke 16). The friends we make on earth by the good we do will one day receive us with joy in the eternal homes (Luke 16:9).

But for the rest, Scripture consistently tells us that at death all fellowship with this earth ends. The dead no longer have a share in anything that happens under the sun (Eccl. 9:5, 6, 10). Whether their children come to honor or are brought low, the dead do not know of it (Job 14:21). Abraham does not know of the children of Israel, and Jacob does not recognize them either; therefore they call to the Lord since he is their Father (Isa. 63:16). Nowhere is there any sign that the dead are in contact with the living: they belong to another realm, one that is totally separate from the earth. Nor does Hebrews 12:1 teach us that the great cloud of witnesses see and watch us in our struggles. For the *martyres* are not eyewitnesses of our struggle but witnesses of faith who serve to encourage us.

For that reason there is no room for the invocation and veneration of saints. By itself there is nothing strange or improper in the idea that the angels and the blessed make intercession for people on earth. Indeed, Protestants frequently also accepted an interest [on their part] in the history of the militant church and a general intercession [on its behalf]. But for that reason it is all the more remarkable that while Scripture so often mentions the intercession of people on earth and specifically recommends and prescribes it (Matt. 6:9f.; Rom. 15:30; Eph. 6:18, 19; Col. 1:2, 3; 1 Tim. 2:1, 2) and further teaches that God frequently spares others for the sake of the elect and upon their intercession (Gen. 18:23ff.; Exod. 32:11ff.; Num. 14:13ff.; Ezek. 14:14, 20; Matt. 24:22, etc.), it never breathes a word about intercession by angels and the blessed in heaven for those who live on earth. With respect to the intercession of angels we have already demonstrated this earlier[47] and concerning the intercession of the blessed dead Roman Catholics themselves admit that it does not occur in Scripture.[48] Only 2 Maccabees 15:12–14 refers, in a vision of Judas, to the intercession of Onias and Jeremiah for their people, which proves only that at that time the Jews were convinced of the intercession of the blessed dead for people on earth.

There is still less basis for the invocation and veneration of the saints. Holy Scripture does say that believers on earth may appeal to each other for intercession (Num. 21:7; Jer. 42:2; 1 Thess. 5:25), but never mentions asking the dead for their intercession; and both angels and human beings expressly refuse to accept the religious veneration that is due only to God (Deut. 6:13; 10:20; Matt. 4:10; Acts 14:10ff.; Col. 1:18, 19; Rev. 19:10; 22:9). Nor is there any reference to the veneration of relics. Even though God sometimes performs miracles through them

(2 Kings 13:21; Matt. 9:21; Luke 6:19; Acts 5:15; 19:12), they must not be the objects of veneration (Deut. 34:6; 2 Kings 18:4; 2 Cor. 5:16). Oswald, accordingly, counts the invocation and veneration of saints among the "dogmas of tradition." Even if one grants a general intercession of the saints for believers on earth, it by no means follows that they may be invoked and venerated for that purpose. Granted, a request for someone's intercession is absolutely not wrong as such and therefore occurs regularly among believers. But such a request always assumes a means of communication and must be conveyed either orally or in writing. And this is precisely what is lacking and diametrically opposed to what Scripture teaches concerning the state of the dead. Rome, therefore, does not dare to say that the invocation and veneration of saints is mandated and necessary, but only that "it is good and useful suppliantly to invoke them."[49]

Theology can in no way make clear how the saints come to know of our prayers, and hence proposes a range of conjectures. Some believe that they are conveyed to them by angels who regularly visit the earth, or that the saints, like the angels, can travel at miraculous speeds and are in a sense ubiquitous. Others are of the opinion that the saints are informed by God himself concerning the content of our prayers or envision all the things they need to know in the consciousness of God. There are also theologians who say that it is not necessary for them to know everything, provided they have a general idea of our needs; or that we need not be concerned about the way they learn of our prayers.[50] Further, Roman Catholics absolutely do not know with certainty which of the dead are in heaven and in the category of perfect saints. The faithful of the Old Testament were first in the limbo of the fathers and, though they were moved to heaven by Christ, they are too far removed from us to be invoked.[51] Concerning some of the New Testament faithful, such as Mary, the apostles, and some of the later martyrs, Rome does assume that they have been taken up into heaven, but this is the case with only a few and even here we may be in error. In earlier times it was the voice of the people that accorded the attribute of sanctity to one who had died; and in some cases it happened that men who possessed this attribute lost it again, as did Clement of Alexandria by the action of Pope Benedict XIV. To prevent these errors, the ecclesiastical act of declaring someone a saint, that is, canonization, has since Alexander III and Innocent III become a prerogative of the apostolic see.[52] In this connection, however, it is a question again whether in this canonization the pope is infallible. And though this may in fact be the case, the pope of course makes rare use of his prerogative. By far the majority of saints are invoked and venerated without it being known precisely whether they are in heaven or are still in purgatory. One has to be content with a moral conviction, and consider in addition that a possible error need not have any bad consequences, and for safety's sake extend the invocation to the "poor souls" in purgatory, which is what is increasingly happening in practice.[53]

In the Church of Rome the invocation of saints is certainly no longer merely a request for their intercession *(ora pro nobis)* but changed gradually into a kind of adoration and veneration. The saints are the objects of religious veneration *(cultus religiosus)*, even if it is not called worship *(latria)* but veneration *(dulia)*. Now there is no doubt that if we should meet angels or the blessed dead, or if we had some kind of personal contact with them, we would owe them respectful homage. But precisely this circumstance does not occur. And consequently all invocation of angels and the blessed dead ends in a kind of religious veneration that is not made right by the name *dulia*. On the road on which Rome is going with this veneration of creatures, there is simply no stopping. Holiness is conceived by it as a superadded gift *(donum superadditum)*, as something substantial that can be communicated in various measure to all creatures, and may then be religiously venerated in proportion. To the degree that a person or thing participates in the divine holiness, they may claim a kind of religious homage *(cultus religiosus)*. First of all possessing this prerogative, then, are Mary, the apostles, martyrs, and saints, but further all and everything that has been in contact with them or still exists in relation to them, hence relics, images, dwellings, and the like. By this principle all creatures can rightfully be religiously venerated "because and to the degree each has a relationship to God," including even the hands of the soldiers who arrested Jesus and the lips of Judas that kissed him.[54] In any case I see no reason why the saints who are on earth should not already be invoked and venerated by Catholic Christians, among them especially the pope, the saint par excellence. "As such there is no objection whatever to extending religious veneration to holiness as it occurs on earth. So then, if one were completely convinced of the godliness of a person, it could as such be venerated as this is done in the case of the saints in heaven. In individual cases it may have occurred privately and perhaps still does."[55] Whatever Oswald further advances against it is based on utility and shows that the veneration of living saints, specifically of the pope, is merely a matter of time in the Roman Catholic Church. The communion of saints degenerates into mutual veneration that crowds the mediator of God and humanity into the background.

Between Death and Resurrection 3

Scripture clearly teaches a distinction between the destiny of the righteous and unrighteous after death but not a great deal about their exact condition. Over the years many have inquired about the possibility of a second chance to respond to the gospel. This idea of a mission station in Hades has no scriptural ground, not even in 1 Peter 3:18–22, which is frequently appealed to. Similarly, the initially attractive notion of postdeath purification, including the Roman Catholic doctrine of purgatory, also has no basis in Scripture. In fact, any and all self-sanctification, in this life or the next, is wholly unnecessary since Christ's perfect obedience fully entitles the believer to eternal life. In a juridical sense all the benefits of Christ are possessed by believers now. Yet their earthly pilgrimage ends only at death when they enter their homeland. When we die, we die to sin. The idea of purgatory is unnecessary as well as illogical; it is not at all clear how purgatory's fires purify and cleanse. Since the doctrine of purgatory is untenable, all offerings and intercessions for the dead are useless and weaken confidence in the sufficiency of Christ's sacrifice and his effectual intercession. Nonetheless, there still is and remains a communion between the church militant on earth and the church triumphant in heaven that cannot be broken. Though the souls of believers in heaven experience no change of status they are confirmed and grow in their knowledge and love of God.

Up until now we have only discussed whether the dead still have any kind of contact with life on earth. Now the question arises whether Scripture teaches us anything about the new relations and conditions in which the dead find themselves on the other side of the grave. What Scripture reports on this subject is not a lot. Still, already in the Old Testament the lines are present which, when extended, lead to a difference in the state of the righteous and the unrighteous after death. The fear of the Lord leads to life, but the ungodly perish and are ruined. And according to the New Testament the rich man immediately enters a place of torment, which, however, is not identical with Gehenna or the abyss. We are not told in Scripture where we must look for it. It is true that

Sheol, Hades, Gehenna, and the abyss are always represented as being below us. But this cannot and must not be understood topographically. The concepts "above" and "below," taken in a local sense, are very relative and in this context have only ethical significance. We locate the kingdom of darkness directly across from the kingdom of light and in accordance with a natural symbolism look for the first below and for the second above us. All fixation of the place of punishment of the dead—in the earth, under the earth, in the sea, in the sun, in the air, or on one of the planets—is mere conjecture. What *can* be stated is that the Beyond is not only a state but also a place, for though souls may not be circumscribed by time and space, they are certainly far from being eternal and omnipresent; they must be somewhere and pass through a succession of moments in time. For the rest it is more in keeping with the sparse data Scripture offers us to abstain from any attempt to determine the place of punishment of the dead. "Do not ask where it is but how you may escape it" (Chrysostom).

Nor do we know anything more about the state in which unbelievers and the ungodly are after death up until the last judgment. All we can say with certainty is that if here already the wrath of God continues to weigh on unbelievers, how much more intensely will it not weigh on them after death, when all the distractions of earthly life are absent and their naked existence is filled with nothing other than the consciousness and sense of that wrath.

A Second Opportunity?

The question has been raised, however, whether on the other side of the grave, for those who have not heard the gospel here on earth or only very dimly, there will not be another opportunity to repent and to believe in Christ. The first ones in the Christian church to give an affirmative answer to that question were Clement and Origen. They inferred from 1 Peter 3:18, 19 that Christ and also the apostles had proclaimed the gospel to the dead in Hades who were susceptible to it. Although Augustine and others refuted this sentiment and though Christ's descent into hell is usually interpreted differently, the idea kept coming back and in the case of many people found acceptance in the nineteenth century when the huge number and rapid increase of non-Christians began to dawn on them. It is indeed a fact of the greatest significance that there have been and still are millions of people who have never had any knowledge of the way of salvation in Christ and therefore never were in a position to embrace him with a believing heart or decisively to reject him. These people cannot be numbered among the unbelievers in a strict sense and Scripture itself says that they must be judged by a different standard than Jews and Christians (Matt. 10:15; 11:20–24; Luke 10:12–25; 12:47, 48; John 15:22; Rom. 2:12; 2 Peter 2:20–22).

From this it does not follow, however, that there is or has to be preaching of the gospel on the other side of the grave. For Scripture never speaks of it with a single word. Many passages that have at times been advanced for this view (such as Matt. 12:40; John 20:17; Acts 2:24, 27, 31; 13:29, 30, 30–37; 1 Tim. 3:16) have not the least evidential value and certainly do not deal with the preaching of Christ in hell. Nor does Ezekiel 16:53–63 open up any perspective on this subject; the Lord there promises that despite the horrors perpetrated in Jerusalem, horrors worse than those in her sisters Sodom and Samaria, he will in the end restore it and accept it in mercy. Now in order to take away all false confidence in God's promise and all pride on the part of Israel, there is added that the Lord will not only restore the fortunes of Jerusalem but also those of Sodom and Samaria (v. 53), so that these too will return to their earlier state. From these data some have concluded that there is a possibility of conversion in the intermediate state. They reason that in Ezekiel's time Sodom and its sisters, that is, the other cities in the Valley of Siddim, had all long ago been destroyed and therefore could not be restored to their former state and be accepted by God in grace if their earlier inhabitants had not been converted by the preaching of the Word of God in Sheol. But this notion is far removed from the text. The Lord here promises only that he will again, despite its harlotry, accept Jerusalem in grace; and, besides, that Sodom and Samaria, which are evidently (cf. v. 61) types of all Gentile nations, will be restored to their former state; that is, in the future Jerusalem will be restored and the Gentile cities will be subject to it. But there is no question of preaching and conversion in Sheol, or of a resurrection and return of the earlier inhabitants of Sodom and Samaria.

The only texts to which one can appeal for a preaching of the gospel in Hades with some semblance of justification are 1 Peter 3:19–21 and 4:6. But these texts, also, do not contain what people wish to read in them. Even if it were true that they speak of a proclamation by Christ after his resurrection to the contemporaries of Noah in Hades, that would only establish the fact that it occurred, but by no means warrant the teaching that there is ongoing preaching of the gospel in Hades to all who have not heard it on earth. The truth, after all, is that Noah's contemporaries were precisely not the kind of people who had never during their lifetime heard the Word of God on earth; on the contrary, they had willfully and maliciously despised the word of Noah, the preacher of righteousness, and had disobeyed the voice of the Lord in the full consciousness of doing so. Accordingly, they were a very special case that provides no warrant for any further conclusions. Also, the aorist *ekēryxen* indicates that this preaching by Christ occurred only once. This preaching, furthermore, cannot have been a proclamation of the gospel unto salvation. If one recalls how severely and consistently Scripture judges all the ungodly and how it always describes the generation of Noah's contemporaries as people who gave themselves up to all kinds of evil and unrighteousness, it becomes preposterous to think that Christ would have proclaimed the gospel of salvation to them above all others. At most, as the old Lutherans explained the text, the reference is to a solemn announcement of his triumph to the denizens of the underworld. In addition, all kinds of difficulties attend such ongoing preaching of the gospel in Hades. According to 1 Peter 3:18, 19, Christ delivered that preaching specifically after he had been made alive and was risen. Did he at that time go physically to Hades? When did he do that? How long did he stay there? And suppose all this were possible—however unlikely it is as such—who then is conducting this preaching in Hades on an ongoing basis after this time? Is there a church in the underworld? Is there an ongoing mission, a calling and ordination to ministry? Are they humans or angels, apostles or other ministers of the Word, who after their death are proclaiming the gospel there? The theory of a mission center in Hades is, in a variety of ways, in conflict with Scripture.

But, as demonstrated earlier,[1] it lacks all support in 1 Peter 3:18–22 as well. All we are told there is that after his resurrection, Christ, made alive in the spirit, went to heaven and by his ascension preached to the spirits in prison and made angels, authorities, and powers subject to him. Nor does 1 Peter 4:6 make any mention of such gospel preaching in Hades. The aorist *euēngelisthē* by its very form refers not to ongoing preaching but to a specific event. That proclamation of the gospel occurred once, and with the intent that those who heard it would be judged like everyone else, "in the flesh," that is, they would die, but might live, as God does, "in the spirit." The preaching of the gospel, therefore, preceded their death; the *nekroi* are those who are now dead but who heard the gospel during their lifetime. The reason why Peter calls these people *nekroi* can be found in the previous verse. There we read that Christ "stands ready to judge the living and the dead." Now then, just as the gospel is preached to the living today, so it was in the past preached to those who are now dead, so that, while they would indeed still die in the flesh [as everyone else does], they would nevertheless even now already live in the spirit in God's presence.

Given these objections, which are derived from Scripture, the entire theory of gospel preaching in the intermediate state collapses. For if it is not in Scripture, theology is not free to advocate it. But there are still many other objections as well. Assuming that the gospel is still being preached in Hades, is that preaching addressed to everyone without distinction? Usually the answer given is "no," and restricts it to those who did not hear of it on earth. This is not only in conflict with their exegesis of 1 Peter 3:18–22 (for if the reference in this passage is to gospel preaching by Christ in Hades, it is addressed precisely to those who *did* hear the gospel through Noah), it also automatically raises the question whether life here on earth is totally immaterial to that preaching of the gospel in Hades. To this question, too, people understandably do not dare to give a negative answer as a rule, for then this life would be completely without value or meaning. For that reason, along with Clement and Origen, they usually say that in the intermediate state the gospel is addressed only to those who are susceptible to conversion— people who, on earth, by their attitude toward the real calling *(vocatio realis)*,[2] have prepared themselves for an acceptance by faith of the gospel.[3] By saying this one in fact again shifts the point of gravity back to this life, and the preaching of the gospel in Hades only brings to light what was already hidden in human hearts here on earth. That is to say, the decision with respect to salvation and perdition is made, not in response to the gospel, but in response to the real calling *(vocatio realis)*, the law. And in essence this is the same opinion that was held also by the Pelagians, Socinians, deists, and the like, namely, that there are three ways to salvation: the law of nature, the Mosaic law, and the law of Christ.

To be added to this is that the theory of a kind of gospel preaching in Hades is based on an array of incorrect assumptions. Basic to it is that it is God's intent to save all humans; that the preaching of the gospel has to be absolutely universal; that all humans must be personally and individually confronted by the choice for or against the gospel; that in making that choice the decision lies in human power; that original and actual sins are insufficient to condemn anyone and that only deliberate unbelief toward the gospel makes a person worthy of eternal ruin. All these assumptions are in conflict with firm scriptural statements and make the theory of gospel preaching in the intermediate state unacceptable. And if, finally, the question is asked whether it is not hard to believe that all those who here on earth, quite aside from any responsibility of their own, failed to hear the gospel are lost, then the answer which has to be given is this: (a) that in this most solemn matter not our feeling but the Word of God decides; (b) that the theory of a preaching of the gospel to the dead in no way relieves the problem, inasmuch as it only helps those who had already prepared themselves for the faith here on earth; (c) that it even aggravates the problem because it pays no attention to the interest of the millions of children who die in infancy and in fact excludes them from the possibility of being saved; and (d) that it takes no account of the sovereign freedom and omnipotence of God, which can save also without the external preaching of the Word, solely by the internal calling and regeneration of the Holy Spirit.

Purification?

The state of deceased believers who have not yet attained full holiness here on earth is conceived by the Church of Rome as a purification of souls by the punishment of fire. The idea of such a state of purification is of pagan origin and occurred especially in two forms. The theory of the transmigration of souls, which is found among the people of India, Egyptians, Greeks, Jews, and the like, holds that before entering the human body the soul has already lived in other bodies; after it has left the human body it also enters new organisms—all with a view to self-purification and ultimately reaching perfection. This theory is too contrary to Scripture for it ever to have found acceptance, aside from a few sects and individual persons, within the bounds of Christianity. It proceeds, after all, from the idea that souls are preexistent, that originally they did not possess a body and are indifferent to all bodies. It is, moreover, in conflict with the doctrine of redemption accomplished by Christ and views purification and perfection as the work of humans themselves. And, finally, it entirely fails to make clear how souls, by repeatedly passing into other bodies, could be freed from sins and trained toward holiness.[4]

Another idea, one that had greater influence on Christian theology, is that souls after death still need to be purified for a time by an assortment of punishments before they can attain the highest level of blessedness. In Parsism we encounter the belief that following the general resurrection there is a three-day period of purification in molten metal that feels gentle to the good but is very painful to the evil.[5] The Jews taught that only the perfectly righteous went immediately to heaven; the others were consigned to Gehinnom, which according to some was a purgatory for all people but in any case it was that for the Jews.[6] Since Origen this conception also filtered out among Christians, there leading to the Catholic doctrine of purgatory or a period of purification, which is accepted by many Protestants.

At first blush this idea is quite appealing. Believers, after all, at the moment of their death are all still saddled with sin; even the most saintly still possess only a small beginning of perfect obedience. This sin that adheres to believers, furthermore, is not rooted in the body but in the soul, which for that reason cannot enter heaven unless it is freed in advance from the guilt of sin and completely purged of its pollution. It is hard to picture how this purification could suddenly take place at, or as a result of, death. Not only is sanctification in this life a slow process; in every domain of life sudden transitions are virtually unknown while gradual growth and development is everywhere. Hence everything favors the idea that after death the souls of believers need to undergo a purification before being taken up into heaven and admitted to the vision of God.

However, no matter what human argumentation would favor such a purgatory, the primary and conclusive objection is that Scripture nowhere speaks of it. Roman Catholic theologians admittedly advance a number of texts, but none of them really serves their purpose. Matthew 5:22 does not breathe a word about a purgatory but does refer to Gehenna. To take "prison" *(phylakē)* in Matthew 5:25 to mean purgatory is arbitrary; it is rather an image of Gehenna, for one who ends up in it has been previously condemned by a judge and will never have a chance to pay off the debt and to leave prison; the "until" *(eōs)* in verse 26 indicates an unfulfillable period (cf. 18:30, 34). In Matthew 12:32 Jesus says that blaspheming against the Holy Spirit will not be forgiven in either this age or the age to come. The words "or in the age to come" only serve to underscore the unpardonability of blaspheming against the Holy Spirit and hence by no means presuppose that some sins can still be forgiven even after this life. But even if this were the case, this text would still not prove anything to support the doctrine of purgatory, for the reference here is to the forgiveness of sin, whereas purgatory is not at all a place for forgiveness but only a place for "paying off" temporal punishments. The text speaks of forgiveness in the age to come, that is, the time after the parousia, while purgatory occurs before the parousia and ends with the last judgment.

According to 1 Corinthians 3:12–15, the work of the ministers of the church must stand up under testing in the day of Christ's parousia. Those who have built on the foundation of Christ with gold, silver, and precious stones, that is, those who in their office and ministry have done solid work, though they will be tested in their work, will receive a reward since the work proves to stand up under the fire of judgment. Those, on the other hand, who have built on the foundation with wood, hay, and straw—which cannot withstand the fire—will suffer the loss of their reward, though they themselves will be saved through the fire of judgment. So, in fact, we read here of a revelatory fire (v. 13), a testing fire (v. 13), and a consuming fire (v. 15); but this is how Paul presents the fire of judgment in the future of Christ and therefore has no room for a purgatory that would purify believers now and end *before* the final judgment. Other texts on which the Church of Rome could base its doctrine of purgatory—if only with some semblance of justification—are nonexistent. Only one passage in the Old Testament apocrypha, 2 Mac-

cabees 12:41–45, shows that the Jews at that time considered offerings
and prayers for the dead who had died in their sins to be a good and
necessary thing—something we know from other sources as well. It is
therefore all the more noteworthy that this folk belief existing among
the Jews is never reported, much less sanctioned, in either the Old or
the New Testament.

The doctrine of purgatory is most closely bound up with justification. By justification the Church of Rome understands the infusion of
supernatural sanctifying grace that in turn enables humans to do good
works and thereby earn eternal life. This grace, however, is subject to
being increased and decreased; one who loses it as a result of mortal sin
and then dies is lost; one who by keeping the precepts and counsels
makes it to perfection in the hour of death immediately enters heaven.
However, one who still has to pay the debt and bear the temporal punishment due to a venial sin or who, after having in the sacrament of penance received back the infused grace lost as a result of a mortal sin is at
his death still in arrears in "paying off" the temporal punishments, is
consigned to purgatory and remains there until he has paid the last
penny. In the Church of Rome justification, sanctification, and glorification is the work of humans themselves, be it on the basis of the supernatural grace infused into them. After receiving it they have to make
themselves worthy of eternal life and the beatific vision of God in
heaven by a condign or full merit;[7] if they fail to achieve this on earth
they must—just as the pagans pictured it—continue the work on earth
in the hereafter until they have attained perfection.

But from Scripture the Reformation again learned to know the justification of sinners by faith and therefore had to come to a rejection of
the fire of purification. Christ accomplished everything; not only did he
bear the punishment, but he also won eternal life for us by his keeping
of the law. And all the benefits that Christ gained by his suffering and
death and that are present and available in him in perfection are immediately conferred on those who believe in truth. He who believes *has*
eternal life. In justification not only the merit of Christ's passive obedience is imputed but also that of his active obedience. In that benefac-
tion believers receive forgiveness, exemption from punishment, and are
not returned to the prefall state of Adam, who with the power granted
him had to keep the law and earn eternal life. On the contrary: on the
basis of Christ's perfect obedience they are immediately entitled to eternal life; the holy works accomplished by Christ are credited to them;
they do not, by keeping the law, have to earn eternal life, but do good
works based on the principle of eternal life already granted to them in
faith. Accordingly, sanctification here is not self-preparation for
heaven, or self-perfection, but solely the unfolding in believers of what

they already possess in Christ, a walking in the good works that God in Christ prepared [for them] (Eph. 2:10). God therefore does not have to wait for any more good works before he can receive believers in heaven, inasmuch as in Christ that heaven is at once opened to everyone who believes. Those who believe have forgiveness and eternal life; they are ready and fit for heaven and need not go through a purgatory either here or hereafter. Even the suffering they often still—and even as a result of sin—have to bear on earth is not a punishment, a penalty, a required late payment of the demands of the law, but a fatherly chastisement that serves their maturation.

The End of Our Pilgrimage

On a Reformational basis, then, the only question is this: When do believers enter into full possession of the benefits of Christ granted them? Those who believe receive them at once in a juridical sense; in Christ they are entitled to all the goods of the covenant, the whole of salvation. But on earth they do not yet enter into full possession. When, then, does this occur? When do believers cease to be pilgrims and arrive in their homeland? To this question Scripture has but one answer: at death. Nowhere does it represent the godly after death as still being tormented by punishment or suffering due to sin. The godly always express as their certain expectation that at death they will have reached the end of their pilgrimage and entrance into the eternal blessed life in heaven (Ps. 73:24, 25; Luke 23:43; Acts 7:59; 2 Cor. 5:1; Phil. 1:23; 2 Tim. 4:7). After death there is no longer any sanctification; a state of sanctity begins in which the spirits of the righteous made perfect (Heb. 12:23) are clothed in long white garments and stand before the throne and before the Lamb (Rev. 7:2, 4). The story is told of the modest de Saci of Port Royal that he always lived in the fear of God and consequently never dared hope for immediate blessedness after death but at his death cried out: "O blessed purgatory!" But such a state of mind is entirely foreign to the godly of the Old and New Testaments and can only be explained on the assumption that such a person, looking at himself, is blind to the finished work of Christ.

Of course, the manner in which the state of holiness commences immediately at the death of believers cannot be understood or clearly described. Regeneration and sanctification effected here on earth by the Holy Spirit is a mystery as well. But there is no doubt that death serves as a means. Not in the sense of Platonic dualism, as though the soul's mere liberation from the body would already constitute its sanctification, for sin is rooted precisely in the soul. Nor in the sense of sentimental rationalism, which has death, as a messenger of peace, turn people

into angels, for death as such is a revelation of God's wrath and the
wages of sin. But death does serve as such a means according to Scripture, which views it for the believer as a dying to sin. For all discipline
is for our good that we may share God's holiness (Heb. 12:10). Those
who like Christ suffer in the flesh because of sin cease from sin (1 Peter
4:1). But this is especially true of death. The consequence of ethical
death, that is, dying to sin in communion with Christ, is that a person
is freed from and dead to sin and henceforth lives for God in Christ
(Rom. 6:6–11; 8:10; 1 Peter 2:24). And this ethical death culminates in
physical death (Rom. 7:24; 2 Cor. 5:1; Phil. 1:21, 23). Death is an enormous change, a breaking of all ties with this earthly life and an entering
into a new world with totally different conditions and relations. It is not
at all strange that, as he does with all suffering, God should employ
death as a means of sanctifying the soul of the believer and cleansing it
from all the stains of sin.[8] Against this we cannot raise the objection
that such a sanctification is mechanical and occurs in one leap, for
death is the biggest leap a person can take, a sudden relocation of the
believer into the presence of Christ and consequently a total destruction
of the outer "man" and a total renewal of the inner "man."

Add to this that the doctrine of purgatory in no way makes this sanctification of the believer any more understandable. In the first place,
Catholic theology has to accord to death a similar critical significance.
Purgatory, after all, is not a place where sins are still forgiven, but
where still-remaining temporal punishments can be "paid off." So those
who have committed venial sins and did not receive forgiveness for
them in this life must receive it in death. Catholic theologians, accordingly, teach that the soul that dies in venial sin, in death immediately
receives the forgiveness of sin in order subsequently to satisfy in purgatory the temporal punishments stipulated for those sins. It is, thus, not
at all clear how purgatory brings about the sanctification of souls. Aside
from the fact that Catholics usually describe purgatory as a material
fire, which by that token cannot have an "ideal" impact on the soul,
there is the question of how pain as such can sanctify a soul. That would
indeed be possible if by means of the torment repentance, contrition,
conversion, faith, love, and the like could be effected in the soul. But on
the Catholic view that may not be assumed. For purgatory is not a mission center, no institution for conversion, no school of sanctification,
but a place where only temporal punishment can be "paid off." So, on
the one hand, the "poor souls" can no longer sin and take on new guilt,
and on the other they cannot improve themselves either, for all improvement implies merit and in purgatory the possibility of merit is excluded. Consequently, it is impossible for us to form any clear notion of
the state of these "poor souls." If they are to be pictured as still more or

less stained by sin, then on the Catholic view it is impossible to understand how they should not continue to sin and so again completely suffer the loss of the grace received. If this possibility is excluded, then the souls are inherently pure and holy and only still have to bear certain temporal punishments they could not bear on earth; but then it is again incomprehensible that the perfectly righteous could still be temporarily excluded from heaven and subjected to the torments of purgatory. In both cases it remains puzzling how purgatory can be a "purifying fire" *(ignis purgatorius)*; it is nothing but a fire of retribution *(ignis vindicativus)*. Oswald correctly points out that the purifying character of purgatory belongs among the more difficult questions![9]

Finally, various questions remain that the doctrine of purgatory fails to answer. According to Catholic belief, the Old Testament devout went to the limbo of the fathers *(limbus patrum)*. The question is: Is this limbo to be pictured as a purgatory, or did they not need a purgatory? And how are we to think of the purification of those who die shortly before the parousia and consequently can no longer enter purgatory, since it ceases to exist when this world comes to an end? The souls of those who died in earlier ages have much more to endure than those who enter purgatory later, inasmuch as the duration of torment in purgatory becomes increasingly shorter. How do Catholics square this fact with the justice of God and the soul's need for purification? If the answer is that to the extent that the end of the world approaches, sanctification is shifted increasingly to the suffering of the present time and to the moment of death, then one seriously undermines the doctrine of purgatory and comes close to the view adopted by the Reformation against this doctrine.

Intercession for the Dead?

If the doctrine of purgatory is untenable, all offerings and prayers for the dead automatically come down with it. Veneration of the dead by sacrifices and prayers was common among pagans. Intercession for the dead became a practice among the Jews later (2 Macc. 12:40–45) and remains in use to the present.[10] In the Christian church there soon arose the custom of wishing the dead peace, light, and refreshment *(refrigerium)* and to remember them in prayers and at the celebration of the Lord's Supper. In the early period this was done with respect to all who died in the Lord without distinction and these offerings and sacrifices were solely memorial in nature. But gradually a distinction was made between the souls who were immediately taken up into heaven and others who still had to spend time in purgatory. Communion with the first then gradually began to be practiced by invocation and veneration; with the second, by intercessions, good works, indulgences, and Masses for the soul.[11] In the ancient Catholic sense—as prayer to God that he would increase the blessedness of those who died in Christ and hear their prayers for the living, and simultaneously as commemoration of and communion with the dead—intercession for the dead was also approved by the Greeks, the Lutherans, Hugo Grotius, many Anglicans, and certain more recent theologians.[12]

But the Reformed rejected this intercession for the dead on the ground that their lot was unalterably decided at death.[13] The fact is that neither the Old nor the New Testament breathes a word about such intercession. The only passage to which appeal can be made is 1 Corinthians 15:29, where Paul mentions those who had themselves baptized *hyper tōn nekrōn*. However, from this it cannot be inferred that such a baptism was received by the living for the benefit of the dead. There is no evidence whatever that such a practice existed in Paul's time or later. True, Tertullian and others report that this custom was found among the followers of Cerinthus and Marcion; but in the first place the correctness of this report is subject to doubt and, second, [if it is correct] the implication is that it was a heretical practice that never found acceptance in the Christian church. Those who would use the text to ground the right to pray for the dead should first of all begin by baptizing the living on behalf of the dead, so that that baptism could benefit them. Paul cites the dead as the reason why the living had themselves baptized. Because those who had died in Christ would rise again, because of what they stood for and on their behalf, the living who were believers had themselves baptized. The apostle here is only expressing the thought that baptism presupposes belief in the resurrection of Christ and of believers. Take away the resurrection and baptism becomes an empty ceremony.

Intercession for the dead, therefore, has no basis whatever in Scripture, as Tertullian for that matter already recognized. For after he had discussed various church practices, including sacrifices for the dead (*De Corona Militus*, ch. 3), he added in chapter 4: "If, for these and other such rules, you insist on having positive scriptural injunction, you will find none. Tradition will be held forth to you as the originator of them, custom as their strengthener, and faith as their observer."[14] Because there is no prescription of the Father we have to content ourselves with the custom of the mother, that is, the church, which thus again receives a position alongside of and above the Word of God. Since, then, intercession for the dead cannot stand the test of Scripture, the question concerning its utility and comfort is no longer appropriate. All the same, these two things are hardly demonstrable either. For though it seems a beautiful thing that the living can help the dead by their intercessions and make up for the wrong they have perhaps done to them during their lifetime, in fact this church practice takes Christian piety in a totally wrong direction. It gives the impression that—contrary to Matthew 8:22—caring for the dead is of greater value than love for the living; it credits one's own works and prayers with a meritorious expiatory power that is effective even on the other side of the grave and benefits the dead; it is based on and conducive to the doctrine of purgatory, which on the one hand, especially among the rich, fosters unconcern and on the other hand perpetuates the uncertainty of believers; and in the minds of Christians it weakens confidence in the sufficiency of the sacrifice and intercession of Christ.[15]

Communion with the Church Triumphant

Although there is no room for the veneration of saints and intercession for the dead, there still is and remains a communion between the church militant on earth and the church triumphant in heaven that cannot be broken. Believers on earth, when they became Christians, came to the heavenly Jerusalem above, which is the mother of us all; to the innumerable angels who serve and praise God there; to the assembly of the firstborn, that is, the devout of the Old Testament who are enrolled in heaven and have their citizenship there; to the spirits of the just, that is, the Christians who have already died and reached perfection, the consummation; to Christ the mediator of the New Testament and to God the judge of all (Heb. 12:22–24).

This communion does not imply that there has to be direct interaction between the members of the militant and triumphant segments of the church, for though this is lacking also between the different persons and peoples who lived at different times and places on earth, humankind is still an organism made up of one blood. The personal contacts that every believer has here on earth are limited to a few persons, but believers are nevertheless members of one holy catholic Christian church. The unity that binds all believers together, the dead as well as the living, is anchored in Christ, and through him in fellowship with the same Father, in the possession of the same Spirit, and in joint participation in the same treasures of salvation. The love that remains even when faith and hope disappear permanently unites all believers with Christ and each other. And that love expresses itself on our part in the fact that we remember with deep respect the saints who have preceded us; speak of them worthily; imitate their faith and good works and, spurred on by their example, run with patience the course that is set before us; feel one with them and live in anticipation of going to them, that together with them and all created beings we may magnify the Lord.

Among the forms in which the communion of the church militant with the church triumphant manifests itself, the hope of reunion occupies a large place. Rationalism, indeed, has made appalling misuse of this fact. It seemed as if the blessedness of heaven consisted not in fellowship with Christ but in the sentimental enjoyment of one another's presence. But nevertheless there is here a good and true element. The hope of reunion on the other side of the grave is completely natural, genuinely human, and also in keeping with Scripture. For Scripture does not teach us a naked immortality of spectral souls but the eternal life of individual persons. Regeneration does not erase individuality, personality, or character, but sanctifies it and puts it at the service of God's name. The community of believers is the new humanity that bears within itself a wide range of variety and distinction and manifests the richest diversity in unity. The joy of heaven, to be sure, first of all consists in communion with Christ but, further, in the fellowship of the blessed among themselves as well. And just as this fellowship on earth, though it is always imperfect, does not infringe on the fellowship of believers with Christ but rather reinforces and enriches it, so it is in heaven. Paul's highest desire was to depart and to be with Christ (Phil. 1:23; 1 Thess. 4:17). But Jesus himself represents the joy of heaven by the image of a meal at which all the guests sit down with Abraham, Isaac, and Jacob (Matt. 8:11; cf. Luke 13:28). The hope of reunion is not bad in itself, therefore, as long as it remains subordinate to the desire for fellowship with Christ.

Nor is it absurd to think that the blessed in heaven yearn for the believers who are on earth. After all, they have a store of memories of the persons and conditions they knew on earth (Luke 16:27–31). The souls under the altar cry out for vengeance on account of the blood that had been shed (Rev. 6:10). The bride, that is, the entire community of believers both in heaven and on earth, pray for the coming of the Lord Jesus (Rev. 22:17). Although Scripture gives us no warrant for believing that the blessed in heaven know everything that happens here on earth, still it is likely that they know as much about the church militant on earth as the latter does about them. And that small amount of knowledge, added to the knowledge that they possess from memory and that is perhaps regularly augmented by statements made by angels and the recently deceased, is sufficient to prompt them to think with ongoing warm interest about this earth and the mighty struggle taking place here. An added ingredient is that the state of the blessed in heaven, however glorious, still for various reasons bears a provisional character. After all, at this stage they are only in heaven and restricted to heaven and not yet in possession of the earth, the inheritance of which has been promised them along with that of heaven. Further, they are deprived of the body and this incorporeal existence is not, as dualism must hold, a gain but a loss, not an increase but a diminution of being, inasmuch as the body is integral to our humanity.

Finally, the part cannot be complete without the whole; the fullness of Christ's love can only be known in communion with all the saints (Eph. 3:18, 19); the one group of believers cannot be made perfect without the other (Heb. 11:40). For that reason there is still room in the case of the blessed in heaven for faith and hope, for longing and prayer (Rev. 6:10; 22:17). Like believers on earth, they eagerly await the return of Christ, the resurrection of the dead, and the restoration of all things. Only then has the end been reached (1 Cor. 15:24). This idea is so much in the foreground in Scripture that by comparison the intermediate state shrinks into a brief span of time of which no account whatever is taken at the final judgment. It is nowhere stated that also that which has been accomplished by the dead in the intermediate state will be judged before the judgment seat of Christ on the last day. That judgment exclusively concerns that which has been done in the body, whether good or evil (2 Cor. 5:10): to that extent the universal judgment is identical with the personal and particular judgment.

However, this still gives us no warrant to conclude with Kliefoth[16] that the souls after death live outside space and time and are denied all development or progress. For though there is certainly no progress like that on earth, and still less a possible change for good or ill, still genuinely existing living souls cannot possibly be without activity unless one thinks of them as being in a coma. The dead remain finite and limited and can exist in no way other than in space and time. Undoubtedly, on the other side of the grave the dimensions of space and the computations of time are very different from those on earth, where we measure by the mile and by the hour. Also, the souls who dwell there do not become eternal and omnipresent as God is; like the angels they must have a specific whereabouts *(ubi definitivum)*, cannot be in two places at the same time, are always somewhere in a specific location, in Paradise or heaven, and so on. Similarly, they are not elevated above all structured time, that is, above all succession of moments, inasmuch as they have a past they remember, a present in which they live, and a future toward which they are moving. The rich man knows that his brothers are still alive (Luke 16:28); the souls under the altar eagerly anticipate a day of vengeance (Rev. 6:10); the bride longs for the coming of Christ (Rev. 22:17); those who come out of the great ordeal serve God night and day (Rev. 7:15); and there is no rest day or night for those who have worshiped the beast (Rev. 14:11).

If, then, the souls exist under some form of space and time, they cannot be conceived as being totally inactive. Jesus indeed says that in the night of death no one can work (John 9:4), and heavenly blessedness is often represented in Scripture as a state of being at rest (Heb. 4:9, 10; Rev. 14:13). But just as it is not inconsistent to say that God rests from his work of creation (Gen. 2:2) and still always works (John 5:17), or that Christ had accomplished his work on earth (John 17:4) and nevertheless prepares a place in heaven for his own (John 14:3), so it is not contradictory to claim that believers rest from their labors and nevertheless serve God in his temple. Though their work on earth is finished, this does not alter the fact that they still have other works to do in heaven. Scripture teaches this plainly. Those who have died in the Lord are with Jesus (Phil. 1:23), stand before the throne of God and of the Lamb (Rev. 7:9, 15), cry out and pray, praise and serve him (Rev. 6:10; 7:10, 15; 22:17). Anyway if they, being conscious, know God, Christ, the angels, and one another, they are by that very fact engaging in activities of intellect and will, increasing in knowledge, and being confirmed in love. If Paul can say that believers on earth, by seeing the glory of the Lord in the mirror of his Word, are being transformed into the same image from one degree of glory to another (2 Cor. 3:18), how much more will that be the case when they are admitted into his immediate presence and see him face to face? There is no change in their state, nor is there any development in an earthly sense, not even sanctification as in the church militant, for holiness itself is the possession of all. However, just as Adam before the fall and Christ himself in his humanity, though perfectly holy, could still increase in grace and wisdom, so in heaven there is an ongoing confirmation of one's state, an ever-increasing degree of conformity to the image of the Son, a never-ending growth in the knowledge and love of God.

Moreover, all have their own task and place. Roman Catholics assume that after death Old Testament believers waited in the limbo of the fathers and were not released until Christ freed them at his descent into hell; and they also believe that infants, who were not yet baptized when they died, will be received neither in hell nor in heaven but in a separate "receptacle," the limbo of infants. But Scripture presents no basis for either of these two "limbos." It is of course logical that those who lose sight of the unity of the covenant of grace, and view the benefits acquired by Christ as a new substance that did not exist before, are compelled to make the devout of the Old Testament wait in the limbo of the fathers for this acquisition and impartation of Christ's benefits. But those who acknowledge the unity of the covenant and view the benefits of Christ as the gracious benevolence of God which, with a view to Christ, could be imparted already before his suffering and death—they have no need for a *limbus patrum*. Under the provisions of the Old Testament the way to heavenly blessedness was the same as under the New

Testament, even though there is indeed a difference in the light by which they walked then and now.

In the same way there is no room on the other side of the grave for a limbo of infants *(limbus infantum)*; for the children of the covenant, whether baptized or unbaptized, go to heaven when they die; and so little has been disclosed to us about the fate of those outside the covenant that we had best abstain from any definite judgment.[17] Still, contained in the theory of the *limbus patrum* and the *limbus infantum* is the true idea that there are varying degrees both in the punishment of the ungodly and in the blessedness of the devout. There is distinction of rank and activity in the world of angels. There is diversity among all created beings and most abundantly among humans. There is distinction of place and task in the church of Christ; on earth every believer is given his or her own gifts and charged with his or her own task. And in death the works of each one follow him or her who dies in the Lord. Undoubtedly this diversity is not destroyed in heaven but, on the contrary, purified of all that is sinful and multiplied abundantly (Luke 19:17–19). Still this difference in degree detracts nothing from the blessedness each enjoys in keeping with his or her own capacity. For all will be at home with the same Lord (2 Cor. 5:8), are taken up in the same heaven (Rev. 7:9), enjoy the same rest (Heb. 4:9), and find joy in the same service of God (Rev. 7:15).

Part 2

The Return of Christ

Visions of the End

4

The universe is finite and its history will come to an end. Those who live without God and without hope find this hard to accept and often turn to illusory dreams of progress or give up in despair. The Old Testament hope is based on an anticipated restoration of the earth as the kingdom of God. The expected day of the Lord brings judgment as well as salvation and is ushered in by the Messiah, David's Son. Prophetically prefigured in the return from Babylonian captivity, the conversion of Israel and renewal of temple worship, the final expression of Israel's hope is cosmic—the Gentiles share in the full blessing of a cleansed and transformed earth. While the Old Testament regards the messianic kingdom as the full establishment of the kingdom of God, it also gives hints of a greater reality breaking through—the eternal, spiritual reign of God. The concrete, earthly character of Old Testament hope, politicized by intertestamental Judaism, gave rise to chiliasm, which posits a twofold return of Christ and a double resurrection. The first establishes an earthly millennial kingdom, the second the final consummation. The major objection to chiliasm is that it overlooks the New Testament's own spiritual application of Old Testament prophecy. It is the Old rather than the New Covenant that is the real intermezzo in salvation history.

Just as it is appointed for humans to die once, so also there must come an end to the history of the world. Science as well as religion has always been convinced of this. Granted: a few people, such as Aristotle in antiquity and Heinrich Czolbe, Friedrich Mohr, and others in modern times, believed that this world was eternal and had neither beginning nor end. But today it is generally agreed that this opinion is untenable. There are many considerations that establish the finite duration of the world beyond all doubt. According to calculations, the rotational speed of the earth decreases by at least one second every 600,000 years. However small this decrease is, after billions of years it nevertheless brings about on earth a reversal in the relation between day and night, which brings all life to an end. Further, the rotation of the earth is continually being slowed by the alternation of high and low tides, the influence of which shifts parts of the earth and decreases the supply of kinetic energy. The earth therefore moves ever closer to the sun and must ultimately disappear in it. Furthermore, the space in which the planets move is not totally empty but filled with ether or rarefied air, which, however weakly, holds back the planets' movement, decreases their rotational speed, causes their orbit to shrink, and thus brings them into ever closer proximity to the sun.

Neither can the sun last for ever. Whether its heat is produced by infalling meteorites or constant shrinkage or chemical processes, the sun gradually uses up that heat, contracts, and moves toward its end. According to Thompson, the sun's diameter decreases thirty-five meters a year and, since it has been shining some twenty million years now, it has only some ten million years left. While kinetic energy, after all, can convert itself into heat, heat cannot be converted into kinetic energy unless it flows out upon a colder body. Therefore, once the temperature has become everywhere the same, the conversion of heat ceases, and the end of things has come. Consequently, the question is simply whether the sun or the earth will last longer. If it is the sun, the earth will ultimately be swallowed up by it and everything will end in conflagration. If it is the earth, the heat supply will one day be exhausted and life will expire in a death of extreme cold.[1]

Various other arguments for a finite world have been advanced as well. Because of its chemical affinity with minerals the earth's supply of water has to grow increasingly smaller. Water and oxygen are increasingly bound up in solids. The earth's products—coal, wood, peat, nutriments—decrease. The earth, however rich in resources, will one day be exhausted and this will occur all the sooner as the human race expands and the danger of overpopulation threatens. Accordingly, from the viewpoint of science, there is absolutely no room for an optimistic outlook on the future. Numerous people, nevertheless, have yielded to such an outlook and dreamed of steady progress and a future paradise of mankind in the present world *(Diesseits)*. Humanists and materialists vie with each other in fostering such illusions. On the basis of the principle of cosmic evolution they believe that their professional prophecies cannot go wrong. In their opinion, by the increase of ideal goods such as science, art, and morality, or by progress in material prosperity, that is, by an abundance of food, shelter, and clothing, the happiness of mankind will one day be fully realized. Kant, Lessing, Herder, Fichte, Schelling, and the like, envision a future in which the ethical kingdom of God will embrace all human beings. All will participate in the Enlightenment, and full humanity will be the principle of the life of everyone.

Even Darwin, at the end of his book on *The Origin of Species* and in the final chapter of his *Descent of Man*, expresses the hope that humanity, which has already risen so far above its animal origins, is moving toward a still higher destiny in the distant future. In that future, says Pierson,[2] the most refined human beings will no longer crave marriage but a man will live with his wife as with his sister, and sensuality will no longer be the death of the zest for living. Others claim that in the case of a highly civilized people marriage will eventually assume the form of a double marriage and two friends will jointly marry two women. Even more extravagant are the expectations of the Socialists, these millenni-alists of unbelief, who think that in the future state of their dreams all sin and struggle will have vanished and a carefree life of contentment will be the privilege of everyone.

But, as we have already stated, there is not much ground on which to base these expectations. And even if a time of increased prosperity and greater happiness were to dawn, what would be the advantage if, as science teaches, all evolution would still finally end in death? At the end of his history of culture Fr. von Hellwald[3] proves helpless to give even the slightest answer to the question for what purpose everything happened—to what end humanity, with all of its struggles and striving, its refinement and development, existed. And Otto Henne Am Rhyn ends his history of culture with the prediction that one day the whole of humankind along with its culture will disappear without a trace. "One day everything we have accomplished will be nowhere to be found." And in the face of that prospect he can only console himself with the thought that it will be a long time before we will get there.[4] Those who live without God and without hope, and have to expect everything from the present world *(Diesseits)*, from immanent cosmic forces, are with-out hope in the world as well.

Even culture cannot be conceived as endless. One may arbitrarily as-sume the passage of billions of years in the past or future of the world but cannot picture it concretely as being filled with history. If humanity were to last a billion years, a "textbook" on world history, which gave 10 pages to a century, would comprise no fewer than 200,000 volumes, each volume calculated at 500 pages; or 20,000 volumes if it devoted only one page to every century; or still 500 volumes if no more than one line was given to each century. And that is how it would be with every-thing that forms the content of our culture. Humanity is finite, and therefore human civilization cannot be conceived as endless either. Both for the earth and for our race an infinite period of time is an ab-surdity, even more palpably so than the foolishness of the millions of years known to us from pagan mythologies. From the perspective of sci-ence, there is much more reason to accept the pessimism of Schopen-hauer and Ed. von Hartmann, which stakes the salvation of the world on combating the alogical will by logical representation, on the absolute negation of will, that is, on the annihilation of the world itself. But even then there is not the slightest guarantee that the absolute will's negation will succeed and not pass over into another world process and ever and again start over ad infinitum. Many Greek philosophers believed that many other worlds preceded this one and that many others would follow it. Even the Pythagoreans and Stoics were of the opinion that everything would return to precisely the same state in which it existed in this world and had existed in previous worlds. Also today many people have returned to such notions,[5] although Windelband rightly calls it a painful idea that "in the periodic return of all things the human personality, with all its activities and suffering, will return as well."[6]

A Religious Perspective on the End

Religion has never been at peace with this idea of an endless development or the total ruination of the world. There are various reasons why it was kept from adopting these philosophical theories. It is obvious that all such theories fail to do justice to the value of personhood and tend to sacrifice it to the world as a whole. They further fail to appreciate the significance of the life of religion and morality and assign to it a position far below that of culture. And finally, for the present as well as for the future, they only build upon forces immanent in the cosmos and take no account whatever of a divine power that governs the world and ultimately, by direct intervention, causes the world to fulfill the purpose laid down for it. All religions, therefore, have another outlook on the future. All of them more or less clearly know of a struggle between good and evil; all of them cherish the hope of the victory of the good in which the virtuous are rewarded and the wicked are punished; and as a rule they consider that future attainable in no other way than by a manifestation of supernatural forces.[7]

Persian religion even expected the appearance at the end of the third world period of the third son of Zarathustra, Saoshyant, who would introduce a thousand-year kingdom of peace and complete the redemptive work of his Father.[8] Among the Muslims, along with belief in the return of Jesus, there gradually arose the expectation of a Mahdi who would take believers back to the golden age of the "four righteous Khalifs."[9] In Israel future hopes were based on the foundation of the covenant God had established with Abraham and his seed. For this covenant is everlasting and is not nullified by human unfaithfulness. Even in the law God repeatedly testifies to the people of Israel that when they violate his covenant he will visit them with the most severe punishments, but afterward will again have compassion on his own. When on account of its sins Israel is scattered among the nations and its land is devastated, in that day the Lord will arouse his people to jealousy by his acceptance of other peoples, bring them to repentance and lead them back to their own country, bless them with innumerable spiritual and material blessings, and bring vengeance on all their enemies (Lev. 26; Deut. 4:23–31; 30:1–10; 32:15–43). Following the promise to the house of David that it will be made sure and that its throne will be established forever (2 Sam. 7:16; 23:5; 1 Chron. 17:14), what increasingly gains prominence in Israel's future hopes is that its conversion and restoration will be brought about by nothing other than the anointed king of the house of David. These ideas were further developed in prophecy and, despite the peculiar features they bear in each of the prophets, assume increasingly firmer forms.

In the expectation that the Old Testament fosters with respect to the future of the people of God, we can clearly discern the following components. All the prophets proclaim to Israel and Judah *a day of judgment and punishment*. The *yôm YHWH*, the time in which the Lord will have compassion on his people and inflict vengeance on their enemies, was viewed very differently by the prophets than by the people. The people misused this expectation and thought that—quite apart from their own spiritual state—Yahweh would protect them from all danger (Jer. 29; Ezek. 33:23ff.; Amos 5:18; 6:13). But the prophets said that the day of the Lord would be a day of judgment for Israel as well. The people would be exiled and its land devastated (Isa. 2:11ff.; 5:5ff.; 7:18; Jer. 1:11–16; Hos. 1:6; 2:11; 3:4; 8:13; 9:3, 6; 10:6; 11:5; 13:12; 14:1; Joel 2:1ff.; Amos 2:4ff.; 5:16, 18, 27; 6:14 etc.; Mic. 3:12; 4:10; 7:13; Hab. 1:5–11; Zeph. 1:1–18, etc.).

Still, that punishment is *temporary*. After many days (Hos. 3:3), after a few days, that is, after a short while (Hos. 6:2), after seventy years (Jer. 25:12; 29:10), after 390 years for Israel and forty years for Judah (Ezek. 4:4ff.), there will be an end to it. God's chastisement of his people is measured (Isa. 27:7ff.; Jer. 30:11). He only leaves it for a short while; his wrath is for a moment but his lovingkindness is forever (Isa. 54:7, 8). He loves his people with an everlasting love and will therefore again have compassion (Jer. 31:3, 20; Mic. 7:19). He cannot utterly destroy his people, though he shakes it as with a sieve (Amos 9:8, 9). His heart recoils within him (Hos. 11:8 RSV). He remembers his covenant (Ezek. 16:60). He will redeem his people, not for the sake of Israel but for his name's sake, for his fame among the Gentiles (Deut. 32:27; Isa. 43:25; 48:9; Ezek. 36:22ff.).

At the end of the time of punishment God sends the *Messiah* from the house of David. Obadiah still speaks in general of saviors who protect the community that has escaped to Mount Zion (vv. 17, 21; cf. Jer. 23:4; 33:17, 20, 21, 22, 26). Amos says that after Israel's judgment God will again raise up the fallen booth of David (9:11). Hosea expects that the children of Israel will repent and seek the Lord and David as king as well (1:11; 3:5; cf. Jer. 30:9; Ezek. 34:23, 24; 37:22–24). Micah prophesies that Israel will not be saved from the power of its enemies until, at Bethlehem, the ruler from the royal house of David is born (5:1, 2). The fact that, like David, he will come forth from Bethlehem, not from Jerusalem, is proof that the royal house of David has lost the throne and has relapsed into a state of lowliness. Isaiah, accordingly, says that a shoot will come out from the stump of Jesse (11:1, 2); Ezekiel expresses the same idea by saying that the Lord will take a tender sprig from the topmost branch of the highest cedar (17:22). God will cause him to shoot forth from the house of David like a branch (Isa. 4:2; Jer. 23:5, 6; 33:14–17), so that in token of this he will also bear the name "Branch" (Zech. 3:8; 6:12). Born in Israel's time of suffering, this son of David will grow up in poverty (Isa. 7:14–17). Though he is a king, he is just, gentle, humble, and therefore he will come riding on the foal of a donkey (Zech. 9:9). He will unite royal dignity with both prophetic dignity (Deut. 18:15; Isa. 11:2; 40–66; Mal. 4:5) and priestly dignity (Ps. 110; Isa. 53; Jer. 30:21; Zech. 3; 6:13). The kingdom he comes to establish is one of righteousness and peace (Pss. 72, 100; Isa. 11, 40–66; Mic. 5:9). He himself is and wins righteousness and salvation for his people (Ps. 72; Isa. 11, 42, 53; Jer. 23:5, 6, etc.). Therefore his appearance is not delayed until after the day of judgment but precedes it. Judah is not redeemed until God gives David a branch (Isa. 9:1–16; 11:1ff.; Jer. 23:5, 6; 33:14–17).

Among the benefits to be conferred on his people by this Anointed One is, first of all, the *return from* the land of *exile*. The land, the people, the king, and God belong together. For that reason the restoration of Israel begins with its return from exile (Isa. 11:11; Jer. 3:18; Ezek. 11:17; Hos. 11:11; Joel 3:1; Amos 9:14; Mic. 4:6, etc.). That return, according to Isaiah's depiction of it, will be extraordinarily splendid. The wilderness will blossom like a rose. Mountains will be leveled and valleys filled up. There will be a paved road on which not even the blind can go astray (35:1–9; 41:17–20; 42:15, 16; 43:19, 20, etc.). Both Israel and Judah will take part in that return (Isa. 11:13; Jer. 3:6, 18; 31:27; 32:37–40; Ezek. 37:17; 47:13, 21; 48:1–7, 23–29; Hos. 1:11; 14:2–9; Amos 9:9–15). But the return from Babylonian captivity was only a very partial fulfillment of this expectation. For that reason the postexilic prophets view it as only a beginning of the realization of the promises. They detach their expectation from a return from exile and, except for Zechariah (8:13), no longer speak of the ten tribes. The returned exiles viewed themselves as representative of the whole of Israel (Ezra 6:17).

All the prophets, for that matter, at the same time view Israel's return from exile as an ethical return, that is, as a *conversion*. Gathering to-

gether from among the nations and circumcision of the heart go together (Deut. 30:3–6). By no means all of them were to return and turn
to the Lord. Many, the majority in fact, will perish in the judgment that
the day of the Lord will bring on Israel. While the Lord will not completely destroy the house of Jacob, he will in fact shake it as in a sieve
and bring about the death of sinners by the sword (Amos 9:8–10). When
he brings Israel and Judah back, he will first lead them into the desert
and purge out the ungodly (Ezek. 20:34ff.; Hos. 2:13). Then many men
will fall so that seven women will take hold of one man (Isa. 3:25–4:1).
The destruction is firmly resolved; only a mere remnant will return (Isa.
4:3; 6:13; 7:3; 10:21; 11:11). The Lord will thrash the children of Israel
and then gather them up one by one (Isa. 27:12). He will destroy the
proud but rescue a poor and wretched people (Zeph. 3:12), and keep
alive his work (Hab. 3:2). One from a city and two from a family will be
brought back (Jer. 3:14); two-thirds will be cut off, but one-third will be
purified (Zech. 13:8, 9). Those who remain, however, will be a holy people to the Lord to whom he betrothes himself forever (Isa. 4:3, 4; 11:9;
Hos. 1:10, 12; 2:15, 18, 22). The Lord forgives them all their iniquity,
cleanses them from all their uncleanness, gives them a new heart, pours
out his Spirit on them all, removes all idolatry and sorcery from their
midst, and establishes a new covenant with them (Isa. 43:25; 44:21–23;
Jer. 31:31; Ezek. 11:19; 36:25–28; 37:14; Joel 2:28; Mic. 5:11–14; Zech.
13:2, etc.). The unclean will no longer dwell among them (Isa. 52:1, 11,
12); they will all be righteous (Isa. 60:21); those who are taught by God
will know him, trust in his name, and not do wrong or speak lies (Isa.
54:13; Jer. 31:31; Zeph. 3:12, 13). Everything will be holy, even the bells
of the horses (Zech. 14:20, 21). For the glory of the Lord has risen over
them (Isa. 60:1; Zech. 2:5) and God himself dwells among them (Hos.
2:22; Joel 3:17; Obad. 21; Zech. 2:10; 8:8, etc.).

For Old Testament prophecy these spiritual benefits include the expectation of the restoration of the *temple* and *the temple worship services.* According to Obadiah, there will be a place of refuge on Mount
Zion; there the saviors who protect Israel and will judge its enemies will
dwell (17, 21). Joel prophesies that the Lord will dwell on Zion, his holy
mountain, and that Jerusalem will be holy—no longer accessible to
strangers—and everlasting (3:17, 20). Amos expects that the cities of
Palestine will be rebuilt and inhabited and that Israel will never again
be driven from it (9:14, 15). Micah announces that, though Zion will be
plowed as a field and Jerusalem reduced to a heap of ruins (3:12), still
the mountain of the house of the Lord will be established as the highest
of the mountains and that out of Zion the law will go forth and the word
of the Lord from Jerusalem, and that the Lord will dwell in Zion (4:1, 2;
7:11). The same idea is expressed by Isaiah (2:2), who adds that Zion

and Jerusalem, kingship and priesthood, temple and altar, sacrifices and feast days, will be restored (28:16; 30:19; 33:5; 35:10; 52:1; 56:6, 7; 60:7; 61:6; 66:20–23). In the same way Jeremiah expects that Jerusalem will be rebuilt, the Lord's throne reestablished there, and the temple services renewed (3:16, 17; 30:18; 31:38; 33:18, 21). Haggai predicts that the splendor of the second temple will be greater than that of the first (2:6–10), and Zechariah announces that Jerusalem will be rebuilt and expanded, that the priesthood and temple will be renewed, and that God will dwell in Jerusalem in the midst of his people (1:17; 2:1–5; 3:1–8; 6:9–15; 8:3ff.).

But none of the prophets develops this vision of the future in such meticulous detail as Ezekiel. First, in chapters 34–37, he says that Israel and Judah will again be gathered together by the Lord, that it will be accepted as one people under the one shepherd from the house of David to be the Lord's possession, and will be given a new heart and a new spirit. Having predicted in chapters 38 and 39 that Israel, now back in its own land, must still endure a final attack from Gog of Magog, in chapters 40–48 he presents an elaborate sketch of the Palestine of the future. The land west of the Jordan will be divided by parallel lines in almost equal strips. The top seven will be inhabited by the tribes Dan, Asher, Naphtali, Manasseh, Ephraim, Reuben, and Judah; the bottom five, by Benjamin, Simeon, Issachar, Zebulun, and Gad. Between the upper and lower parts of the territory a strip of land will be reserved for the Lord. In the middle of this 25,000 x 25,000 cubit strip stands a high mountain; and on top of it is built the temple, which is filled with the glory of the Lord, and measures 500 cubits square and is surrounded by an area of 500 cubits on each side. Around this the priests, all of whom must be descendants of Zadok, will receive an allotment 25,000 cubits in length and 10,000 cubits in width to the south, and the Levites will get their allotment, which is equal in size, to the north, while to the east and west a section of the holy strip is assigned to the prince. The city of Jerusalem is separate from the temple and situated south of the land allotted to the priests on a plain that is 25,000 cubits in length and 5,000 cubits in width. In the wall, on each side of the city, are three gates, according to the number of the tribes of Israel. On the great feasts all of Israel comes to the temple to sacrifice, but Gentiles are forbidden access. If Israel thus lives in accordance with God's ordinances it will enjoy immense blessing. From under the threshold of the temple door flows a stream that gets ever deeper, makes the land fertile, and even makes fresh the stagnant waters of the Dead Sea. On its banks on both sides of the river are trees whose fruit is for food and whose leaves are for healing.[10]

Added to these spiritual benefits come a wide range of *material blessings*. Under the Prince of Peace of the house of David Israel will live securely. There will no longer be war: bow and sword will be abolished (Hos. 2:18); horses will be cut off, chariots destroyed, strongholds thrown down (Mic. 5:10, 11), and swords will be beaten into plowshares and spears into pruning hooks. All will sit down under their vine and their fig tree (Isa. 2:4; Mic. 4:3, 4), for the kingdom is the Lord's and he is their stronghold (Joel 3:16, 17; Obad. 21). The land will become extraordinarily fertile, so that the mountains will drip sweet wine and the hills will flow with milk. A fountain issuing from the house of the Lord will irrigate the dry land and turn the desert into a Garden of Eden. Wild beasts will be driven away, enemies will no longer rob the harvest, and all the trees, seasonably refreshed by gentle rains, will bear abundant fruit (Isa. 32:15–20; 51:3; 60:17, 18; 62:8, 9; 65:9, 22; Jer. 31:6, 12–14; Ezek. 34:14, 25, 26, 29; 36:29; 47:1–12; Hos. 2:17, 20, 21; 14:6; Joel 3:18; Amos 9:13, 14; Zech. 8:12; 14:8, 10). An enormous reversal will occur, even in nature: animals will receive a different nature (Isa. 11:6–8; 65:25), heaven and earth will be renewed and the former things will no longer be remembered (Isa. 34:4; 51:6; 65:17; 66:22). Sun and moon will be altered: the light of the moon will be like the sun and the light of the sun will be seven times its normal strength (Isa. 30:26). Indeed, the sun and moon will be no more: there will be continuous day, for the Lord will be the people's everlasting light (Isa. 60:19, 20; Zech. 14:6, 7).

In the human world as well the change will be enormous. Once Israel is gathered, Palestine will resound with people (Mic. 2:12, 13). The descendants of the children of Israel will be like the sand of the sea, and especially the progeny of the house of David and of the Levites will be multiplied (Isa. 9:2; Jer. 3:16; 33:22; Hos. 1:10). On account of the multitude of people and animals, Jerusalem will become immeasurable and will have to be inhabited like villages (Zech. 2:1–4). Various causes underlie this marvelous increase. Many Israelites—after a number of them have been returned—will come to Jerusalem and share in the blessing of Israel (Jer. 3:14, 16, 18; Zech. 2:4–9; 8:7, 8). Indeed, when the Lord's messengers will make this blessing known among the Gentiles, the latter will bring to Jerusalem the Israelites still residing among them in chariots, in litters, on horses, on mules, and on dromedaries (Isa. 66:19, 20). Also the Israelites who have died will share in those blessings. All of Israel can then be said to have been brought back to life (Isa. 25:8; Ezek. 37:1–14; Hos. 6:2). Isaiah (26:19) and Daniel (12:2) specifically announce that the defeated Israelites will arise from the sleep of death and at least in part awaken to everlasting life. And, finally, all the citizens of the kingdom will reach a very advanced age. And there will no longer be in it "an infant that lives but a few days, or an old person who does not live out a lifetime; for one who dies at a hundred years will be considered a youth, and one who falls short of a hundred will be

considered accursed" (Isa. 65:20; cf. Zech. 8:4, 5). There will no longer
be sickness, nor mourning, nor crying (Isa. 25:8, 30:19; 65:19); the Lord
will even destroy death, swallowing it up in victory (25:8).

Finally, the *Gentiles* will share in that blessing of the kingdom of God
as well. Woven throughout Old Testament prophecy is the thought that
God will avenge the blood of his servants on his enemies. The prophets
of God, therefore, announce God's judgments over several peoples: Philistia, Tyre, Moab, Ammon, Edom, Asshur, and Babel. But the final effect of these judgments is not the destruction but the salvation of the
Gentiles: in Abraham's seed all the nations of the earth will be blessed.
Granted: in one prophet it is more the political side of this subjection of
the Gentiles under Israel that comes to the fore, while in another it is
the religious, spiritual side. All of them nevertheless expect that the rule
of the Messiah will be extended to all peoples (cf. Pss. 2, 21, 24, 45, 46,
47, 48, 68, 72, 86, 89, 96, 98, etc.). Israel will, by hereditary right, possess the Gentiles (Amos. 9:12; Rev. 17–21). While they will be judged
(Joel 3:2–15), everyone who calls on the name of the Lord will be saved,
for in Mount Zion is deliverance (Joel 2:32 [cf. KJV]). The Ruler from Bethlehem will be great to the ends of the earth and protect Israel from its
enemies (Mic. 5:3f.).

Still, the Gentiles will go to Mount Zion to discover the ways of the
Lord (Mic. 4:1, 2). After the Lord has "shriveled" all the gods of the peoples (Zeph. 2:11; 3:8) the Gentile inhabitants of the islands will bow
down to him and he will give pure lips to all peoples, enabling them to
call on his name (3:9). Ethiopia will bring gifts to the Lord in Zion (Isa.
18:7). Egyptians and Assyrians will serve him (19:18–25). Tyre will
hand over its profits to the Lord (23:15–18), and on Mount Zion he will
prepare for all peoples a feast of rich food (25:6–10). Indeed, the servant
of the Lord will be a light also to the Gentiles. His messengers will make
known the Lord among the nations of the earth, and he will be served
by them. The Lord's house will be a house of prayer for all peoples. All
will bring their sacrifices there, worship the Lord, and call themselves
after his name. They will pasture Israel's flocks and cultivate its fields,
so that Israelites can completely devote themselves as priests to the service of the Lord (40–66, *passim*). When Israel has been restored and
Jerusalem is the throne of the Lord, all the Gentiles will be gathered
there around the name of the Lord, bless themselves, and boast in the
Lord (Jer. 3:17; 4:2; 16:19–21; 33:9). In the end all peoples will acknowledge that the Lord is God (Ezek. 16:62; 17:24; 25:5f.; 26:6; 28:22; 29:6;
30:8f.). All the Gentiles will bring their treasures to Jerusalem and fill
the house of the Lord with splendor (Hag. 2:7–10). Peoples will come
and say to one another, "Let us go to entreat the favor of the LORD." "Ten
men . . . will take hold of a Jew, grasping his garment and saying, 'Let

us go with you, for we have heard that God is with you'" (Zech. 8:21–23; cf. 2:11, 14:16–19). The people of the holy ones will receive dominion over all the nations of the earth (Dan. 7:14, 27).

The Uniqueness of Old Testament Eschatology

These messianic expectations of the Old Testament, as any reader can see at once, are of a unique kind: they limit themselves to a future blessed state *on earth*. While in the Old Testament it may sometimes happen that a believer will express the hope that after death he will be taken up in eternal glory, this expectation is individual and stands by itself. As a rule, the eye of prophecy is directed toward that future in which the people of Israel will live securely under a king of David's dynasty in Palestine and will rule over all the nations of the earth. An assumption of believers into the heaven of glory at the end of time is not part of the Old Testament outlook. Salvation is expected on earth, not in heaven. In this connection Old Testament prophecy knows only of one coming of the Messiah. It does know that the Anointed One will be born of the house of David when it has fallen into decline, that he will share in the suffering of his people, even that as servant of the Lord he will suffer for his people and bear their iniquities. He will be a totally different king from the rulers of the earth; he will be humble, gentle, doing justice and protecting his people. He will be not only king but also prophet and priest. But in its view of the life of the Messiah, Old Testament prophecy never clearly separates the state of humiliation from the state of exaltation. It gathers up both in a single image. Nor does it make a distinction between a first and second coming and does not position the latter, which is for judgment, a long time after the former, which is for salvation. It is one single coming in which the Messiah bestows righteousness and blessedness on his people and brings it to dominion over all the peoples of the earth. The kingdom he is coming to establish, therefore, is the completed kingdom of God. He himself will in fact govern his people as king, but in that capacity he is still no more than a theocratic king who does not rule in accordance with his own powers but in an absolute sense realizes the rule of God.

Old Testament prophecy makes no temporal distinction between the rule of Christ and the rule of God. It does not expect that the Messiah of the house of David, after having temporarily exercised sovereignty, will turn his kingdom over to God. It does not view the future, which it depicts as being in the messianic kingdom, as an intermediate state that in the end must yield to a divine government in heaven. It regards the messianic kingdom as the final state and clearly views God's judgment over enemies, the repulsion of the final attack, the transformation of nature, and the resurrection from the dead as events that precede the initial and full establishment of this kingdom. And this kingdom is sketched by the prophets in hues and colors, under figures and forms, which have all been derived from the historical circumstances in which they lived. Palestine will be reconquered, Jerusalem rebuilt, the temple with its sacrificial worship restored. Edom, Moab, Ammon, Assyria, and Babylon will be subdued. All citizens will be given a long life and a relaxed setting under vine and fig tree. The [projected] image of the future is Old Testament-like through and through; it is all described in terms of Israel's own history and nation.

But into those sensuous earthly forms prophecy puts everlasting content. In that shell is an imperishable core which, sometimes even in the Old Testament itself, breaks through. Return from exile and true conversion coincide. The religious and political sides of Israel's victory over its enemies are most intimately bound up with each other. The Messiah is an earthly ruler but also an everlasting king, a king of righteousness, an eternal father to his people, a prince of peace, a priest-king. The enemies of Israel are subjected to her but in the process acknowledge that the Lord is God and serve him in his temple. This temple with its priesthood and sacrificial worship are visible proof that all the citizens of the kingdom serve the Lord with a new heart and a new spirit and walk in his ways. And the extraordinary fertility of the land presupposes a total transformation of nature, the creation of a new heaven and a new earth, the home of righteousness.

Later Judaism introduced an assortment of changes in these Old Testament expectations. Robbed of political sovereignty and scattered among the nations, it began increasingly to take account of the future destiny of individuals and broadened its horizon to include humanity and the world as a whole. Someday—it was believed—on the basis of its own strictly law-abiding righteousness, Israel, led by the Messiah, would achieve political dominion over all nations. But this messianic kingdom was of a provisional and temporary kind. In the end it would make way for a kingdom of God, for a blessedness of the righteous in heaven, which would be introduced by the resurrection of all human beings and universal judgment. In that way, the political and religious sides, which in the prophetic vision of the future were most intimately united, were torn apart. In Jesus' day Israel expected a tangible, earthly, messianic kingdom whose conditions were depicted in the forms and images of Old Testament prophecy. But now these forms and images were taken literally. The shell was mistaken for the core, the image of it for the thing itself, and the form for the essence. The messianic kingdom became the political rule of Israel over the nations—a period of external prosperity and growth. And at the end of it [in this scenario] universal judgment could only occur after the general resurrection, when people were judged according to their works and either received the reward of heavenly blessedness or the penalty of hellish pain.

The Rise of Chiliasm

This is how the doctrine of chiliasm arose. Admittedly, a large part of Jewish apocryphal literature continues to adhere to the future expectations of the Old Testament. But frequently, especially in the Apocalypse of Baruch and the fourth book of Ezra, we find the view that the glory of the messianic kingdom is not the last and the highest. On the contrary, after a specific period of time, often calculated—for example, in the Talmud—at four hundred or one thousand years, this kingdom has to make room for the heavenly blessedness of the kingdom of God. Accordingly, chiliasm is not of Christian but of Jewish and Persian origin.[11] It is always based on a compromise between the expectations of an earthly salvation and those of a heavenly state of blessedness. It attempts to do justice to Old Testament prophecy in the sense that it accepts the earthly messianic kingdom predicted by it but claims this kingdom will be replaced after a time by the kingdom of God. It would appear that its strength lies in the Old Testament, but actually this is not the case. The Old Testament is decidedly not chiliastic. In its depiction of the messianic kingdom it describes the completed kingdom of God that is without end and lasts forever (Dan. 2:44), preceded by judgment, resurrection, and world renewal.

Chiliasm, nevertheless, found credence among the Jews and also with many Christians. It surfaced over and over when the world developed its power in opposition to God and brought suffering on the church by persecution and oppression. In the earliest period we encounter it in Cerinthus, in The Testament of the Twelve Patriarchs, in the thought of the Ebionites in Barnabas, Papias, Irenaeus, Hippolytus, Apollinaris, Commodianus, Lactantius, and Victorinus. Montanism, on the other hand, urged caution. Gnostics, the theologians of Alexandria, and particularly Augustine resisted it most vigorously, while the changed situation of the church, which had overcome the world power of the day and increasingly viewed itself as the kingdom of God on earth, gradually prompted it to die out completely. It came up again before and during the Reformation, when many began to view Rome as the harlot of Revelation and the pope as the Antichrist. It revived among the Anabaptists, the David-Jorists, and the Socinians, and since then has not died out again although the official churches rejected it. Over and over political disturbances, the wars of religion, persecutions, and sectarian movements breathed new life into it. In Bohemia it was preached by Paul Felgenhauer and Comenius; in Germany by Jacob Böhme, Ezekiel Meth, Gichtel, Petersen, Horche, Spener, J. Lange, and S. König; in England by John Archer, Newton, Joseph Mede, Jane Leade, and many Independents; in the Netherlands by Labadie, Anthony Bourignan, Poiret, and so on. Even some Reformed theologians tended toward a moderate form of chiliasm. Examples are Piscator, Alsted, Jurieu, Burnet, Whiston, Serarius, Cocceius, Groenewegen, Jac Alting, d'Outrein, Vitringa, Brakel, Jungius, Mommers, and others.[12]

In the eighteenth and nineteenth centuries, under the pressure of societal and political upheavals, it not only found acceptance among Swedenborgians, Darbyists, Irwingians, Mormons, Adventists, and others, but—after the turn toward realism taken by Bengle, Oetinger, Ph. M. Hahn, J. M. Hahn, Hasenkamp, Menken, Jung-Stilling, J. F. van Meyer, and so on—was embraced by many theologians in the churches of the Reformation.[13]

The basic ideas of chiliasm are virtually the same in all its forms. They come down to the assertion that we must distinguish between a twofold return of Christ and a double resurrection. They go on to say that at his first return Christ will overcome the forces of the Antichrist, bind Satan, raise the believers who have died, and gather the church around himself, in particular the community of Israel, now repentant and brought back to Palestine. From within that community he will rule over the world and usher in a period of spiritual florescence and material prosperity. At the end of that time he will return once more to raise all humans from the dead, judge them before his throne of judgment, and decide their eternal destiny. Still, these basic thoughts allow for an assortment of variations. The beginning of the thousand-year reign was variously determined. Following the example of the letter of Barnabas, many Church Fathers, and later the Cocceians as well, taught that it began with the seventh millennium of the world. The "Fifth-monarchmen" had it begin after the fall of the fourth world-kingdom. Hippolytus fixed its beginning in the year 500, Groenewegen in 1700, Whiston in 1715 and later in 1766, Jurieu in 1785, Bengel in 1836, Stilling in 1816, and so on. Its duration was determined at 400 years (4 Ezra), or 500 (Joseph of Nicodemus), or 1,000 (Talmud, etc.), or 2,000 (Bengel), or only 7 (Darby) years. Sometimes it was assigned an indeterminate number of years, and the number given in Revelation 20:2, 3, was consequently taken to be symbolic (Rothe, Martensen, Lange, etc.). A few people believed that before the establishment of a 1,000-year reign there will be no return of Christ (Kurtz), or at least no visible return (Darby), or a return that is visible only to believers (Irving), and that no resurrection of believers should be assumed before the millennium (Bengel).

Many are convinced that, upon his first return, Christ will remain on earth, but others are of the opinion that he will appear for only a short while—to establish his kingdom—and then again withdraw into heaven. According to Piscator, Alsted, and the like, Christ's rule in the millennium will be conducted from heaven. Participating in that rule, then, are the risen martyrs who were either taken up into heaven (Piscator) or stayed behind on earth (Alsted), or all the risen believers who remain here on earth (Justin, Irenaeus, etc.), or those who upon his appearance in the clouds are brought out to meet Christ in the air (Irving), or the people of Israel in particular. The reason is that chiliasts usually expect a national conversion of Israel, and the majority imagine that Israel, upon its conversion, will be brought back to Palestine and be the most important citizens of the thousand-year kingdom there (Jurieu, Oetinger, Hofmann, Auberlen, etc.). Those who assume that after his first return Christ will stay on earth usually fix a rebuilt Jerusalem as his city of residence, although the Montanists at one time thought it would be Pepuza [in Phrygia] and Mormons today think of their Salt Lake valley. The ideas of the restoration of temple and altar, of priesthood and sacrifices, are rejected as a rule as being too obviously inconsistent with the New Testament but were nevertheless still defended by the Ebionites and in more modern times by Serarius, Oetinger, Hess, and others.

Concerning the character and conditions of the thousand-year kingdom, people entertain very different ideas. Sometimes it is depicted as a realm of sensual pleasures (Cerinthus, Ebionites, etc.). Then again it is viewed as more spiritual and all enjoyment of food and drink, marriage, and procreation, is removed from it (Burnet, Lavater, Rothe, Ebrard). Most often the millennium is viewed as a transitional state between this world *(Diesseits)* and the next *(Jenseits)*. It is a realm in which believers are prepared for the vision of God (Irenaeus) or in which they enjoy tranquility and peace, without being totally freed from sin and exempted from death. It is a realm in which nature (Irenaeus) as well as people (Lactantius) will be extraordinarily fertile, and in which, according to a popular notion held later, the church will especially fulfill its mission work to humanity (Lavater, Ebrard, Auberlen, etc.).

All these variations constitute as many objections against chiliasm. It cannot even stand before the tribunal of Old Testament prophecy, a court to which it loves to appeal. Aside from the fact that, as stated earlier, the Old Testament does not view the messianic kingdom as provisional and temporary but as the end-result of world history, chiliasm is guilty of the greatest arbitrariness in interpreting prophecy. It doubles the return of Christ and the resurrection of the dead, although the Old

Testament does not give the slightest warrant for this. It is devoid of all rule and method and arbitrarily calls a halt, depending on the subjective opinion of the interpreter. All the prophets, with equal vigor and force, announce not only the conversion of Israel and the nations but also the return to Palestine, the rebuilding of Jerusalem, the restoration of the temple, the priesthood, and sacrificial worship, and so on. And it is nothing but caprice to take one feature of this picture literally and another "spiritually." Prophecy pictures for us but one single image of the future. And this image is either to be taken literally as it presents itself—but then one breaks with Christianity and lapses back into Judaism—or this image calls for a very different interpretation than that attempted by chiliasm. Such an interpretation is furnished by Scripture itself and we must take it from Scripture.

A Scriptural Reply to Chiliasm

In the Old Testament already there are numerous pointers for a new and better interpretation of the prophetic expectations than chiliasm offers. Even the modern view of the history of Israel recognizes that the Yahwism of the prophets distinguishes itself from the nature religions by its moral character and gradually gave a spiritual meaning to the religious laws and customs in use in Israel. True circumcision is that of the heart (Deut. 10:16; 30:6; Jer. 4:4). The sacrifices pleasing to God are a broken heart and a contrite spirit (1 Sam. 15:22; Pss. 40:6; 50:8f.; 51:17; Isa. 1:11f.; Jer. 6:20; 7:21f.; Hos. 6:6; Amos 5:21f.; Mic. 6:6ff.). The true fast is to loose the bonds of injustice (Isa. 58:3–6; Jer. 14:12). In large part the struggle of the prophets is directed against the external, self-righteous worship of the people. Accordingly, the essence of the future dispensation is that the Lord will make a new covenant with his people. He will give them a new heart and write his law on it. He will pour out his Spirit on all so that they will love him with their whole heart and walk in his ways (Deut. 30:6; Jer. 31:32; 32:38f.; Ezek. 11:19; 36:26; Joel 2:28; Zech. 12:10).

Now it is true that that future is depicted in images derived from the historical circumstances that then prevailed, so that Zion and Jerusalem, temple and altar, sacrifice and priesthood, continue to occupy a large place in it. But we must remember that we ourselves do the same thing and can only speak of God and divine things in sensuous, earthly forms. One reason God instituted Old Testament worship as he did was that we would be able to speak of heavenly things, not in self-made images but in the correct images given us by God himself. The New Testament, accordingly, takes over this language and in speaking about the future kingdom of God refers to Zion and Jerusalem, to temple and altar, to prophets and priests. The earthly is an image of the heavenly. All that is transitory is but an analogy ("Alles Vergängliche ist nur ein Gleichniss").

Nor must we forget that all prophecy is poetry that must be interpreted in terms of its own character. The error of the older exegesis was not spiritualization as such but the fact that it sought to assign a spiritual meaning to all the illustrative details, in the process, as in the case of Jesus' parables, often losing sight of the main thought. When it is stated, for example, that the Lord will cause a shoot to come forth from the stump of Jesse, that he will establish Mount Zion as the highest of the mountains, that of the exiles he will bring back one from a city and two from a family, that he will sprinkle clean water on all and cleanse them from their sins, that he will make the mountains drip sweet wine and the hills flow with milk, and so forth, everyone senses that in these lines one has to do with poetic descriptions that cannot and may not be taken literally. The realistic interpretation here becomes self-contradictory and misjudges the nature of prophecy.

It is also incorrect to say that the prophets themselves were totally unconscious of the distinction between the thing [they asserted] and the image [in which they clothed it]. Not only did the prophets undoubtedly view the above poetic descriptions as imagery but in the names for Sodom, Gomorrah, Edom, Moab, Philistia, Egypt, Asshur, and Babel they repeatedly refer to the power of the Gentile world that will someday be subject to Israel and share in its blessings (Isa. 34:5; Ezek. 16:46f.; Dan. 2:17f.; Obad. 16, 17; Zech. 14:21). Zion often serves as the name for the people, the believing community of God (Isa. 49:14; 51:3; 52:1). And although it is true that Old Testament prophecy cannot conceive the future kingdom of God without a temple and sacrifice, over and over it *transcends* all national and earthly conditions. It proclaims, for example, that there will no longer be an ark of the covenant, since all Jerusalem will be God's throne (Jer. 3:16, 17), that the kingdom of the Messiah will be everlasting and encompass the whole world (Pss. 2:8; 72:8, 17; Dan. 2:44), that the inhabitants will be prophets and priests (Isa. 54:13; 61:6; Jer. 31:31), that all impurity and sin, all sickness and death, will be banished from it (Ps. 104:35; Isa. 25:8; 33:24; 52:1, 11; Zech. 14:20, 21), that it will be established in a new heaven and on a new earth and will no longer need the sun or the moon (Isa. 60:19, 20; 65:17; 66:22). Even Ezekiel's realistic picture of the future contains elements that require a symbolic interpretation: the equal shares assigned to all the tribes, though in numbers they vary widely; the precisely measured strips of land intended for priests, Levites, and the king; the separation of the temple from the city; the high location of the temple on a mountain and the brook that streams out from under the threshold of the east door of the temple toward the Dead Sea; and finally, the artificial way things are put together and the impossibility of implementing them practically—all these features resist a so-called realistic interpretation.

Finally, in Old Testament exegesis the question is not whether the prophets were totally or partially conscious of the symbolic nature of their predictions, for even in the words of classic authors there is more than they themselves thought or intended. It is a question, rather, what the Spirit of Christ who was in them wished to declare and reveal by them. And *that* is decided by the New Testament, which is the completion, fulfillment, and therefore interpretation of the Old. The nature of a tree is revealed by its fruit. Even modern criticism recognizes that not Judaism but Christianity is the full realization of the religion of the prophets.

The New Testament views itself—and there can certainly be no doubt about this—as the spiritual and therefore complete and authentic fulfillment of the Old Testament. The spiritualization of the Old Testament, rightly understood, is not an invention of Christian theology but has its beginning in the New Testament itself. The Old Testament in spiritualized form, that is, the Old Testament stripped of its temporal and sensuous form, is the New Testament. The peculiar nature of the old dispensation consisted precisely in the fact that the covenant of grace was presented in graphic images and clothed in national and sensuous forms. Sin was symbolized by levitical impurity. Atonement was effected by the sacrifice of a slain animal. Purification was adumbrated by physical washings. Communion with God was connected with the journey to Jerusalem. The desire for God's favor and closeness was expressed in the longing for his courts. Eternal life was conceived as a long life on earth, and so forth. In keeping with Israel's level of understanding, placed as Israel was under the tutelage of the law, all that is spiritual, heavenly, and eternal was veiled in earthly shadows. Even though the great majority of the people frequently fixated on the external forms—just as many Christians in participating in the sacraments continue to cling to the external signs—and while devout Israelites with their hearts indeed penetrated to the spiritual core that was hidden in the shell, they nevertheless saw that spiritual core in no other way than in shadows and images.

For that reason the New Testament says that the Old was "a shadow of the things to come but the substance belongs to Christ," *schia tōn mellontōn, to de sōma tou Christou* (Col. 2:17), "a model and shadow of the heavenly sanctuary," *hypodeigmati kai schia latreuousin tōn epouraniōn* (Heb. 8:5). The shadow, while not itself the body, does point to the body, but vanishes when the body itself appears. The New Testament is the truth, the essence, the core, and the actual content of the Old Testament. The Old Testament is revealed in the New, while the New Testament is concealed in the Old *(Vetus Testamentum in Novo patet, Novum Testamentum in Vetere latet)*. For that reason the New Testament frequently refers to "the truth." Over against the law given by Moses stands the truth that came through Jesus Christ (John 1:14, 17). He is the truth (John 14:6) and the Spirit sent out by him is the Spirit of truth (John 16:13; 1 John 5:6). The Word of God he preached is the Word of truth (John 17:17). The benefits of salvation promised and foreshadowed under the Old Testament have become manifest in Christ as eternal and authentic reality. All the promises of God are "yes" and "amen" in him (2 Cor. 1:20). The Old Testament was not abolished but fulfilled in the new dispensation, is still consistently being fulfilled, and will be fulfilled, until the parousia of Christ.

Christ, therefore, is the true prophet, priest, and king; the true servant of the Lord, the true atonement (Rom. 3:25), the true circumcision (Col. 2:11), the true Passover (1 Cor. 5:7), the true sacrifice (Eph. 5:2), and his body of believers the true offspring of Abraham, the true Israel, the true people of God (Matt. 1:21; Luke 1:17; Rom. 9:25, 26; 2 Cor. 6:16–18; Gal. 3:29; Titus 2:14; Heb. 8:8–10; James 1:1, 18; 1 Peter 2:9; Rev. 21:3, 12), the true temple of God (1 Cor. 3:16; 2 Cor. 6:16; Eph. 2:22; 2 Thess. 2:4; Heb. 8:2), the true Zion and Jerusalem (Gal. 4:26; Heb. 12:22; Rev. 3:12; 21:2, 10). Its spiritual sacrifice is the true religion (John 4:24; Rom. 12:1; Phil. 3:3; 4:18).[14] All Old Testament concepts shed their external, national-Israelitish meanings and become manifest in their spiritual and eternal sense. The Semitic no longer needs to be transposed into the Japhetic, as Bunsen wished, for the New Testament itself has given to the particularistic ideas of the Old Testament a universalist and cosmic meaning.

Totally wrong, therefore, is the chiliastic view according to which the New Testament, along with the church composed of Gentiles, is an intermezzo, a detour taken by God because Israel rejected its Messiah, so that the actual continuation and fulfillment of the Old Testament can only start with Christ's second coming. The opposite, rather, is true. Not the New Testament but the Old is an intermezzo. The covenant with Israel is temporary, the law has been inserted in between the promise to Abraham and its fulfillment in Christ, that it might increase the trespass and be a disciplinarian leading to Christ (Rom. 5:20; Gal. 3:24f.). For that reason Paul always goes back to Abraham (Rom. 4:11f.; Gal. 3:6f.), and links his gospel to the promise made to him. Abraham is the father of believers, of *all* believers, not only believers from among the Jews, but also from among the Gentiles (Rom. 4:11). The children of the promise are his offspring (Rom. 9:6–8). In Christ the blessing of

Abraham comes to the Gentiles (Gal. 3:14). Those who belong to Christ are Abraham's offspring and heirs according to promise (Gal. 3:29).

In the days of the Old Testament the people of Israel were chosen for a time that salvation might later, in the fullness of time, be a blessing for the whole world. Israel was chosen, not to the detriment of but for the benefit of the nations. From its earliest beginning the promise to Adam and Noah had a universalist thrust and, after having put aside its temporary legalistic form under Israel, has, in Christ, fully revealed this before all the nations. The curtain has been torn, the dividing wall has fallen, the handwriting of the law has been nailed to the cross. Now Gentile believers, along with Jews, as fellow heirs, fellow citizens, fellow saints, fellow members of the household of God, have been brought near in Christ and are built upon the same foundation of apostles and prophets (Eph. 1:9–11; 2:11–22).

Therefore the New Testament is not an intermezzo or interlude, neither a detour nor a departure from the line of the Old Covenant, but the long-aimed-for goal, the direct continuation and the genuine fulfillment, of the Old Testament. Chiliasm, judging otherwise, comes in conflict with Christianity itself. In principle it is one with Judaism and must get to where it attributes a temporary, passing value to Christianity, the historical person of Christ, and his suffering and death, and only first expects real salvation from Christ's second coming, his appearance in glory. Like Judaism, it subordinates the spiritual to the material, the ethical to the physical, confirms the Jews in their carnal-mindedness, excuses their rejection of the Messiah, reinforces the veil that lies over their mind when they hear the reading of the Old Testament, and promotes the illusion that the physical descendants of Abraham will as such still enjoy an advantage in the kingdom of heaven. Scripture, on the other hand, tells us that the true reading and interpretation of the Old Testament is to be found with those who have turned in repentance to the Lord Christ (2 Cor. 3:14–16). It tells us that a person is a Jew who is one inwardly and that circumcision is a matter of the heart (Rom. 2:29). It teaches that in Christ there is neither man nor woman, neither Jew nor Greek, but that they are all one in Christ Jesus (1 Cor. 12:13; Gal. 3:28; Col. 3:11). The Jewish person who becomes a Christian was not but becomes a child of Abraham by faith (Gal. 3:29).[15]

Israel, the Millennium, and Christ's Return 5

The chiliast expectation that a converted nation of Israel, restored to the land of Palestine, under Christ will rule over the nations is without biblical foundation. Whatever the political future of Israel as a nation, the real ekklēsia, the people of God, transcends ethnic boundaries. The kingdom of God in the teaching of Jesus is not a political reality but a religious-ethical dominion born of water and the Spirit. The salvation rejected by Israel is shared by the Gentiles, and the community of Christbelievers has in all respects replaced national Israel. New Testament passages, such as Romans 11, which initially seem to teach the contrary, in fact confirm the teaching that God's promises are fulfilled in the spiritual offspring of Abraham, even though they may be only a remnant. Furthermore, the New Testament nowhere suggests that the church of Christ will ever achieve earthly power and dominion such as that of Old Testament Israel. Instead, like its master, the pilgrim church can expect a cross of persecution and suffering. The New Testament does not recommend virtues that lead believers to conquer the world but rather patiently to endure its enmity. John's Apocalypse assures the suffering church of all times that it shares the certainty of Christ's victory even in the face of terrible anti-Christian apostasy, lawlessness, and persecution. Revelation 20, in analogy with the rest of Scripture, confirms this conclusion rather than lending support to chiliast dreams of world rule. Also, Revelation 20 does not teach the chiliast doctrine of a twofold resurrection; the "first" resurrection simply refers to those faithful who die and immediately live and reign with Christ in heaven. When human apostasy and wickedness reach the apex of power and the world is ripe for judgment, Christ the king will suddenly appear to bring about the end of world history. Jesus' disciples are to be watchful of the signs but they are also forbidden to calculate. All believers ought at all times to live as though the coming of Christ is at hand.

Although in the previous chapter we generally established that the New Testament is antichiliastic,[1] we do need to demonstrate this in greater detail. Chiliasm includes the expectation that shortly before the return of Christ a national conversion will occur in Israel, that the Jews will then return to Palestine and from there, under Christ, rule over the nations. In this connection there is some difference among chiliasts over whether the conversion will precede the return or vice versa.[2] Since it is hard to imagine that the dispersed Jews will first be converted successively and then jointly conceive the plan to go to Palestine, some believe that the Jews will first gradually return to Palestine and then later be jointly converted to Christ there. Others attempt to combine the two views in such a way that first a large part of the Jewish people will go to Palestine and that, after having first restored the city and the temple and the temple services and then converted to Christ, they will be gradually followed by their remaining fellow Jews. And they point out that this expectation is already in the process of being fulfilled. Thousands of Jews already live in Palestine. The question of the Near East is approaching solution, for Turkey owes its existence to the mutual jealousies of the great powers. Once Turkey is destroyed there is every chance that Palestine will be assigned to the Jews to whom by rights it belongs. Furthermore, in the hearts of many Jews, as is evident from the Zionism that has emerged in recent years, there is a longing to return to Palestine and to form an independent state there. Finally, the greatly improved modes of transportation—which they read Nahum (2:3, 4) and Isaiah (11:16; 66:20) as having predicted—make such a return simple and convenient.

However we may view these political combinations, the New Testament furnishes not the slightest support for such an expectation. When the fullness of time had come, the Jews, considered as a nation, were on the same level as the Gentiles. Together they were worthy of condemnation before God, because they sought to establish a righteousness of their own based on the law and rejected the righteousness that is through faith (Rom. 3:21). For that reason God sent John to them with the baptism of repentance, thus telling them that, though they were circumcised and though they baptized proselytes, they were guilty and unclean before him and needed rebirth and conversion as much as the Gentiles to enter the kingdom of heaven. By baptism John already separated the true Israelites from the bulk of the people, and Jesus followed in his tracks. He took over John's baptism and had it administered by his disciples. Indeed, initially, like John, he publicly proclaimed that the kingdom was drawing near. But he understood that kingdom very differently from his contemporaries. He did not understand by it a political but a religious-ethical dominion and taught that not physical descent from Abraham but only rebirth from water and spirit gave a person access to the kingdom of heaven. As a result he gradually gathered around him a group of disciples that distinguished and separated itself from the Jewish people. And these were the true *ekklēsia*, the real people of God, as Israel should have been but now in its rejection of the Messiah proved itself not to be.

This separation between the Jews and the New Testament *ekklēsia* became increasingly sharper. Granted, there were many who believed in Christ but the people [as a whole], led by the Pharisees and scribes, rejected him. Though a rising for some, for many he was to be a falling and a sign that was opposed (Luke 2:34). He came to his own people but they did not accept him (John 1:11). Jesus himself says that "prophets are not without honor except in their own country" (Matt. 13:57). Over and over he experienced that the Jews did not wish to come to him (John 5:37–47; 6:64); he testified that they would die in their sin (8:21), that they were children of their father the devil (8:44), plants not planted by the Father (Matt. 15:13, 14), and regarded their unbelief, not as an accidental, unforeseen circumstance, but as the fulfillment of prophecy (Matt. 13:13; John 12:37f.). Not only did Jesus not expect anything *from* the Jews in the present, in the future also he expected nothing *for* them. On the contrary, he announced the total destruction of the city and the temple so that not one stone would be left upon another (Matt. 22:7; 23:37–39; Mark 13; Luke 2:6f.; John 2:18–21; 24:1f.). During his entry into Jerusalem he wept over the city (Luke 19:41–44). On the Monday before his death, on his way to Bethany, he cursed the fig tree which, while it did not yet bear fruit but did already have leaves, was an image of pseudo-pious, self-righteous Israel, and said, "May no one ever eat fruit from you again" (Mark 11:12–14).

On the occasion of his going to the cross he commanded the women not to weep over him but to weep over Jerusalem (Luke 23:28). He even proclaimed that the salvation rejected by Israel would be shared by the Gentiles. The kingdom of God will be taken from Israel and given to a people who produce the fruits of that kingdom (Matt. 21:43). The vineyard will be rented out to other tenants (Matt. 21:41). Invited to the wedding are the people out on the main streets (Matt. 22:9). The lost son takes precedence over the older son (Luke 15). Similarly, Jesus states that many will come from the east and the west and sit down in the kingdom of heaven with Abraham, Isaac, and Jacob (Matt. 8:10–12); that he has other sheep not of this sheepfold (John 10:16). He rejoices that, as certain Greeks desire to see him, he will soon, like a grain of wheat, fall into the earth and die and so bear much fruit (John 12:24). Accordingly, after his resurrection he instructs his disciples to preach the gospel to all nations (Matt. 28:18).

In the case of the apostles we encounter the same judgment concerning Israel. As Jesus' witnesses they must indeed begin their work in Jerusalem but then continue to the ends of the earth (Acts 1:8). Peter therefore immediately brings the gospel to the Jews (Acts 2:14; 3:19; 5:31), but then learns in a vision that from then on no one is unclean but that anyone who fears God, no matter of what nation he has been born, is acceptable to him (Acts 10:35, 43). Paul always begins his preaching among the Jews but when they reject it he turns to the Gentiles (Acts 13:46; 18:6; 28:25–28). "First the Jew but then also the Greek" is the rule he observes on his missionary journeys (Rom. 1:16; 1 Cor. 1:21–24). For both Jews and Gentiles are worthy of condemnation before God and need the same gospel (Rom. 3:19f.). There is but one way to salvation for all, faith—the faith as it was practiced by Abraham even before the law came, and was reckoned to him as righteousness (Rom. 4:22; Gal. 3). Those of the Jews who reject Christ are not really true Jews (Rom. 2:28, 29). They are not the "circumcision" but the "mutilation" (Phil. 3:2). They are the irregulars, idle talkers, deceivers, who must be silenced (Titus 1:10, 11). They have killed the Lord Jesus and their own prophets as well. They persecute believers, do not please God, and oppose everyone. They hinder the apostles from speaking to the Gentiles. Thus they constantly fill up the measure of their sins, so that now God's wrath has reached its limit and is being discharged upon them (1 Thess. 2:14–16). The Jews who slander the church of Smyrna, though they say they are Jews, are not; rather they are a synagogue of Satan (Rev. 2:9; 3:9). Real Jews, the true children of Abraham, are those who believe in Christ (Rom. 9:8; Gal. 3:29, etc.). This is the New Testament's judgment concerning the Jews. The community of believers has in all respects replaced carnal, national Israel. The Old Testament is fulfilled in the New.[3]

Difficult Passages on Israel and the Church

Only a few passages seem to be at variance with this consistent teaching of Scripture and to mean something different. The first is Matthew 23:37–39 (Luke 13:33–35), where Jesus tells the inhabitants of Jerusalem that their house will be left to them desolate, and that they will not see him again until they say, "Blessed is the one who comes in the name of the Lord." Here Jesus in fact expresses the expectation that one day, namely, at his return, the Jews will recognize him as the Messiah. Now, if from another text we were certain of a millennium and a conversion coincident with it, then this passage could be explained in light of it. But since this is not the case, not even in Revelation 20, as will be made clear later, this passage can only refer to an acknowledgment of the Messiah by the Jews at Christ's coming again for judgment. And until then—Jesus expressly states—Jerusalem will be left desolate. Jesus therefore in no way expects a rebuilding of the city and the temple before his return.

A second passage to be considered is Luke 21:24, where Jesus says that Jerusalem will be trampled on by the Gentiles until the times of the Gentiles are fulfilled. The conjunction "until" *(achri)* does not suggest the implication that with the onset of the period described by it the opposite will occur (the Jews will rebuild and inhabit Jerusalem). But even if this were the case, Jesus is not saying that the trampling of Jerusalem will end before his parousia, for after having pronounced judgment over Jerusalem he immediately proceeds to discuss the signs that will occur before and at his return (Luke 21:25f.). The times of the Gentiles continue until his return. Again, if the New Testament taught a twofold return of Christ, this passage could be interpreted in terms of it, but it will become evident in a moment that there is no ground in the New Testament for this position.

The third text that comes up in this connection is Acts 3:19–21. In this passage Peter calls the Jews to repentance that their sins may be wiped out, times of refreshing *(kairoi anapsuxeōs)* may come from the presence of the Lord, and he, that is, God, may send the Messiah appointed for the Jews, that is, Jesus, who must remain in heaven until the time of the restoration of all things. Some think that the "times of refreshing" referred to here will begin when the Jewish people are converted and all things are again restored in the millennium in keeping with their original destiny and that these "times" will then last until the second return of Christ. But there are serious objections against this interpretation. The times of universal restoration *(chronoi apokatastaseōs pantōn)* can hardly be understood of the restoration of natural and moral relations expected by chiliasts in the millennium. We are clearly told that these times occur at the end of Jesus' stay in heaven. Until that time, then, Jesus will be at his Father's right hand and, since Scripture knows of only one return of Christ, the times of the restoration of all things will coincide with the consummation of the world. In addition, the expression "the restoration of all things" *(apokatastasis pantōn)* is much too strong for the restoration of the Jewish kingdom expected by chiliasm. Accordingly, the times of refreshing are not identical with but precede the times of the restoration of all things. Peter, after all, in speaking of the conversion of the Jews, refers to a twofold purpose: that times of refreshing may come for them and that God may send them the Christ appointed for them. The "times of refreshing" take place before the return of Christ and refer either to the spiritual peace that is the result of repentance and the forgiveness of sins or to certain future times of divine blessing and favor. The latter is most probable because the times of refreshing are not immediately associated with the forgiveness of sins but with the mission of Christ. Then what Peter says here is this: "Repent, O Jews, that your sins may be wiped out, so that for you, too, as a people who have handed over, rejected, and killed Christ (vv. 13–15), times of refreshing may come from the presence of the Lord, and God may afterward send the Christ who was appointed for you in the first place (v. 26) in order, also for your salvation, to restore all things." Whether such times will ever come for the Jews Peter does not say. That depends on their conversion, a conversion of which nothing is said to suggest that it is to be expected.

"All Israel" in Romans 11

The final passage to be considered is Romans 11:11–32. In Romans 9–11 Paul deals with the awesome problem of how God's promise to Israel can be squared with the rejection of the gospel by the greater majority of the people of Israel. In response, the apostle replies in the first place that the promise of God concerns not the carnal but the spiritual offspring of Abraham and works this out in great detail in chapters 9 and 10. In the second place he remarks that God still has his elect also in Israel and therefore has not rejected that people. Paul himself is proof of this and many others with him. Though many have become hard and blind, the elect have received salvation: there has consistently been a remnant chosen by grace (11:1–10). But this hardening that has come over the great majority of the people of Israel is not God's final goal. In his hand it is rather a means to bring salvation to the Gentiles in order that they, accepting that salvation in faith, may in turn arouse Israel to jealousy (vv. 11–15). After admonishing believers from the Gentiles not to boast of their advantage (vv. 16–24), Paul further develops this thought, saying that a hardening has come over a part of Israel until the *plērōma* of the Gentiles, the full number of those from their midst who were destined for salvation, has come in. And in that way, in keeping with God's promise, all Israel will be saved. Hence, though now the unbelieving Jews are enemies of God as regards the gospel in order that the salvation they have rejected should come to the Gentiles, as regards election they are beloved for the sake of their ancestors, for God's promises are irrevocable. Therefore, just as things were with the Gentiles, so will they go with the Jews who are hardened. First the Gentiles were disobedient and now receive mercy, so now the Jews, too, are disobedient that through the mercy shown to the Gentiles, they may receive mercy as well. For God has imprisoned all, Gentiles and Jews, in disobedience so that he may be merciful to all (vv. 25–32).

Most interpreters think that the question whether God has rejected his people (v. 1) has not been fully answered by the assertion that in Israel God always has his elect, the people who, in the course of centuries, are successively brought in (vv. 1–10). They judge, therefore, that everything that follows in chapter 11 is not just a further explication of, but an addition to, the answer given in verses 1–10, a new answer that only now fully disposes of the objection that God rejected his people. By "all

Israel" *(pas Israēl)* they therefore understand the whole of the people of Israel which in the last days will repent and turn to the Lord.

But no matter how commonly held this explanation is, there are weighty objections to it. If in 11:25–32 it were the intent of the apostle to give a new, supplementary answer he would render his reasoning at the end inconsistent with its beginning and starting point. In 9:6f., after all, he stated that the promises of God have not failed because they concern the spiritual offspring of Abraham and will still consistently find their fulfillment in this spiritual offspring (11:1–10). It is a priori very unlikely that Paul later reconsidered this reasoning, supplementing and improving it in the sense that the promises of God are not fully realized in the salvation of spiritual Israel but will be fully realized only when in the last days a national conversion of Israel takes place. In any case, in 9:1–10:11 Paul does not breathe a word about such an expectation for the people of Israel, nor is there any expression here that prepares or intimates it. Nor does even 11:11–24 as yet contain anything that points to it. Granted, 11:11–15 is understood by many in that sense. But even if these words were to be understood, not hypothetically as an element in an argument, but as the description of a fact, they convey no more than the idea that Israel's rejection of Christ was a great gain for the Gentiles for by it the reconciliation effected by Christ's death fell to the Gentiles. God's *acceptance* of Israel will then be a much greater boon to the Gentiles, for when Israel has reached its *plērōma*, the full number of its elect, and also the *plērōma* of the Gentiles has entered in, that will bring about life from the dead: the resurrection from the dead of the new humanity. The Gentile world owes its reconciliation, mediately speaking, to Israel's failure; to Israel's fullness *(plērōma)* it will someday owe its life from the dead.

If in 11:26 Paul is seeking to convey a new fact, the manner in which he does it is very odd indeed. For he does not say *and then*, or *thereupon*, that is, after the fullness of the Gentiles has come in, all Israel will, but "and in *that way* all Israel will be saved" *(kai outōs pas Israēl sōthēsetai)*. That can only mean: in the way described in the preceding verses. Just prior to this, in verse 25, Paul stated that a hardening has come over only a part *(apo merous)* of Israel. Believers among the Gentiles might perhaps begin to think—as Israel used to think—that they alone were the elect people of God and that Israel was totally rejected. But Paul says that this is not so. No: Israel as such has not been rejected. Among them there has always been a remnant chosen by grace. True enough, some branches have been broken off, and in their place a wild olive shoot has been grafted in, but the stem of the tame olive tree has been preserved. When the *plērōma* (fullness) of the Gentiles comes in, also the *plērōma* of Israel is brought in, and *in that way* all Israel is saved.

This fact, that a hardening has come *upon a part* of Israel, Paul calls a mystery (*mystērion*, 11:25). Elsewhere he frequently calls by that name the fact that now the Gentiles are fellow heirs and fellow citizens with the saints, fellow members of the household of God, and here he describes with the same word the fact that the Jews have only in part become hardened and that God continually brings numerous elect from among them into his church. For that *partial* hardening will last until the *plērōma* of the Gentiles will have come in. Never, up until the end of the ages, will God totally reject his ancient people; he will always bring to faith in Christ, alongside a part from the Gentile world, a part from Israel as well. The Gentiles, but also the Jews, had deserved a very different fate. But this is the great mystery: that God is rich in mercy; that he gathers his elect from every nation, also that of the Jews who rejected him; that he imprisoned all in disobedience that he might be merciful to all. That mystery sends the apostle into ecstasy and causes him to marvel at and adore the depth of God's wisdom and knowledge (11:33–36).

All Israel *(pas Israēl)* in 11:26 is not, therefore, the people of Israel that at the end of time will be converted in mass. Nor is it the church of the Jews and the Gentiles together. But it is the *plērōma* that in the course of centuries will be brought in from Israel. Israel will continue to exist as a people alongside the Gentiles, predicts Paul. It will not expire or disappear from the earth. It will remain to the end of the ages, produce its *plērōma* for the kingdom of God as well as the Gentiles, and keep its special task and place for that kingdom. The church of God will be gathered out of all peoples and nations and tongues. Paul does not calculate how large that *plērōma* from Israel will be. It is very possible that in the last days the number of the elect from Israel will be much greater than it was in Paul's, or in later, or in our time. There is not a single reason for denying this. The spread of the gospel among all peoples rather prompts us to expect that both from Israel and from the Gentiles an ever-increasing number will be saved. But that is not what Paul intends to say: he does not count, but weighs. A full *plērōma* will come from the Gentile world, as well as from Israel, and that *plērōma* will be all Israel *(pas Israēl)*. In that *plērōma* all Israel is saved, just as in the church as a whole the whole of humanity is being saved.

It is also the case that a conversion of Israel other than the one indicated by Paul is hard to conceive. For that matter, just what is a national conversion and how and when will it take place in the case of Israel? One cannot of course have the least objection—the continued existence of the people of Israel in the light of prophecy rather argues for it—to the fact that from Israel as well a very large number of people are still being brought to faith in Christ. But however large this number may be, it remains a remnant chosen by grace (Rom. 11:5). Certainly not even the most fervent chiliast thinks that at some point in the future all Jews without exception will be converted. And even if he did believe this, thinking that in that way alone Romans 11:26 would be completely fulfilled, then such an endtime national conversion would still not help the millions of Jews who, throughout the ages and right up until the end, died in unbelief and hardness of heart. Were a person really to think that God's promise to Israel can only be fulfilled if—not a selection *(eklogē)* from the people but—the nation itself were brought into the fold, he or she would come into conflict with the history in question. Always, throughout all the ages, also in the days when Israel as a nation was the people of God, it was never more than a small segment of the people who truly served and feared God. And this is how it is not only in the case of the Jews, but also in the case of the Gentiles. It is always "a remnant chosen by grace" which, from within Christian nations, obtains salvation in Christ.

Further, there is no room left in Paul's sketch of the future for a national conversion of Israel such as chiliasts expect. For he expressly states that a hardening has come on part of Israel *until* the full number *(plērōma)* of the Gentiles has come in and that *in that way* (not *after that*) all Israel will be saved (11:25, 26). Therefore, the hardening on part of Israel will last until the *plērōma* from the Gentile world has come in and, after that, according to chiliasts, the national conversion of Israel has to occur. The question is: Is there, then, a lapse of time between the coming of the *plērōma* from the Gentile world and the end of the ages? If so, are there still Gentile nations in that period and is there not a single person from among them that turns to the Lord? The truth is, the coming in of the *plērōma* of the Gentiles cannot be conceived as temporally antecedent to the salvation of all Israel. For Romans 11:26 does not mention a new fact that takes place *after* the coming in of the full number of the Gentiles. But the coming in of the full number of the Gentiles and the salvation of all Israel run parallel because a hardening has come on only a part of Israel.

In conclusion it should be noted that, even if Paul expected a national conversion of Israel at the end, he does not say a word about the return of the Jews to Palestine, about a rebuilding of the city and a temple, about a visible rule of Christ: in his picture of the future there simply is no room for all this.[4]

An Interim Millennial Age?

In our discussion of the expectations that the New Testament fosters with regard to the future of the people of Israel we left undecided the question whether the New Testament, in passages other than the ones cited in this connection so far, perhaps taught the existence of an interim state between this dispensation and the consummation of the ages. We acknowledged that if that were the case Matthew 23:37–39, Luke 21:24, and Acts 3:19–21, although by themselves give us no reason whatever for the acceptance of a transitional period, could nevertheless be understood and explained along those lines. We now face the question, therefore, whether according to Jesus and the apostles there still awaits the church a period of power and glory that precedes the general resurrection of the dead and the event of world judgment. If this were so, we would expect clear mention of it in the eschatological discourse that Jesus gave his disciples in the final days of his life (Matt. 24; Mark 13; Luke 21). But in this discourse not a word is said, not even an allusion is made, about such a kingdom. True, chiliasts try to insert their millennium in one part or another of the discourse, saying, for example, that Christ's first coming is mentioned in Matthew 24:27 and his second coming in verse 30, but this exegesis is certainly without any foundation.

In his eschatological discourse Jesus responds to two questions put to him by his disciples. They are: (1) when will the things he has said concerning Jerusalem—namely, that not one stone of the temple will be left upon another—take place? and (2) what will be the sign of his coming and of the consummation of the world?

Jesus replies to the question by first dealing with the early signs (Mark 13:1–8; cf. Matt. 24:1–8; Luke 21:5–11), then with the fate of the disciples (Mark 13:9–13; cf. Matt. 24:9–14; Luke 21:12–18), and finally with the catastrophe in Judea (Mark 13:14–23; cf. Matt. 24:15–26; Luke 21:20–24). The second question, the one concerning the parousia of Jesus and the consummation of the world, is answered in Mark 13:24–31 (cf. Matt. 24:29–35; Luke 21:25–33). And in this connection Jesus links his parousia immediately with the destruction of Jerusalem. In the fall of this city he sees the announcement and preparation of the consummation of the world (Matt. 24:29; "immediately" *[eutheōs];* Mark 13:24: "in those days" *[en ekeinais tais hēmerais]).* He even states that "this generation will certainly not pass away until all these things have taken place" (Matt. 24:34; Mark 13:30; Luke 21:32).

However this expectation on the part of Jesus of his early parousia—an event immediately following the destruction of Jerusalem—is to be understood (on which more later), in any case it is clearly evident that in this discourse there is no room for a thousand-year kingdom. Jesus first sums up (Mark 13:1–8) a number of general signs by which the disciples can tell that all things, specifically the destruction of Jerusalem and the end of the world, are approaching in tandem. These general signs *(signa communia)* are the rise of pseudo-Christs; wars and rumors of wars; the disturbance and rebellion of nations against nations, along with earthquakes and famine, and the like; then the preaching of the gospel in the entire world as a testimony to all the nations (Matt. 24:14; Mark 13:10). And finally, as a prelude to the drama of the end, the things that happen in Judea and Jerusalem (Matt. 24:15–28; Mark 13:14–23). Then follow the signs that immediately precede the parousia (the *signa propria*): the darkening of sun and moon, the falling down of the stars, and the shaking of the powers in the heavens (Mark 13:24, 25).

Immediately linked with Christ's parousia, then, are the judgment, the separation of the good and evil, the end of the world (Mark 13:26, 27). Consonant with this is what Jesus says in Matthew 13:37–43, 47–50: the growth, side by side, of wheat and weeds, and the catching in a single net of all kinds of fish, events that continue to the end of the age until the time of the harvest and the judgment of the world. Jesus only knows of two aeons: the present and the future aeons. In the present aeon his disciples cannot expect anything other than oppression and persecution and must forsake all things for his sake. Jesus nowhere predicts a glorious future on earth before the end of the world. On the contrary, the things he experienced are the things his church will experience. A disciple is not above his teacher, nor a slave above the master. Only in the age to come will his disciples receive everything back along with eternal life (Matt. 19:27–30; cf. Matt. 5:3–12; 8:19, 20; 10:16–42; 16:24–27; John 16:2, 33; 17:14, 15, etc.). Accordingly, when the disciples in Acts 1:6 ask Jesus whether this is the time he will restore the kingdom to Israel, he does not deny it but tacitly admits that this will happen someday. But he says that the Father has set the times or seasons for this by his own authority and that in this period the disciples have the calling to act as his witnesses from Jerusalem to the ends of the earth.

The whole New Testament, which was written from the viewpoint of the "church under the cross," speaks the same language. Believers, not many of whom are wise, powerful, or of noble birth (1 Cor. 1:26), should not expect anything on earth other than suffering and oppression (Rom. 8:36; Phil. 1:29). They are sojourners and foreigners (Heb. 11:13); their citizenship is in the heavens (Phil. 3:20); they do not look at the things that can be seen (2 Cor. 4:18), but mind the things that are above (Col. 3:2). Here they have no lasting city but are looking for the city that is to come (Heb. 13:14). They are saved in hope (Rom. 8:24) and know that if they suffer with Christ they will also be glorified with him (Rom. 6:8; 8:17; Col. 3:4). Therefore, along with the entire groaning creation, they wait with eager longing for the future of Christ and for the revelation of the glory of the children of God (Rom. 8:19; 1 Cor. 15:48f.), a glory with which the sufferings of the present time are not worth comparing (Rom. 8:18; 2 Cor. 4:17). Nowhere in the New Testament is there a ray of hope that the church of Christ will again come to power and dominion on earth. The most it may look for is that, under kings and all who are in high positions, it may lead a quiet and peaceable life in all godliness and dignity (Rom. 13:1; 1 Tim. 2:2). Therefore, the New Testament does not first of all recommend the virtues that enable believers to conquer the world but, while it bids them avoid all false asceticism (Rom. 14:14; 1 Tim. 4:4, 5; Titus 1:15), lists as fruits of the Spirit the virtues of love, joy, peace, patience, kindness, generosity, faithfulness, gentleness, and self-control (Gal. 5:22; Eph. 4:32; 1 Thess. 5:14f.; 1 Peter 3:8f.; 2 Peter 1:5–7; 1 John 2:15, etc.).

It is a constant New Testament expectation that to the extent to which the gospel of the cross is spread abroad, to that extent the hostility of the world will be manifested as well. Christ is destined to be a rising for many but also to be a falling for many, and to bring out into the open the hostile thoughts of many. He has come into the world for judgment *(crisis)* that those who do not see may see and that those who see may become blind (Matt. 21:44; Luke 2:34; John 3:19–21, 8:39; Rom. 9:32, 33; 1 Cor. 1:23; 2 Cor. 2:16; Heb. 4:12; 1 Peter 2:7, 8). In the last days, the days that precede the return of Christ, the wickedness of human beings will rise to a fearful level. The days of Noah will return. Lust, sensual pleasures, lawlessness, greed, unbelief, pride, mockery, and slander will erupt in fearful ways (Matt. 24:37f.; Luke 17:26f.; 2 Tim. 3:1; 2 Peter 3:3; Jude 18). Among believers as well there will be extensive apostasy. Temptations will be so powerful that, were it possible, even the elect would be caused to fall. The love of many will grow cold and vigilance diminish to the extent that the wise will fall asleep along with the foolish virgins. Apostasy will be so general that Jesus can ask whether at his coming the Son of man will still find faith on earth (Matt. 24:24, 44f.; 25:1f.; Luke 18:8; 1 Tim. 4:1).

John's Apocalypse

The Book of Revelation, which John wrote, is in agreement with this. The letters to the seven churches do indeed deal with concrete conditions prevailing in those churches at the time and are first of all addressed to those churches, to incite them to watchfulness and to prepare them for the coming persecutions and the return of Christ. Still their intent and import are clearly much broader. The number seven, which in Revelation is consistently charged with symbolic meaning, already points in that direction. It is the number of completeness and makes the seven churches, which have here been selected from among the many churches in Asia Minor, appear as types of the Christian church as a whole. The letters addressed by John to the churches did not first have a separate existence and were not sent separately to the respective churches. Rather, they belong together, were composed together and joined to each other, and are addressed to the whole church: "let anyone who has an ear listen to what the Spirit is saying to all the churches." But though the letters therefore undoubtedly have a significance that reaches far beyond the seven churches referred to by name and existing at the time in Asia Minor, this significance does not consist in that they describe successive periods in the history of Jesus' church and together make up a little compendium of the whole history of the church. Instead, they depict church conditions that were then present and are at the same time typical for the church of Christ as a whole, conditions that may recur over and over in the church and will recur especially at the end of history. For it is clear that they were all written under the impression of approaching persecution and the speedy return of Christ. They all contain a reference to the parousia and with a view to it exhort the churches to be watchful and faithful. They serve to call an increasingly worldly Christianity back to its first love, to arouse it from apathy, and with an eye to the crown awaiting it, to equip it for battle and to prompt it to persevere, with unyielding loyalty, even unto death.

For the day of the Lord is drawing near. After describing the conditions that existed in the church of Christ of his time and would exist, especially toward the end of the world, John proceeds to report the things that are about to happen (4:1). The book of God's decrees concerning the end of all things is opened in heaven by the Lamb (chs. 4 and 5) and in particular that which relates to the very end of time (ch. 10) and concerns all the nations of the earth (10:11) is shown to John by an angel. John alternately positions the reader on earth and in heaven. In heaven, for there everything has already been settled and determined; there honor is already being brought to God and to the Lamb; there the battle has, as it were, already been fought and won (chs. 4 and 5). There the souls of the martyrs are already clothed in long white garments and await the fulfillment of their number (6:9–11). There John proleptically sees the whole multitude of the redeemed standing before the throne (7:9–19). There the prayers of the saints have already been heard by God (8:1–4). There, proleptically as well, the 144,000 who were sealed (7:1–8) have been taken up; as firstfruits they precede the rest (14:1–5), and have gained victory over the beast and his image (15:1–4). There the whole multitude of the redeemed are already bringing glory and honor to God since the marriage of the Lamb has come (19:1–8).

The church on earth therefore does not need to be afraid of the judgments with which God in the end visits the world. The 144,000 servants of God out of every tribe of the sons of Israel are sealed in advance (7:1–

8). The temple and the altar and those who worship there are not abandoned to the heathen, and the two witnesses who prophesied there,
though they were killed, are also raised up and taken up into heaven
(11:1–12). The Christian church, though persecuted by Satan for
Christ's sake, finds a place of refuge in the wilderness (12:1–14). In principle, the battle has been decided. For Christ has been taken up into
heaven (12:5) and Satan has been defeated by Michael and his angels
and thrown from heaven down to earth (12:7–11). Now he has but little
time left on earth (12:12), and takes advantage of it. He effects the rise
of the beast from the sea or from the bottomless pit (11:7; 13:1; 17:8)
and gives it power and glory. This beast is the Roman Empire (13:1–10).
It is supported by another beast, the beast of the earth, that is, the false
prophet, false religion, the Antichrist (13:11–18). This "beast" comes to
full development in a single person, who can therefore himself be called
"the beast" (13:3, 12, 18; 17:8, 10, 11) and who has his center in the city
of "Babylon," that is, Rome, the great harlot, who rules over all the nations (chs. 17, 18). But this massive development of power is futile. By
opening the seven seals, by blowing the seven trumpets, by emptying
the seven bowls, God displays his wrath, visits nature and humanity
with his judgments, and makes preparations for the final judgment.
First "Babylon" falls (ch. 18). Then Christ appears (19:11–16) and conquers the beast from the sea and the beast of the earth (vv. 19–21), and
soon Satan as well (20:1–3).

Now it is very peculiar that this last victory over Satan occurs in two
phases. First he is bound for a thousand years and thrown into the bottomless pit; then he again deceives the nations and makes war against
the church. But then he is overcome for good and thrown into the lake
of fire and brimstone (20:1–10). Proponents of chiliasm find in this per-
icope—aside from the Old Testament—their most powerful support,
while opponents are not a little perplexed at this passage and have
tested all their exegetical skills on it. The idea that, following the con-
quest of the world empire, a final attack from the side of the nations still
has to be repulsed is one that John undoubtedly borrowed from Ezekiel.
The latter expects that Israel, having returned to its own land and living
there in security, will once more be attacked by Gog of the land of Magog, the chief prince of Meshech and Tubal, that is, the nation of the
Scythians allied with a variety of other nations from the north, east, and
south. The attack ends, however, when God himself in his wrath destroys these nations on the mountains of Israel (chs. 38, 39). In 38:17 the
Lord says that, by the ministry of his prophets, he had already spoken
of these nations earlier. And indeed these earlier prophets proclaimed
that the Lord in his day would judge not only those historic nations in
the midst of whom Israel lived and with whom it came in contact, but

all the pagans living afar off as well (Isa. 25:5–8; 26:21; Jer. 12:14–16; 30:23, 24; Joel 2:32; 3:2, 11f.; Mic. 4:5, 11; 5:6–8;). A very similar prophecy clearly occurs in Zechariah, which in chapters 12–14 sketches how against the day of the Lord Jerusalem will be besieged by the nations and how these will then be judged by the Lord. And Daniel not only regards Antiochus Epiphanes as the personified embodiment of the world empire that is hostile to God, but also expects that this hostile power will rise up once more and thus become ripe for judgment (11:40f.).

The expectation of prophecy was therefore twofold: it first envisioned a victory of the people of God over the nations in whose midst it lived, and then a victory over the nations that up until then had not yet appeared on the stage of world history. This double expectation passed into the apocryphal literature[5] and also into the New Testament. The first expectation is, of course, in the foreground. The appearance of Christ arouses and activates the anti-Christian principle. Jesus speaks of false prophets and false Christs (*pseudoprophētai* and *pseudochristoi*), who position themselves against him and his kingdom (Matt. 7:15; 24:5, 24; Mark 13:21, 22; Luke 17:23). In 2 Thessalonians 2, to moderate the impatience of the Thessalonians relative to their expectation of Jesus' speedy return, Paul points out that that day of Christ will not come unless the apostasy and the Man of Sin come first. The latter cannot yet come because there is something restraining him. Indeed at work already is the mystery of lawlessness (*to mystērion tēs anomias*); only the Man of Sin cannot come until he who now restrains him is removed from their midst. Only then will the lawless one (*anomos*) be revealed but he will also immediately be slain by Jesus (2:6–8). The Apocalypse sees anti-Christian power embodied in the beast from the sea, the Roman Empire, whose center is the city of Rome and whose head is a specific emperor; and, parallel to this, in the beast of the earth, false prophecy that seduces people into worshiping the world empire and its emperor. In his letters John first calls this adversary of Christ by the name of Antichrist (*antichristos*), in 1 John 2:18 probably even without the article; and he sees his essence realized in those who in principle deny the coming of Christ in the flesh (1 John 2:22; 4:2, 3; 2 John 7).

The representations of Antichrist, in Scripture, are therefore diverse. Daniel sees his type in Antiochus Epiphanes. Jesus detaches the anti-Christian principle from the Old Testament antithesis between Israel and the nations and sees it embodied in many false Christs and many false prophets who will rise up after and against him. Paul has the Man of Sin arise from a general apostasy and calls him the lawless one (*anomos*) and the opponent (*antikeimenos*) of Christ but also depicts him with features derived from Daniel as the one "who exalts himself above every so-called god or object of worship, so that he takes his seat in the temple of God, declaring himself to be God" (2 Thess. 2:4). John, in his letters, expresses the belief that Antichrist has come in the heretics of his days. And the Apocalypse, in turn, sees his power emerge in the world empire supported by false prophecy. From this it is evident that in seeing the word "Antichrist" we must not think exclusively of one person in particular, or of a group of persons, say, the heretics of the first centuries, the Roman Empire, Nero, the Jews, Mohammed, the pope, Napoleon, and the like. Scripture clearly teaches that the power of Antichrist has its own history, manifests itself at different times and in different ways, and finally evolves in a general apostasy and the breakdown of all natural and moral ties that now still hold back such apostasy, and then embodies itself in a world empire that utilizes the false church and apotheosizes itself by deifying the head of that empire. Christ himself, by his appearing, then destroys this anti-Christian power in its highest and latest manifestation.[6]

But, with this, complete victory has not yet been achieved. In the nature of the case the anti-Christian principle can only become active in those nations that have known the gospel and have finally, in conscious and deliberate hostility, rejected it. But there have always been, still are today, and will be until the end of time, nations which, like lopped-off branches of a tree, lie outside the history and culture of humankind. Jesus does say (Matt. 24:14) that the end will not come until the gospel has been preached throughout the entire inhabited world as a testimony to all nations. But certainly this prophecy does not imply that someday Christianity will be the dominant religion in all nations, or that it will be known to all people individually, for history teaches that millions of people and countless nations, also in the centuries following Christ's coming on earth, have died and disappeared without having had any knowledge of the gospel. But Jesus' saying only means that the preaching of the gospel will get through to all nations. It by no means defines the measure in which, or the limits to which, this will happen. Nor is this prophecy realized at one time, but successively in the course of centuries, so that many nations that once walked in the light of the gospel have later been deprived of it again. Whereas in the present century the gospel is spreading among pagans, in Christian nations apostasy is increasing at a rapid rate. It is therefore more than likely that toward the time of the parousia many peoples on earth will be deprived of the knowledge of Christ.

The Millennium in Revelation 20

It is this reality that is reflected in the twentieth chapter of John's Revelation. Because we read there of a thousand-year binding of Satan and of martyrs living and ruling with Christ in that time, many have believed that here, in clear, undeniable language, a thousand-year reign is being taught. In fact, however, this interpretation of Revelation 20, though it is in accord with the analogy of apocryphal literature, is not in accord with the analogy of Scripture. Revelation 20 as such contains nothing of all the things that belong to the essence of chiliastic belief.

The reasons for this latter statement are as follows. To begin with, the chapter does not say a word about a conversion and return of the Jews, of the rebuilding of Jerusalem, of a restoration of the temple and temple worship, of an initial renewal of the earth. These things, rather, are excluded. For even if the 144,000 in chapter 7 are to be understood as referring to the *plērōma* from Israel and are distinct from those mentioned in 14:1, what this would mean is nothing other and nothing more than that also many Christians from among the Jews will remain firm in the great tribulation and assume a place of their own among the multitude standing before the throne of God. But it in no way states that they will arise from the dead and live in Jerusalem. Christians, in this book, are the real Jews and the Jews who harden themselves in unbelief are a synagogue of Satan (2:9). Although the earthly Jerusalem is occasionally called the holy city and the temple in Jerusalem is called the temple of God (11:1, 2), still that Jerusalem is allegorically called "Sodom" and "Egypt" (11:8). The true Jerusalem is above (3:12; 21:2, 10) and there, too, is the temple of God (3:12; 7:15; 11:19, etc.), the ark (11:16), and the altar (6:9; 8:3, 5; 9:13; 14:18; 16:7). And that Jerusalem does not come down from heaven in Revelation 20 but only in Revelation 21.

Second, the life and rule of the believers who remained faithful in the great tribulation take place in heaven, not on earth. Not a word is said about the earth. John saw the angel who binds Satan come down from heaven (20:1); the thrones he saw (20:4) are located in heaven (4:4; 11:16), and the souls of the martyrs are seen here (20:4), as in every other passage, in heaven (6:9; 7:9, 14, 15; 11:12; 14:1–5; 18:20; 19:1–8). Christ already on earth made believers kings and priests to God (1:6). That is what they *are* in heaven (5:10) and they expect that one day they will be that on earth as well (5:10), but this expectation is only fulfilled in the new Jerusalem that comes down from above. Then they will be kings forever (22:5). But now, in heaven, this kingship is temporary: it lasts a thousand years.

Third, John also does not know of a physical resurrection that precedes the millennium and a second that follows it. Such a first resurrection is not taught anywhere in Scripture. There is indeed mention of a spiritual resurrection from sin (John 4:25, 26; Rom. 6:4, etc.). There is also a resurrection from the dead *(anastasis ek nekrōn)* that refers to individual cases, like the resurrection of Christ (1 Peter 1:3; cf. Acts 26:23; 1 Cor. 15:23) or only to believers (Luke 20:35, 36; Acts 4:2), but in that case it is absolutely not distinguished temporally by a thousand-year reign from the universal resurrection from the dead *(anastasis nekrōn)* (Matt. 22:31; John 5:28, 29; Acts 24:15; 1 Cor. 15:13, 42). True, some writers have tried to find this distinction in 1 Corinthians 15:20–28 and 1 Thessalonians 4:13–18 but they do so erroneously. In 1 Corinthians 15:20–28 Paul is most certainly dealing only with the resurrection of believers, while he does not breathe a word, nor does he need to, about that of the ungodly. But of the resurrection of believers he clearly states that it will occur at the time of Christ's parousia, and that *then* the end comes, when he delivers the kingdom to the Father (vv. 23, 24). One could indeed infer from this passage that, according to Paul, there is no resurrection of the ungodly, but one could not possibly derive from it that the latter is separated by a thousand-year reign from that of believers. For the resurrection of believers is immediately followed by the end and the delivering up of the kingdom, because all [God's] enemies have been vanquished and the last enemy, death, has been destroyed.

Nor is there any hint of such a prior physical resurrection of believers in 1 Thessalonians 4:13–18. In Thessalonica people were worried about the lot of those who died in Christ—we do not know why. Chiliasts think that, while the Thessalonians did not doubt the resurrection and eternal life of those who died in Christ, they believed in two resurrections, one before and one after the thousand-year reign, and were worried that the believers who had already died would only rise again in the second resurrection and would therefore have no part in the glory of the thousand-year reign. But this opinion is farfetched and has no support whatever in the text. If in fact there was a first resurrection of believers one would expect rather that the church in Thessalonica would not be worried about the lot of the dead, for these would of course be precisely the kind who would share in that first resurrection. And if someone were to respond by saying that the information that there is a prior resurrection of believers is precisely what the Thessalonians did not know, then the apostle could simply have informed them in a few words. But he does not do this at all. He does not speak of a first and second resurrection. He only asserts that the believers who will still be alive at Jesus' coming will have no advantage over those who already died in Christ earlier. We do not know in what respect the Thessalonians thought that the latter would be at a disadvantage by comparison with the former. But it does not matter. The fact is that this is what they thought in Thessalonica. And over against this idea Paul now says that this is not the case. In fact, through Jesus who will raise them from the dead, God will cause the now-dead believers to be immediately with him (with Jesus) in his future, so that he will, as it were, bring them along with him. And the believers who are left and alive will by no means have an advantage over them, inasmuch as the resurrection of the dead comes first and then all believers, both the resurrected and the transformed, will be caught up together in the clouds to meet the Lord. The text, therefore, does not say anything about a first and second resurrection.

If, then, such a twofold resurrection occurs nowhere else in Scripture, we will do well not to find it too quickly in Revelation 20. And in reality it does not occur there either. We only read in verses 4 and 5 that the souls of the believers who remained faithful in the great tribulation live and reign as kings with Christ a thousand years and that this is the first resurrection. John clearly says that he saw the souls *(tas psychas)* of the martyrs (cf. 6:9) and makes no mention of the resurrection of their bodies. He further says that the souls lived and reigned immediately as kings with Christ a thousand years—not that they arose or were resurrected or entered into life. He speaks further of the rest of the dead *(hoi loipoi tōn nekrōn)* and therefore assumes that the believers whose souls he saw in heaven still in a sense belong to the dead but nevertheless lived and reigned. By contrast he does not say of the rest of the dead, as the Authorized Version [Dutch: *Statenvertaling*] has it, that they did not come to life again, but that they did *not* live *(ouk ezēsan)*. And finally he emphatically adds that this "living" and "ruling" of the souls of the believers who remained faithful, by contrast to the "not-living" of the rest of the dead, is the first resurrection.

One can, as it were, feel the contrast: the first resurrection [of which John speaks] is not the one accepted by some—even in John's time—as though a physical resurrection of believers would precede the thousand-year reign. Rather, the first resurrection consists in the "living" and "reigning" in heaven with Christ of the believers who remained faithful. The believers to whom John is writing and who are soon going to encounter the tribulation must not think that they will only experience salvation at the end of time. No: "blessed are the dead who die in the Lord *from now on" (ap arti)*. They immediately gain rest from their labors. Upon their death they immediately receive a crown. They live and reign in heaven with Christ from the moment after their death, and can therefore face the coming tribulation with confidence. The crown of life awaits them (2:10). Here, in 20:4, 5, John is repeating, in brief, what he wrote earlier to the seven churches. The promises there given to believers if they persevered to the end all come down to the assertion that he who conquers will be crowned. "To everyone who conquers, I will give permission to eat of the tree of life" (2:7); ". . . I will give some of the hidden manna" (2:17); ". . . I will give authority over the nations" (2:26); ". . . I will also give the morning star" (2:28); ". . . will be clothed

. . . in white robes" (3:5); ". . . I will make you a pillar in the temple of
my God" (3:12); eats the Last Supper with Jesus (3:20). In a word: to
"one who conquers I will give a place with me on my throne" (3:21).
What John saw earlier in the form of a promise he now sees in the form
of fulfillment in chapter 20: those who remain faithful until death immediately live and reign with Christ on his throne in heaven. And *that*
is the *first* resurrection.

But John adds a further statement and by it confirms the above interpretation. For he says: "Blessed and holy is he who shares in the first
resurrection. Over such the second death has no power, but they shall
be priests of God and of Christ and reign with him a thousand years."
According to 20:14, the second death is nothing other than the reality
of being thrown into the lake of fire. Whatever may be the lot of the rest
of the dead mentioned in verse 5, in any case the believers who remained faithful, who live and reign with Christ, are secured against the
second death. They already have the crown of life and already eat the
manna of life and therefore need not fear the judgment to come. "Whoever conquers will not be harmed by the second death" (2:11), which
goes into effect at the final judgment. If John had conceived the first
resurrection in a chiliastic sense, namely, as a physical resurrection of
believers before the thousand-year reign, he would not have had to furnish such consolation to believers. He could have confined himself to
saying that they would rise again *before* the thousand-year reign. But
no; in a sense the believers continue to belong to the category of the
dead up until the final judgment. But this is no hardship: if they persevere to the end they will be immediately crowned and though the *first*
death still reigns over their bodies, they cannot be hurt by the *second*
death.

Against this interpretation it may be advanced that John nevertheless
speaks clearly of a thousand-year reign of believers with Christ, even if
it is in heaven, and that he situates it after the return of Christ (19:11–
16) and the fall of the world empire and the false prophet (19:20). Still
this objection is not as serious as it sounds.

The location of the vision in Revelation 20 following that of chapter
19 has no bearing whatever on the chronological sequence of events.
Generally speaking, the art of writing, in distinction, say, from the art
of painting, can only narrate consecutively events that are actually si-
multaneous. Scripture is no exception. It frequently relates successively
things that in reality occurred side by side. In the prophets it often happens that they see and describe consecutively things that happen or will
happen simultaneously or even in a totally different order. This is especially the case, as it is increasingly being recognized, in the Book of Revelation. The letters to the seven churches do not furnish a description

of ecclesiastical conditions succeeding each other in that same order. The seven seals, the seven trumpets, and the seven bowls do not constitute a chronological series but run parallel and in each case take us to the end, the final struggle of the anti-Christian power. And so in itself there is no objection to the assumption that that which is narrated in Revelation 20 runs parallel to the events of the previous chapters.

It needs to be recognized that in reference to the world empire that he depicts, John is thinking of the Roman Empire. Prophecy in the Old as well as in the New Testament is not concerned with things high in the sky but has a historical basis and views the actual powers in the midst of which it exists as the embodiment of the struggle of world empires against the kingdom of God. The Book of Daniel, for example, leads up to Antiochus Epiphanes and regards him as the personification of hostility against God and his people. John similarly derives from the Roman Empire of his day the features he needs for his world empire. Although everything that has been written beforehand has been written for our instruction, the Revelation of John is nevertheless primarily a book of consolation for "the church under the cross" of his own time to urge it to persevere in the struggle and to encourage it by picturing the crown awaiting it. If John privately believed that in the Roman Empire he was seeing the very last development of world empire and that Christ would come in just a few years to put an end to it, that would not in any way be unusual or something at variance with the spirit of prophecy. We are not bound by John's personal opinion but by the word of his prophecy. And the prophecy that throws its light on history is in turn interpreted and unveiled by history.

If privately John really believed that in a few years the Roman Empire would be destroyed by the appearing of Christ, it was in any case his opinion that this would not spell the end of world history, for in that case there would be no room for the reign of believers with Christ in heaven alongside it and this reign could only begin after that time. But this "contemporary-historical" *(zeitgeschichtliche)*[7] view of things, however much truth there is in it, does not completely convey the thought of John's Revelation. For it is clearly evident that in chapter 19 the history of the world has reached its end. Babylon has fallen (ch. 18); God reigns as king (19:6); the marriage of the Lamb has come (19:7–9); Christ has appeared (19:11–16); the last battle of all the kings of the earth and their armies has been fought (19:17–19); the world empire and the false prophet have been destroyed and thrown into the lake of fire, which, as the second death, is not opened until after the judgment (19:20; cf. 20:14); and the rest were slain (19:21). The nineteenth chapter therefore clearly runs on to the same end of the world as that depicted in 20:10–15. There is no material left for a sequel to world history. The "contemporary-historical" *(zeitgeschichtliche)* exegesis leaves the origin of the nations that appear in 20:3, 8 unexplained or would otherwise come into conflict with 19:17–21. However, just as the letters to the seven churches and similarly the seven seals, trumpets, and bowls first of all relate to conditions and events in John's day but then have further implications for the church of all times and for the history of the world as a whole, so it is true of the world-empire depicted in Revelation that it is modeled on the Roman Empire of the first centuries but does not achieve its full realization in that empire. It keeps rising again and again and must always again succumb to the appearance of Christ until it finally exerts its utmost powers, exhausts itself in a final gargantuan struggle, and is then forever annihilated by the coming of Christ.

If this view is correct, the vision of Revelation 20 is not intended to relate to us the things that will occur in chronological order after the events of Revelation 19, but has a place of its own and reports to us things that run parallel with the preceding. The ultimate ending of the history of the world to be narrated, it turns out, is twofold: one ending of the historic nations in which Christianity is openly active, and another of the barbaric nations which—as Revelation 20:8 clearly tells us—"are at the four corners of the earth," and have therefore lived away from the center of history and outside the circle of mankind's culture. The world-empire and false prophecy could only arise and function among the former, for anti-Christianity presupposes familiarity with the gospel. The latter only succeed in making a fierce assault on the church of Christ. But it is the same Satan who works both over there and over here. Over and over, having been forced back and defeated among culture-producing nations, he forges a new instrument for the battle against Christ from among the barbaric peoples. First, he is thrown from heaven; then he works on earth and raises up a world-empire against Christ; and finally he summons up the barbaric nations from around the world to fight the final battle against Christ. But all this occurs, not in chronological sequence, but in a logical and spiritual sense.

The thousand years, as is generally recognized today, are symbolic. They contrast with the few days during which the believers who remained faithful are oppressed and persecuted here on earth (12:17), but also with the completed glory that is eternal (22:5). They denote the holy, blessed rest of believers who have died and are in heaven with Christ as well as the longing with which they look for the day when their blood will be avenged (6:10), while on earth the struggle of world-empire and the international world against Christ continues. And after John in Revelation 20:1–9 has told the history of the barbaric nations up to the very end with which that of the culture-producing nations in 19:17–21 concluded as well, he picks up the thread of both visions and relates the ultimate end of world history as a whole. In 19:21 people are slain by the sword of Christ; in 20:9 they are consumed by fire from heaven. But after the world-empire, the false prophet, and Satan have been condemned and thrown into the lake of fire (19:20; 20:10), all the dead arise and are judged according to their works (20:11–15).

The Return of Christ

The teaching of Scripture unfolded up to this point makes clear that the course and outcome of world history are very different from the way people usually imagine them. It is most certainly true of the end of things, if anywhere, that God's ways are higher than our ways and his thoughts higher than our thoughts. The kingdom of God, although analogous to a mustard seed and leaven and a seed that sprouts and grows aside from any knowledge and involvement of human beings (Matt. 13:31, 33; Mark 4:27), nevertheless does not reach its completion by way of gradual development or an ethical process. According to the incontrovertible testimony of Scripture, the history of humankind, both in the case of culture-producing and of uncultured nations, rather ends in a general apostasy and an appalling final struggle of a coalition of all satanic forces against God and his kingdom.

But then, in any case, the end is here. The world, in time and with the power given it by God, has done nothing, as in the days of Noah, other than make itself ripe for judgment; at the apex of its power it suddenly collapses at the appearance of Christ. In the end a catastrophe, a divine act of intervention, terminates the rule of Satan here on earth and brings about the completion of the unshakable kingdom of heaven. Just as in the case of a believer perfection is not the fruit of a slowly progressing process of sanctification but sets in immediately after death, so also the perfection of humanity and the world comes about, not gradually, but suddenly by the appearance of Christ.

It is specifically Christ who is appointed by the Father to bring about the end of the history of humankind and the world. And he is appointed to this role because he is the Savior, the perfect Savior. The work he completed on earth is only a part of the great work of redemption he has taken upon himself. And the time he spent here is only a small part of the centuries over which he is appointed as Lord and King. Anointed by the Father from all eternity he began to engage in his prophetic, priestly, and royal activity immediately after sin came into the world. He continued that activity throughout all the revolving centuries since. And one day, at the end of the times, he will complete it. That which he acquired on earth by his suffering and death he applies from heaven by his Word and the working of his Spirit; and that which he has thus applied, he maintains and defends against all the assaults of Satan, in order one day, at the end, to present it without spot or wrinkle, in total perfection, to his Father who is in heaven. Accordingly, the return of Christ unto judgment is not an arbitrary addition that can be isolated from his preceding work and viewed by itself. It is a necessary and indispensable component of that work. It brings that work to completion and crowns it. It is the last and highest step in the state of his exaltation.

Because Christ is the Savior of the world he will someday return as its Judge. The crisis or judgment *(krisis)* he precipitated by his first coming he consummates at his second coming. The Father gave him authority to execute judgment *(krisin poiein)* because he is the Son of man (John 5:27). Eschatology, therefore, is rooted in Christology and is itself Christology, the teaching of the final, complete triumph of Christ and his kingdom over all his enemies. Along with Scripture we can go back even further. The Son is not only the mediator of reconciliation *(mediator reconciliationis)* on account of sin, but even apart from sin he is the mediator of union *(mediator unionis)* between God and his creation. He is not only the exemplary cause *(causa exemplaris)* but also the final cause *(causa finalis)* of creation. In the Son the world has its foundation and example and therefore it has in him its goal as well. It is created through him and for him as well (Col. 1:16). Because the creation is *his* work it cannot and may not remain the booty of Satan. The Son is the head, Lord, and heir of all things. United in the Son, gathered under him as their head, all creatures return to the Father, the fountain of all good. The second coming is therefore required by his first coming. It is implied in the first; in time, by inner necessity, it will proceed from the first; it brings the first coming to its full effect and completion and was therefore comprehended in a single image with the first coming by Old Testament prophecy.

Not only is the second coming ideally and logically linked with the first; there is between them a real bond as well. Just as the Old Testament was a continual coming of God to his people until in Christ he came to live bodily among them, so the dispensation of the New Testament is a continued coming of Christ to his inheritance in order in the end to take possession of it forever. Christ is not only he who was to come in the days of the Old Testament and actually came in the fullness of time. He is also the coming one *(ho erchomenos)* and the one who will come *(ho erchomenos hēxei,* Heb. 10:37; cf. Rev. 1:4, 8, etc.). Christ's second coming is the complement of the first. This ideal and real connection between the first and second comings of Christ also explains the manner in which the New Testament speaks of the time of his parousia.

An entire series of texts posits this parousia as being very close at hand. Jesus links the prophecy of the consummation immediately to that concerning the destruction of Jerusalem (Matt. 24:29f. and par.). Paul considers it possible that he and his fellow believers will still experience the parousia of Christ (1 Cor. 15:51; 1 Thess. 4:15). And all the apostles assert that they are in the last days, that the future of the Lord is at hand, and derive from this expectation a motive for vigilance (Rom. 13:11; 1 Cor. 10:11; Heb. 3:14; 6:11; 10:25, 37; James 5:7–9; 1 Peter 1:6, 20; 4:17; 5:10; 1 John 2:18; Rev. 1:3; 3:11, 20; 22:7, 10, 12, 20).

The Timing of Christ's Return

Errors have been made in both directions in the interpretation of this New Testament expectation of the early return of Christ. The New Testament absolutely contains no doctrine concerning the time of Christ's return. It by no means establishes as a fact that Christ's return will occur or immediately after the destruction of Jerusalem. Many interpreters have indeed inferred this from Matthew 10:23; 16:28; 24:34; 26:64 and parallels, but mistakenly so. For it cannot be reasonably doubted that Jesus spoke of his coming in various senses. In John 14:18–24 (cf. 10:16–24) he speaks to his disciples of his coming in the Spirit after Pentecost or, according to other interpreters, of his coming after the resurrection when he will again appear to his disciples for a little while. In Matthew 26:64, before the [Jewish] Council, Jesus not only confirmed his messiahship with an oath but also stated that he would convince them of it because they would from that time on *(ap arti)* see him sitting at the right hand of God's power and coming on the clouds of heaven.

Elsewhere also there is mention of such a coming in glory. Matthew 16:28 (cf. Mark 9:1; Luke 9:27) leaves no room for doubt about this. Jesus says here that some of his bystanders will not taste death before they see the Son of Man coming in his kingdom. A moment earlier he had admonished his listeners to be concerned above all about the salvation of their souls, underscoring this admonition by saying that the Son of Man would come in the glory of his Father and repay everyone for what they have done. And this would not even be very long—he added in verse 28 by way of explanation—for even before all his bystanders had died, the Son of Man will come in his kingdom *(en tē basileia autou)*, that is, with the royal power and dignity the Father will give him. For by his resurrection and ascension Christ was appointed by the Father to be head, king, and Lord (Acts 2:33; 5:31); and from that time on, in the measure in which his kingdom is founded and extended on earth, he is continually coming in his royal dignity. In Mark 9:1 and

Luke 9:27 the phrase is therefore explained by saying that many will not taste death before they have seen the kingdom of God, or have seen it come with power. Matthew 10:23 can be explained in the same way: the disciples are told they will not have gone through all the towns of Israel before the Son of Man comes. Although this coming is not in any way explained further, it cannot possibly refer to the parousia because in that case Jesus would be contradicting himself. In any case in Matthew 24 he has his parousia come after the destruction of Jerusalem. Jesus does not say how long after this appalling event his coming will occur. But in his prophecy he does indeed tie it to the fall of Jerusalem. The translation of *eutheōs* in Matthew 24:39 by "suddenly" instead of by "immediately" entails no change in this, for in the words following we are clearly told that the signs of the parousia will come immediately *(eutheōs)* after the tribulation of those days ("in those days after that tribulation," Mark 13:24; cf. Luke 21:25–27).

This is confirmed by Matthew 24:34 (cf. Mark 13:30; Luke 21:32), where Jesus says that "this generation will not pass away until all these things take place." The words "this generation" *(hē genea autē)* cannot be understood to mean the Jewish people, but undoubtedly refer to the generation then living. On the other hand, it is clear that the words "all these things" *(panta tauta)* do not include the parousia itself but only refer to the signs that precede and announce it. For, after predicting the destruction of Jerusalem and the signs and his return and even the gathering of his elect by the angels, and therefore actually ending his eschatological discourse, Jesus proceeds in verse 32 to offer a practical application. Here he states that just as in the case of the fig tree the sprouting of leaves announces the summer, so "all these things" are signs that the end is near or that the Messiah is at the door. Here the expression *panta tauta* clearly refers to the signs of the coming parousia, not to the parousia itself, for else it would make no sense to say that when "these things" occur, the end is "near." In verse 34 the words "all these things" *(panta tauta)* have the same meaning. Jesus therefore does not say that his parousia will still occur within the time of the generation then living. What he says is that the signs and portents of it as they would be visible in the destruction of Jerusalem and concomitant events would begin to occur in the time of the generation then living. Of this Jesus is so sure that he says that while heaven and earth will pass away his words will by no means pass away. For the rest, however, Jesus abstains from all attempts at further specifying the time. His intent is not to inform his disciples of the precise moment of his parousia, but to urge them to be watchful. And for that reason he does not say when he will come, but what the signs of the times are that announce his coming. Taking notice of the signs of the times is a duty for Jesus' disciples; the calculation of the precise time of his coming is forbidden to them and also impossible. The first demands that Jesus shed his light on the events that will occur; and so he does, as all the prophets before him, and as after him all his apostles have done.

For this reason he does not say either that many centuries will still elapse between the destruction of Jerusalem and his parousia. That would immediately again have rendered the admonition to be watchful powerless. As prophecy has at all times done, so Jesus announces the approach of the end *in* the events of his time. And the apostles follow his example when, in heresy and deception, in ordeals and judgments, in Jerusalem's fall and Rome's empire, they depict for us the early messengers of Christ's return and the initial fulfillment of his prophecy. For all believers ought at all times to live as though the coming of Christ is at the door. "The proximity of the parousia is, so to speak, only another way of expressing its absolute certainty."[8] But for the same reason, the calculation of the precise moment of the parousia is also inappropriate for Christians. After all, Jesus deliberately left this completely uncertain. His coming will be sudden, unexpected, surprising, like that of the thief in the night (Matt. 24:43; Luke 12:39; cf. "like a trap," Luke 21:35).

Many things have to happen before the end comes (Matt. 24:6). The gospel must be preached throughout the whole world (Matt. 24:14). The bridegroom is delayed and the master of the servants for a long time stayed in a far country (Matt. 25:5, 13, 19). Weeds and wheat must grow together until the harvest (Matt. 13:30). The mustard seed must grow into a tree and the leaven must leaven the whole batch of dough (Matt. 13:32, 33). In fact, once, when dealing with the topic of the parousia, Jesus expressly stated that the day and the hour of his coming are not known to anyone, neither to angels nor humans, indeed, not even to the Son of Man (Mark 13:32). Even after his resurrection Jesus still testifies that the Father has fixed the times and seasons for the establishment of his kingdom by his own authority (Acts 1:7). All the apostles echo this language. Christ comes like a thief in the night (1 Thess. 5:1, 2; 2 Peter 3:10; Rev. 3:3; 16:15). He will not appear until after Antichrist has come (2 Thess. 2:2f.). The resurrection is scheduled to occur in a fixed sequence, first that of Christ, then that of believers at his coming (1 Cor. 15:23). And that future is delayed inasmuch as the Lord uses another standard for measuring time than we and wishes in his patience that all should come to repentance (2 Peter 3:8–9).

The Manner of Christ's Return

About the *manner* of Jesus' return Holy Scripture speaks as soberly as it does about its timing. In the New Testament Christ's second coming is

frequently referred to with the name *parousia* ("coming"), either absolutely (Matt. 24:3) or further described as "the coming of the Son of
Man" or as "the coming of our Lord Jesus Christ" (Matt. 24:27, 37, 39;
1 Thess. 3:13; 4:15; 5:23, etc.) or as "the coming of the day of God"
(2 Peter 3:12). The word *parousia* as such does not really include the
idea of return but indicates that Jesus, after having been absent and hidden for a time (Acts 3:21; Col. 3:3, 4) and having then come back (Matt.
16:27; 24:30, etc.; cf. Luke 19:12, 15), will again be and remain present.
For that reason *parousia* alternates with *epiphaneia* ("manifestation";
1 Tim. 6:14; Titus 2:13), *apokalypsis* ("revelation"; Luke 17:30; 1 Cor.
1:7; 2 Thess. 1:7; 1 Peter 1:7, 13), and *phanerōsis* ("appearance"; Col. 3:4;
1 Peter 5:4; 1 John 2:28); in 2 Thessalonians 2:8 we even read of "the
manifestation of his coming" *(hē epiphaneia tēs parousias autou)*.

This parousia is a work of God insofar as God will send his Anointed
and to that end fixes the times and seasons (Acts 1:7; 3:20; 1 Tim. 6:14–
16). But it is also an act of Christ himself as Son of Man to whom the
Father has given authority to execute judgment and who must rule as
king until all his enemies have been put under his feet (John 5:17; 1 Cor.
15:25). Since upon his departure from earth he was taken up in heaven,
at his parousia he will return from heaven (Phil. 3:20; 1 Thess. 1:10;
2 Thess. 1:7; Rev. 19:11). And as at his ascension a cloud enclosed him
and hid him from the eyes of his disciples (Acts 1:9), so, in the language
of the Old Testament, he is also described as returning on the clouds of
heaven, which like a triumphal chariot will carry him down to earth
(Matt. 24:30; 26:64; Mark 13:26; 14:62; Luke 21:27; Rev. 1:7; 14:14). For
he does not return in the form of a servant but with great power and
with his own and the Father's glory (Matt. 16:27; 24:30; Mark 8:38;
13:26; Luke 22:27; Col. 3:3, 4; 2 Thess. 1:9, 10; Titus 2:13), as King of
kings and Lord of lords (Rev. 17:14; 19:11–16), surrounded by his angels (Matt. 16:27; 25:31; Mark 8:38; Luke 9:26; 2 Thess. 1:7; Rev. 19:14),
by his saints among whom the blessed in heaven are perhaps included
(1 Thess. 3:13; 2 Thess. 1:10; Jude 14). Although on account of its unexpected character, his parousia is comparable with the breaking into a
house of a thief in the night, it will nevertheless be visible for all human
beings on earth and be like the lightning that flashes from one side of
the sky to the other (Matt. 24:27; Luke 17:24; Rev. 1:7) and be announced by the voice of an archangel and the trumpet of angels (Matt.
24:31; 1 Cor. 15:52; 1 Thess. 4:16).

In connection with their doctrine of the ascension, Lutherans said
that the return of Christ was not subject to a succession of moments but
consisted solely in the sudden return to visibility of the body of Christ,
which at his exaltation had once become invisible and ubiquitous. Although they generally recognized that the return of Christ was visible

and local, they only meant by this that, by a special disposition of God *(singularis Dei dispositio)* and for the special purpose of judgment, Christ's human nature would become visible for a while at a specific place, without thereby relinquishing its presence elsewhere.[9] But Reformed theologians attributed to Christ's return a physical, local, and temporal character. They even recognized that this return, however sudden, was still subject to a succession of moments *(successiva)*. Also at the highest step of his exaltation, at his return for judgment, Christ would maintain his true human nature.[10]

Part **3**
The Consummation

The Day of the Lord 6

The day of our Lord's return brings about the resurrection of believers, the judgment of unbelievers, and the renewal of creation. The general resurrection restores the temporary rupture of body and soul at the time of death and places all human beings before God's judgment seat. Believers are comforted by this bodily redemption, which represents Christ's final deliverance from sin and its consequences and brings them into the full joy of communion with their Lord. As our Lord's own resurrection shows, the final resurrection maintains continuity between the earthly body and the glorified resurrection body. Persons retain their individual identities. Precisely how this happens we do not know and should not speculate; what is important is the substantial unity as well as qualitative distinction between what the Apostle calls the "natural body" and the "spiritual body" (1 Cor. 15). Because the resurrection body is re-formed rather than created wholly anew, burial rather than cremation is the preferred mode of Christian care of the dead. After the resurrection comes the judgment. While there is already an immanent judgment upon sin in our world and history, it is a pantheistic error to reduce world judgment to world history. The final judgment will be a global and public vindication of the gospel and Christ's rule. The objections to eternal punishment of the wicked and the various alternatives to it such as hypothetical and unconditional universalism as well as conditional immortality appeal naturally to human sentiment but finally have no ground in Scripture. The clear teaching of Scripture, along with firm conviction about the integrity of God's justice, should be sufficient and deter us from undue speculation. God will be God and will be glorified.

The day of the Lord or the day of our Lord Jesus Christ (*yôm YHWH, hē hēmera tou kuriou hemōn Iesou Christou,* Matt. 24:36f.; Luke 17:24f.; 21:34; Acts 17:31; 1 Cor. 1:8; 5:5 etc.) begins with the appearance of Christ on the clouds. By speaking of a "day" Scripture does not by any means intend to convey that all the things that fall under the heading of "the last things"—Christ's return, the resurrection of the dead, the final judgment—will occur in a time frame of twelve or twenty-four hours. In Old Testament times the day of the Lord was the

131

time in which God, in a marvelously glorious way, would come to his people as king to redeem it from all its enemies and to settle it with him in Jerusalem in peace and security. In that event of God's coming began the great turning point in which the old aeon passed into the new and all conditions and connections in the natural and human world changed totally. In later Jewish thought the idea was that in the day of the Lord the present world aeon would pass into the future world aeon, which would then frequently be still further differentiated in three generations or in the days of the Messiah, lasting 40 or 100 or 600 or 1,000 or 2,000 or 7,000 years, and the subsequently beginning eternity.[1]

According to the New Testament, the last part of the present aeon *(aiōn outos)* began with the first coming of Christ so that now we live in the last days or the last hour (1 Cor. 10:11; Heb. 1:2; 9:26; 1 John 2:18) and the aeon to come *(aiōn mellōn)* starts with his second coming (Matt. 19:28; Mark 10:30; Luke 18:30; 20:35; 1 Cor. 15:23; Heb. 2:5, etc.). And this age to come *(aiōn mellōn)* begins with the day of the Lord *(hēmera tou kuriou)*, that is, the time in which Christ appears, raises the dead, executes judgment, and renews the world. In the New Testament this period is never represented as lasting long. Paul says in 1 Corinthians 15:52, for example, that the transformation of believers still living and the resurrection of believers who have died will occur in a moment, in the twinkling of an eye (cf. 1 Thess. 4:15–17). The resurrection and the last judgment are intimately associated as in a single act (Luke 14:14; 2 Cor. 4:14; Rev. 20:11–13). Judgment is fixed on a day (Matt. 10:15; 11:22, etc.) and even on an hour (Rev. 14:7). But this last term is proof that Scripture is in no way minded to fit all the events associated with Christ's parousia precisely into a time frame of twenty-four hours or sixty minutes: the word "hour" *(ōra,* originally "season") often refers to a much longer period of time than an hour of sixty minutes (Matt. 26:45; John 4:21; 5:25; 16:2, 32; Rom. 13:11; 1 John 2:18). The events that are destined to occur in the parousia of Christ are so comprehensive in scope that they are bound to take considerable time. The inventions of the past century—for the purpose of mutual contact, the exercise of community, hearing and seeing things at a great distance—have shrunk distances to a minimum; and it is likely that they are a mere beginning and prophecy of what will be discovered in the centuries ahead. The doctrine of the last things certainly has to reckon with all these things. Still, such events as the appearance of Christ so that all will see him, the resurrection of all the dead and the transformation of those still living, the rendering of judgment on all people according to their deeds, and the burning and renewal of the world, are such immense occurrences that they can only take place over a certain period of time.

The Resurrection of the Body

The first event that follows the appearance of Christ is the resurrection of the dead. This event is not the result of an evolution of bodies in general, or of the resurrection body implanted in believers by regeneration and sacrament in particular but the effect of an omnipotent, creative act of God (Matt. 22:29; 1 Cor. 6:14; 15:38; 2 Cor. 1:9). The Father specifically carries out this work by the Son, whom he has "granted . . . to have life in himself" (John 5:26; 6:27, 39, 44; 1 Cor. 6:14; 2 Cor. 4:14; 1 Thess. 4:14). He is the resurrection and the life, the firstborn of the dead (John 11:25; Acts 26:23; 1 Cor. 15:20; Col. 1:18; Rev. 1:5), and must of necessity, therefore, bring about the resurrection of his own (John 6:39, 40; 1 Cor. 15:20–23, 47–49). Undoubtedly Scripture teaches a general resurrection, a resurrection not only of believers but also of unbelievers and of all human beings (Dan. 12:2; Matt. 5:29, 30; 10:28; John 5:29; Acts 24:15; Rev. 20:12, 13), and attributes this resurrection to Christ as well (John 5:29). But it very rarely speaks of this general resurrection, the reason being that it is very differently related to Christ than the resurrection of believers. The resurrection of the dead in general is only obliquely a fruit of the work of Christ. It has become a necessity only because a temporal death has occurred; and this temporal death is separated from eternal death by God's gracious intervention. Originally the punishment of sin was death in its full scope and severity. But because, out of the fallen human race, God chose for himself a community for eternal life, he immediately delayed temporal death already in the case of Adam and Eve, allowed them to reproduce themselves from generation to generation, and only at the end of the ages consigns those who have disobeyed his law and his gospel to eternal perdition. The general resurrection, therefore, only serves to restore in all human beings the temporary rupture of the bond between soul and body—a rupture that occurred only with a view to grace in Christ—to place them all before the judgment seat of God as *human beings,* in soul and body, and to let them hear the verdict from his mouth. The Father also brings about this general resurrection through Christ, because he not only gave life to the Son but also the authority to execute judgment, and this judgment must strike the whole person, in both soul and body (John 5:27–29).

The resurrection of the dead in general, therefore, is primarily a judicial act of God. But for believers this act is filled with abundant consolation. In Scripture the resurrection of the believing community is everywhere in the foreground, so much so even that sometimes the resurrection of all human beings is left out of consideration or deliberately omitted (Job 19:25–27; Ps. 73:23–26; Isa. 26:19, 20; Ezek. 37; Hos.

6:2; 13:14; Mark 12:25; 2 Cor. 5; 1 Thess. 4:16; Phil. 3:11). This is the real, the true resurrection won directly by Christ, for it is not just a re-union of soul and body, but an act of vivification, a renewal. It is an event in which believers, united in soul and body, enter into communion with Christ and are being re-created after God's image (Rom. 8:11, 29; Phil. 3:21). For that reason Paul has the resurrection of believers coincide with the transformation of those who are left alive. The latter will have no advantage over the former, for the resurrection will take place prior to the transformation, and together they will go forth to meet the Lord in the air (1 Cor. 15:51, 52; 2 Cor. 5:2, 4; 1 Thess. 4:15–17).

In this resurrection the identity of the resurrection body with the body that has died will be preserved. In the case of the resurrections that occur in the Old and New Testaments the dead body is reanimated. Jesus arose with the same body in which he suffered on the cross and which was laid in the tomb of Joseph of Arimathea. At the time of Jesus' death many bodies of the saints were raised and came forth from their tombs (Matt. 27:52). In the resurrection of the last day all who are in the tombs will hear Jesus' voice and come forth (John 5:28, 29). According to Revelation 20:13, the dead will return to earth from the tombs, from the sea, from the realm of the dead and Hades. And Paul teaches that the resurrection body proceeds from the body that has died, just as from the grain that has been sown God raises up new grain (1 Cor. 15:36f.).

In the Christian religion this identity of the resurrection body with the body that was laid aside at death is of great significance. In this respect it is, in the first place, diametrically opposed to all dualistic theories according to which the body is merely an incidental dwellingplace or prison of the soul. The essence of a human being consists above all in the most intimate union of soul and body in a single personality. The soul belongs by nature to the body and the body belongs by nature to the soul. Although the soul does not itself create the body, it nevertheless has its own body. The continuity of an individual human being is maintained as much in the identity of the body as in the identity of the soul.

In the second place, Christ's redemption is not a second, new creation but a re-creation. Things would have been much simpler if God had destroyed the entire fallen world and replaced it with a completely new one. But it was his good pleasure to raise the fallen world up again and to free from sin the same humanity that sinned. This deliverance consists in the reality that Christ delivers his believing community from all sin and from all the consequences of sin, and therefore causes it to completely triumph over death as well. Death is the last enemy to be annihilated. And the power of Christ is revealed in the fact that he not only gives eternal life to his own but, in consequence, also raises them on the last day. The rebirth by water and Spirit finds its completion in the rebirth of all things (Matt. 19:28). Spiritual redemption from sin is only fully completed in bodily redemption at the end of time. Christ is a complete Savior: just as he first appeared to establish the kingdom of heaven in the hearts of believers, so he will one day come again to give it visible shape and make his absolute power over sin and death incontrovertibly manifest before all creatures and bring about its acknowledgment. "Corporeality is the end of the ways of God" ("Leiblichkeit ist das Ende der Wege Gottes").

Directly connected with this truth is the care of the dead. Cremation is not to be rejected because it is assumed to limit the omnipotence of God and make the resurrection an impossibility. Nevertheless, it is of pagan origin; it was never a custom in Israel or in Christian nations, and militates against Christian mores. Burial, on the other hand, is much more nearly in harmony with Scripture and creed, history, and liturgy, with the doctrine of the image of God that is also manifest in the body, with the doctrine of death as a punishment for sin, and with the respect that is due to the dead and the resurrection on the last day. Christians do not, like the Egyptians, artificially conserve corpses; nor do they mechanically destroy them, as many people desire today. But they entrust them to the earth's bosom and let them rest until the day of the resurrection.[2]

The Christian church and Christian theology, accordingly, vigorously maintained the identity of the resurrection body with the body that had died. It frequently swung over to another extreme and not only confessed the resurrection of the *flesh* but even at times taught that in the resurrection the totality of matter *(totalitas materiae)* that once belonged to a body was assembled by God from all corners of the earth and brought back, in the same manner and measure as was once there, to the various parts of the body.[3] But this notion is open to serious objections.

First, it leads to a variety of subtle and curious inquiries that are of no value for the doctrine of the resurrection. The question that is then pursued is whether the hair and the nails, the blood and the gall, the semen and the urine, the intestines and the genitals will all rise again and be composed of the same—in number and kind—atoms of which they were composed in this life. In the case of the physically handicapped, people who lacked one or more parts, and in the case of children who died in infancy and sometimes even before birth, this idea led to no little embarrassment. In all these and similar cases, whether they wanted to or not, people had to resort to the assumption that resurrection bodies would be augmented with components that did not belong to them earlier. Hence the resurrection cannot consist in a return to and the vivification of "the totality of matter."

Second, physiology teaches that the human body, like all organisms, is subject to a constant process of metabolism, so that after a period of seven years not a single particle would still be present of those that made up the substance of the body before that time. The chemicals of which our bodies consist, like oxygen, hydrogen, nitrogen, and so on, are the same as those that occur in other creatures around us, but they constantly change. This change is sufficient proof that the identity of human bodies cannot consist in that they are always composed of the same chemicals in number. It is enough that they consist of the same chemicals in kind.

Third, this is reinforced by the many kinds of metamorphoses that nature exhibits in all its domains. As a result of the impact of air, water, heat, and the like, plants are transformed into peat and coal, carbons into diamond, clay into claystone, and rock into fertile soil. In the plant and animal world, within the limits of the various species, there is endless variety. And during the time of its existence every organism undergoes a series of changes. The maggot becomes a fly; every larva passes from an undeveloped into a more developed state; an embryo passes through various stages and then arrives at extrauterine existence; the caterpillar becomes a pupa and then a butterfly, and so on. We do not know what it is that remains the same under all these metamorphoses. Both matter and form change. In the whole organism there seems to be nothing stable. Still the identity is maintained, an identity that is therefore independent of the coarse mass of materials, its transformation and its quantity.

If we now relate these facts to what Scripture teaches us about the resurrection, we see a chance to maintain the substantial unity as well as the qualitative distinction between the present and the future body. For, strictly speaking, Scripture does not teach the resurrection of the *flesh*, but of the *body*. From the resurrections Scripture reports and from the resurrection of Christ we may indeed—not as far as the form and manner is concerned but as to the essence of it—draw conclusions about the resurrection of the dead in the last days. For in the case of all these resurrections the body still existed as a whole and Christ's body had not even been given over to corruption (Acts 2:31). But the bodies of those who rise in the parousia are totally decomposed and scattered in all sorts of ways and have passed into other creatures. In this case we can hardly speak of flesh in a literal sense, for flesh is always animated. That which is no longer alive and animated therefore also ceases to be flesh and returns to dust (Gen. 3:19). Job can indeed say—assuming now that this translation is correct—that from his flesh he will see God

(19:26), and after his resurrection Jesus can testify that a spirit has no flesh and bones as he had (Luke 24:39).

However, this is still not sufficient to prove the resurrection of the *flesh* in the strict sense of this word. For though the flesh of which Job's body consisted was indeed the substratum for the resurrection body, it did not for that reason form the substance of it. And Jesus arose with the same body in which he died and which had not even seen corruption, and remained moreover in a transitional state up until his ascension, so that he could still eat food as well. Paul certainly teaches very clearly that flesh and blood, being perishable, cannot inherit the kingdom of God, which is imperishable (1 Cor. 15:50). Holsten, Holtzmann, and others have altogether mistakenly inferred from this that, according to Paul, the deceased body does not rise at all and that the actual resurrection occurs already at the time of a person's death. For the apostle expressly attests his faith in the bodily resurrection and defends it against those in the church of Corinth who denied it both in the case of Jesus and that of believers. And he is also thoroughly convinced that the very same body that is laid in the grave is raised again in the resurrection. At the same time he asserts that the resurrection is not a rehabilitation but a re-formation.[4] The body rises, not as a body of flesh and blood—weak, perishable, mortal—but as a body that is clothed in imperishability and glory. While the body composed of flesh and blood is the seed from which the resurrection body springs (1 Cor. 15:35–38), there is nevertheless a big difference between the two. Even on earth there is a lot of difference in kinds of "flesh" in the case of organic beings and in "substance" in the case of inorganic creatures (vv. 39–41). Similarly, there is an important difference between the present body and the future body, as is evident from the contrast between Adam and Christ (vv. 42–49). The first is a natural body *(sōma psychikon)* composed of flesh and blood, a body that is subject to change and animated by a soul *(psychē)*, but the latter is a spiritual body *(sōma pneumatikon)*. Though it is a true body, it is no longer controlled by a soul but by the spirit *(pneuma)*. It is no longer composed of flesh and blood; it is above the sex life (Matt. 22:30) and the need for food and drink (1 Cor. 6:13). In these respects it is distinguished even from the body that humans possessed before the fall; it is immortal, imperishable, spiritualized, and glorified (1 Cor. 15:42f.; Phil. 3:21).

Therefore, according to Paul, the identity of the resurrection body with the body entrusted to the earth is independent of body mass and its constant change. All organisms, including human bodies, are composed of the same materials in kind, not in number. And therefore it is absolutely not necessary for the resurrection body to consist of the same atoms in terms of number as those of which it consisted when it was laid in the grave. But for the resurrection body's identity with the flesh-and-blood body laid in the grave it *is* required that it have the same organization and shape, the same basic configuration and type, which marked it here as the body of a specific person. In all the metamorphoses to which all creatures are subject their identity and continuity are preserved. While after death the bodies of humans may disintegrate and in terms of their material mass pass into all sorts of other organisms, on earth something remains of them that constitutes the substratum of the resurrection body. Just what that is we do not know and will never be able to discover. But the oddness of this fact vanishes the moment we consider that the ultimate components of things are totally unknown to us. Even the most minute atom is still amenable to analysis. Chemical analysis continues endlessly but never reaches the utterly simple. Still, in the case of all organisms and therefore also in the case of the human body, there has to be something that keeps its identity in the ever-ongoing process of metamorphosis. Then what is so absurd about believing that such an "organic mold" or "pattern of individuality" of the body remains even after death to serve as "seed" for the resurrection body? For according to Scripture it is a fact that the resurrection body does not, along with the blessed, come down from heaven, nor is it composed of spiritual or celestial elements. The resurrection body does not come from heaven but from the earth. It is not a self-generated product of the spirit *(pneuma)* or the soul *(psychē)* but arises from the body that was laid in the grave at death. Accordingly, it is not spiritual in the sense that its substance is spirit *(pneuma)*, but is and remains material. That matter, however, is no longer organized into perishable flesh and blood but into a glorified body.[5]

The Judgment

After the resurrection comes the judgment, an event that is pictured in the Old Testament as a victory of the Messiah over all Israel's enemies but is described in the New Testament more spiritually as a judicial work of Christ in which he judges and sentences all people in accordance with the law God gave them. The first time, to be sure, Jesus came on earth, not to judge the world, but to save it (John 3:17; 12:47). Still, immediately at his appearance he produced a judgment *(krisis)* whose purpose and result is that those who do not see can see and that those who see may become blind (3:19, 20; 9:39). As Son of Man Jesus continually exercises judgment when to those who believe already he grants eternal life here on earth and allows the wrath of God to continue to rest on those who do not believe (3:36; 5:32–38). Undoubtedly there is, therefore, an internal spiritual judgment at work, a crisis that is realized from generation to generation. It is an immanent judgment this side of the Beyond that takes place in the consciences of human beings. Here on earth faith and unbelief already bear their fruit and bring their reward. Just as faith is followed by justification and peace with God, so unbelief leads to a progressive darkening of the mind and hardening of the heart and a yielding to all kinds of unrighteousness. Indeed, even apart from the antithesis between faith and unbelief, virtue and vice each bears its own fruit. Also in the natural life good and evil bring their own reward, not only in the excusing or accusing voice of conscience, but also in the external prosperity or adversity often associated with them. Scripture and history vie with each other in teaching that blessing and curse, compassion and anger, signs of favor and judgment, alternate in the lives of people and nations. There is great truth in the poet's saying that "the history of the world is the judgment of the world" ("die Weltgeschichte ist das Weltgericht"—Schiller).

Still, though in part this saying is true, it is also false. It is pantheistic, not theistic, in origin and undermines all judgment instead of confirming and honoring it. For if the history of the world is the judgment of the world, it totally ceases to be a judgment and becomes a natural process. This natural process is not at all concerned about the awesome contrast between good and evil and forces it back, and that only for a time, into the hidden recesses of the conscience. For then there is no longer a God who can make the natural order subservient to the moral order. All that remains is the power of nature, which controls the entire physical world and which soon shrinks to a minimum and eliminates the restricted domain that had initially been reserved for the moral rule of the good. For the good is not a power that can withstand the power of nature if it lacks grounding in an omnipotent God, who is the Creator of both the natural and the moral order. Indeed, against this pantheism always objects that, after all, the good should be done for its own sake and not from a hope of reward or fear of punishment.

But the desire of the soul for the triumph of the good, the victory of justice, has nothing at all in common with the self-centered wish for earthly happiness and the satisfaction of the senses. On the contrary, though Scripture takes account of the reality that humans are sensuous beings and holds before their eyes a reward that is "great in heaven" [Matt. 5:12], that reward is always subordinate to the honor of God's name and acquired by Christ, along with the good works in which believers walk [Eph. 2:10]. It is precisely the devout who with eager longing await the day in which God will glorify his name before the eyes of all creatures, and in their cause brings about the triumph of his own over all opposition. And this desire becomes all the stronger as the blood that cries out for vengeance runs over the earth in wider and deeper streams, as injustice triumphs, as wickedness increases, as falsehood flourishes, and as Satan's domain expands and rises up against the realm of righteousness. All of history cries out for world judgment. The whole creation longs for it. All people witness to it. The martyrs in heaven cry out for it with a loud voice. The believing community prays for the coming of Christ. And Christ himself, the Alpha and the Omega, says: "See, I am coming soon; my reward is with me, to repay according to everyone's work" [Rev. 22:12–13]. So, however firmly Scripture—especially in the Gospel of John—recognizes spiritual judgment that is operative throughout history, it nevertheless speaks of a final judgment as well, the judgment that brings about the triumph of the kingdom of Christ over all unrighteousness. The history of the world may be *a* judgment of the world, but *the* judgment of the world will take place at the end of time when Christ comes to judge the living and the dead.

In this connection Scripture repeatedly attributes this judgment to the Father (Matt. 18:35; 2 Thess. 1:5; Heb. 11:6; James 4:12; 1 Peter 1:17; 2:23; Rev. 20:11, 12). Still he accomplishes this work by Christ, to whom all judgment has been given, whom he has appointed as judge (John 5:22, 27; Acts 10:42; 17:31; Rom. 14:9), and who will therefore summon all human beings before his judgment seat and judge them according to what they have done (Matt. 25:32; Rom. 14:9–13; 2 Cor. 5:10; 2 Tim. 4:1, 8; 1 Peter 4:5; Rev. 19:11–21). For Christ is the Son of Man who already precipitated a crisis by his appearance, continues it in history, and completes it at the end of time. Their relation to him decides the eternal weal or woe of human beings. In his judgment of the living and the dead he celebrates his highest triumph and realizes the consummation of his kingdom and the total subjection of all his enemies. For that reason the main issue in the final judgment is that of faith or unbelief. For faith in Christ is the work of God par excellence (John 6:29; 1 John 3:23). Those who believe do not come into judgment (John 5:24); those who do not believe are already condemned and remain under God's wrath (John 3:18, 36).

Therefore, the standard in the final judgment will in the first place be the gospel (John 12:48); but that gospel is not opposed to, and cannot even be conceived apart from, the law. The requirement to believe, after all, is itself grounded in the law and the gospel is the restoration and fulfillment of the law. In the final judgment, therefore, all the works performed by people and recorded in the books before God are considered as well (Eccles. 12:14; 2 Cor. 5:10; Eph. 6:8; 1 Peter 1:17; Rev. 20:12; 22:12). Those works, after all, are expressions and products of the principle of life that lives in the heart (Matt. 7:17; 12:33; Luke 6:44) and encompass everything effected by humans, not in the intermediate state but in their bodies, not the deeds alone (Matt. 25:35f.; Mark 9:41, 42;

Luke 6:35; 14:13, 14; 1 Cor. 3:8; 1 Thess. 4:6, etc.) but also the words (Matt. 12:36) and the secret purposes of the heart (Rom. 2:16; 1 Cor. 4:5). For nothing remains hidden and everything will be revealed (Matt. 6:4, 6, 18; 10:26; Eph. 5:11–14; 1 Tim. 5:24, 25). In the final judgment, therefore, the norm will be the entire Word of God in both its parts: law and gospel.

But in connection with this, Scripture nevertheless clearly states that consideration will be given to the measure of revelation that any given person has received. Those who knew the will of the Lord and did not do it will be given "a more severe beating" (Luke 12:47). It will be more tolerable for Tyre and Sidon in the day of judgment than for Jerusalem and Capernaum (Matt. 10:15; 11:22, 24; Mark 6:11; Luke 10:12, 14; Heb. 2:3). Those who did not hear the gospel are not judged by it but by the law. The Gentiles who did not know the Mosaic law but sinned against the law known to them by nature perish apart from the Mosaic law whereas Jews are judged above all by this law (Rom. 2:12). Although Scripture views the judgment as extending to all humans without exception (Matt. 25:32; Acts 17:31; Rom. 2:6; 14:10; 2 Cor. 5:10; 2 Tim. 4:1; Rev. 20:12), it nevertheless makes a distinction between the nations that knew the gospel and finally produced anti-Christianity, and the other nations that never heard of Christ and therefore first learn of him at his parousia. It further speaks in particular of the judgment of evil angels, and of the role the good angels and believers play in the final judgment.

It is not at all easy to gain a clear picture of that judgment. There is certainly not exclusively an internal and spiritual event occurring solely in the human conscience. It is definitely a judgment that is realized externally as well and is visible to all creatures. However much the image and the reality may be intertwined, the appearance of Christ, the resurrection, and everything associated with the judgment are drawn too realistically to give us the freedom to spiritualize everything. That being the case, the execution of this judgment also requires a place and a space of time, for Scripture prompts us to think of it as occurring successively. The angels accompany Christ at his coming on the clouds to be of service to him in the execution of the sentence. They gather the righteous, separate the evil from the righteous, and drive them away (Matt. 13:30, 49; 24:31). He is surrounded, moreover, by the blessed (1 Thess. 3:13; 4:16; 2 Thess. 1:10; Jude 14; Rev. 17:14; 19:14). Following the resurrection of the believers who died and the transformation of those who remain alive, they are together caught up in the clouds to meet the Lord in the air (1 Thess. 4:17). Just as Christ's resurrection and ascension were disjoined and even separated by a period of forty days, so it is not impossible that the resurrection and transformation of believers at the end of time will not yet, at one stroke, confer on them the full glory that they will receive after the renewal of the world in a new heaven and a new earth. However this be, the resurrection and transformation of believers includes, as it did for Christ, their justification.

Scripture does indeed say that all humans without distinction, hence also believers, must appear before the judgment seat of Christ. But it also attests that those who believe in him are not condemned and do not come into judgment for they already have eternal life (John 3:18; 5:24); that the believers who have died are already with Christ in heaven and clothed in long white garments (2 Cor. 5:8; Phil. 1:23; Rev. 6:11; 7:9, 14); and that Christ is coming to be glorified in his saints and to be marveled at in all who believe (2 Thess. 1:10). Before pronouncing his verdict on the evil angels, on the anti-Christian world, and on barbaric peoples, Christ has already positioned the sheep at his right hand and is surrounded by his angels and his saints. This is also evident from 1 Corinthians 6:2, where Paul expressly states that the saints will judge the world and the angels. This statement may not be watered down into an act of endorsement by believers of the judgment Christ pronounces over the world and the angels but, as the context shows, specifically indicates that the saints will participate in [Christ's] judgment of the world and the angels. For that matter, Jesus already promised his twelve disciples that they would sit with him on twelve thrones, judging the twelve tribes of Israel (Matt. 19:28; Luke 22:30). And around the throne of God John saw thrones in heaven on which were seated the elders of the church (Rev. 4:4; 11:16; 20:4, 6). For Christ and his church are one: that in which the world and the angels have wronged the believing community is counted as having been done against him (Matt. 25:40, 45; Mark 9:41, 42). This judgment of Christ and his church is even extended to the good angels (1 Cor. 6:3), for the angels are ministering spirits sent forth to serve, for the sake of those who are to obtain salvation (Heb. 1:14). The angels will, therefore, receive a place in the future kingdom of God in accordance with the service they have rendered in relation to Christ and his church. Accordingly, in John's vision, Christ, surrounded by his armies, goes out to meet the anti-Christian forces (Rev. 19:11–21). The church triumphant takes part in the royal reign of Christ (Rev. 20:4–6). And Christ finally annihilates all opposition when he judges the nations who are at the four corners of the earth (Rev. 20:7–10).[6]

The Place of Punishment

In the New Testament the place to which the wicked are consigned is called Gehenna. The Hebrew *(gē hinnôm)* was originally the name for the valley of Hinnom, which was located southeast of Jerusalem and, according to Joshua 15:8, 18:16, served as the boundary line between two tribes. Under Ahaz and Manasseh this valley became a site for the worship of Molech in whose honor children were slain and burned (2 Kings 16:3; 21:6; 2 Chron. 28:3; 33:6; Jer. 32:34, 35). Under Josiah this place was destroyed, therefore, and declared unclean by the priests (2 Kings 23:10). Jeremiah prophesied that here a terrible bloodbath would be inflicted on the Israelites and the Topheth valley would be called the Valley of Slaughter (Jer. 7:32; 19:6). And the Apocryphal book of Enoch predicted that in this valley the wicked would be gathered up for judgment. For this reason the name "Gehinnom" was later transferred to the place of punishment for the wicked after death. According to others, however, the transfer had another reason. According to later Jews, after the valley of Hinnom had been destroyed by Josiah, it was used for dumping and burning all kinds of trash. Just as Gan Eden referred to the place where the righteous lived after death, Gehinnom became the name of the place to which the unclean and the ungodly were consigned to suffer punishment in the everlasting fire.

Fire, for that matter, was from ancient times the revelation and symbol of the anger and wrath of the Lord. Israel's God is a consuming fire, an eternal flame (Deut. 4:24; 9:3; Isa. 33:14). He spoke to the children of Israel from the midst of the fire (Deut. 4:12, 33; 5:4, 22–26; 9:10; 10:4; cf. Exod. 3:2). His wrath is a red-hot fire flaming forth from his nostrils (Pss. 18:8; 79:5; 89:46; Jer. 4:4). Fire coming forth from the presence of the Lord consumes the offering (Lev. 9:24). By fire he destroyed Nadab and Abihu (Lev. 10:2), complainers from among his people (Num. 11:1; Ps. 106:18), the descendants of Korah (Num. 16:35), the regiments of fifty sent out against Elijah (2 Kings 1:10ff.). And one day he will come in a blaze of fire to do justice on earth and to punish the wicked (Deut. 32:22; Pss. 11:6; 83:14; 97:3; 140:10; Isa. 30:33; 31:9; 66:15, 16, 24; Jer. 4:4; 15:14; 17:4; Joel 2:30; Amos 1:4ff.)—a fire burning to the depths of Sheol (Deut. 32:22), a fire that will never be quenched (Isa. 66:24) and that burns forever (Jer. 17:4).

This representation [of judgment] then passed into the New Testament. Gehenna, the place of punishment after the day of judgment, is distinct from Hades *(hadēs)*, the underworld *(phylakē)*, and the pit *(abyssos)* but identical with the furnace of fire *(kaminos tou pyros)* (Matt. 13:42, 50) and the lake of fire *(limnē tou pyros)* (Rev. 19:20; 20:10, 14, 15; 21:8). It is a place destined for the beast from the pit and for the false prophet (Rev. 19:20), for Satan and his angels (Rev. 20:10), for Death and Hades (Rev. 20:14), and for all the wicked (Rev. 20:15; 21:8). And these are all hurled into it *after* the resurrection (Matt. 5:29, 30; 10:28), and *after* the final judgment (Rev. 19:20; 20:10, 14, 15; 21:8). Before that time Hades, the prisonhouse (*phylakē*, 1 Peter 3:19; Rev. 20:7), or the pit *(abyssos)* were their abode, and the punishment of everlasting fire or the dimness of the outer darkness was still reserved for them (Matt. 8:29; 25:41, 46; 2 Peter 2:17; Jude 13). Burning in that Gehenna is everlasting, unquenchable *fire* (Matt. 18:8; Mark 9:43, 44, 48). This is where the *worm* that does not die keeps gnawing (Mark 9:44, 48) and the *torment* never ends (Matt. 25:46; 2 Thess. 1:9; Rev. 14:11). It is a Gehenna or *furnace of fire* (Matt. 5:22; 13:42, 50; 18:9) and at the same time a place of extreme, outer *darkness* (Matt. 8:12; 22:13; 25:30; 2 Peter 2:17; Jude 13; cf. Deut. 5:22; Ps. 97:2, 3). It is located "outside" (Rev. 22:15), in the *depths* so that one is thrown down into it (Matt. 5:29, 30; Rev. 19:20; 20:10, 14, 15).

This place is far from the marriage table of the Lamb (Matt. 8:11, 12; 22:13), far from fellowship with God and with Christ (Matt. 7:23; 25:41; Luke 13:27, 28; 2 Thess. 1:9); it is rather in the company of Satan and his angels (Matt. 25:41; Rev. 20:10, 15). The *wrath of God* in all its terror is manifested there (Rom. 2:5–8; 9:22; 1 Thess. 1:10; Heb. 10:31; Rev. 6:16, 17). Consequently Gehenna is not only a place of privation but also of sorrow and pain, in both soul and body; a place of *punishment* (*kolasis;* Matt. 25:46; Rev. 14:10, 11), of *weeping (klauthmos)* and *gnashing of teeth* (*brygmos tōn odontōn;* Matt. 8:12; 13:42, etc.), of *anguish* and *distress* (*thipsis* and *stenochōria;* Rom. 2:9; 2 Thess. 1:6), of *destruction* (*apōleia;* Matt. 7:13; Rom. 9:22; Phil. 1:28; 3:19; 2 Peter 3:7; Rev. 17:8, 11), of *corruption* (*phthora;* Gal. 6:8), of *ruin* (*olethros;* 1 Thess. 5:3; 2 Thess. 1:9; 1 Tim. 6:9). Gehenna is the realm of the second death (Rev. 2:11; 20:6, 14, 15; 21:8).

On this firm scriptural basis the Christian church built a doctrine of the eternity of hellish punishment. Accordingly, in theology as well as in the pulpit, in poetry as well as in the graphic arts, people frequently vied with each other in offering graphic descriptions and realistic portrayals of the pains experienced in the eternal fire in both soul and body.

Alternatives to Eternal Punishment

Nevertheless, from time to time objections were raised against this doctrine. After the Enlightenment of the eighteenth century introduced a milder assessment of sin and crime, abolished instruments of torture, moderated punishments, and aroused a sense of humanity on all sides, there also arose a very different view of the punishments of hell. Many people either altered their idea of them or rejected them altogether. The grounds on which people argue against the eternity of hellish punishment always remain the same. [They are as follows:]

a. Eternal punishment is incompatible with the goodness, love, and compassion of God, and makes him a tyrant who takes pleasure in inflicting pain and torment and who prepares praise for himself out of the everlasting moans of millions of unfortunate creatures.

b. Eternal punishment is incompatible with the justice of God, since it is unrelated and in no way proportionate to the sin in question, which, however appalling, is nevertheless limited and finite in character. It is inconceivable that God, who is perfect love and supreme justice, will punish human beings, even if they have sinned a thousand years, with everlasting torment.

c. Such eternal punishment is also unimaginable and inconceivable. Scripture speaks of fire, and a worm, and darkness, but these are all images. Taken literally, they are mutually exclusive. But aside from this, what is the value of an eternal punishment that has no purpose other than to torment the sinner for ever and ever? What is its utility for those who suffer it since in the nature of the case it excludes the possibility of true repentance and only impels them to keep sinning? What glory does it bring to God's name if it does not overcome and destroy sin but only perpetuates it forever? And how is it possible that the unredeemed continually harden themselves under the burden of such an eternal punishment without ever coming to repentance and self-humiliation before God?

d. Scripture, accordingly, does not teach an eternal and endless punishment in hell. It does indeed speak of eternal pain, and the like, but here as elsewhere the word "eternal" does not mean "endless" but refers to a period of time the limit of which eludes our perception or calculation: a thing is eternal (*aiōnios*) if it exceeds a longer or shorter age (*aiōn*). This is even reinforced by the fact that "eternal" (*aiōnios*), used in the positive sense of the benefits of salvation, say, of life, especially denotes an inner quality by which all these saving benefits are represented as being nonperishable. By contrast the condition of the lost is described in terms of "destruction" (*apōleia*), "corruption" (*phthora*), "ruin" (*olethros*), "death" (*thanatos*), which suggests that in this condition they cannot continue to exist forever but will either be utterly annihilated or at some point totally restored.

e. For the latter Scripture offers hope when it teaches that Christ is the propitiation for the sins of the whole world (Col. 1:19, 20; 1 John 2:2), and that God desires all humans to be saved that way (1 Tim. 2:4; 4:10). "For as all die in Adam, so all will be made alive in Christ" (Rom. 5:18; 1 Cor. 15:22). Now God gathers up all things under Christ as head (Eph. 1:10), so that someday every knee will bow before Christ (Phil. 2:10) and God may be all in all (1 Cor. 15:28). God has imprisoned all in disobedience so that he may be merciful to all (Rom. 11:32).

If for now we ignore pantheism and materialism, which deny all immortality and eternity, then, on the basis of the above considerations, the following three hypotheses can be constructed with regard to the final end of the ungodly.

In the first place there are those who teach that a possibility of repentance remains open, not only in the intermediate state right up until the final judgment,[7] but also thereafter and for all eternity. Whether there is a hell and eternal punishment, therefore, depends totally on the persons involved and their free will. If they persist in opposing the call to conversion, they will dig themselves ever deeper and more firmly into sin and prolong their punishment. However, since the preaching of faith and repentance never stops and the human will continues to be free, an eternal punishment in hell becomes extremely improbable and people rather flatter themselves with the hope that in the end all will repent and enter into eternal life. Hence in Scripture eternal pain only means that those who wait so long before repenting always retain the memory of their stubborn recalcitrance and will eternally rank behind those who believed the gospel in this life. What this hypothetical universalism comes down to, therefore, is a theory of ongoing purgation and a renewal of the doctrine of the migration of the soul. In the main, the difference between them is only that metempsychosis has this purgation occur in the present world *(Diesseits)* whereas hypothetical universalism situates it in the next *(Jenseits)*. This doctrine found acceptance especially among eighteenth-century rationalists but many contemporary theologians defend it as well.[8]

This sentiment of an ongoing repentance and purgation naturally leads to the theory of the so-called universalists, who think that in the end all creatures will participate in eternal salvation and glory. That which is desired and hoped for in the former is expected as certain and proclaimed as dogma by the latter. The doctrine of the return of all things into God already occurs in Indian and Greek philosophy; from there it passed into Gnosticism and Neo-Platonism and was for the first time represented in Christian theology by Origen. While Origen indeed repeatedly mentions an eternal punishment in hell, he only regards it as a practical doctrine necessary for the ignorant but viewed very differently by the "knowers" (Gnostics). For, according to Origen, all spirits were originally created alike by God but the acts of the free will produce unlikeness and bring about the transfer of human souls to a material world for the purpose of purgation and union with bodies. This process of purgation also continues after death and the final judgment until, from and through the greatest possible diversity, this likeness again emerges and all spirits return to God in the same condition in which they were originally with him. However, because the free will ever remains the same, it can equally well return from the evil to the good as from the good to the evil, and so there is a continual alternation of apostasy and restoration of all things, an endless creation and annihilation of the material world.[9] In antiquity this notion of the restoration of all things found acceptance with Gregory of Nazianz, Gregory of Nyssa, Didymus, Diodorus of Tarsus, Theodore of Mopsuestia, and others.[10] In the Middle Ages Scotus Erigena, Amalric of Bena, and the Brothers and Sisters of the Free Spirit adhered to it. After the Reformation it was held by Denck and numerous Anabaptists, Jane Leade, J. W. Petersen, Ludwig Gerhard, F. C. Oetinger, Michael Hahn, Jung-Stilling, Swedenborg, and so on; and in modern times by Schleiermacher and many others.[11]

A much better reception, however, was accorded a third opinion known as conditional immortality. Although an earlier theology very frequently spoke of immortality in a spiritual sense as a gift acquired by Christ, still hardly a soul thought of denying the natural immortality of the soul. The Socinians, under the influence of their abstract supernaturalism, were the first to teach that souls were not by nature immortal but only became immortal by a gift of God in the case of obedience. From this it followed that, by virtue of a natural perishability, the wicked and the demons must one day cease to exist. Although Socinus did not yet say this clearly, his followers taught in plain terms that the second death consisted in annihilation. And according to Crell, Schmalz, and others, this event did not take place at or shortly after death but only after the general resurrection and the judgment of the world.[12] This doctrine was taken over from the Socinians by Locke, Warburton, Whiston, Dodwell, Walter, and others, and in the nineteenth century by Rothe and Weisse.[13] It began to catch on and to gain adherents, however, particularly after it was advocated by Edward White in his *Life in Christ*.[14] This book produced numerous reactions, evoking not only serious dissent but also broad endorsement. Today, conditionalism has a great many defenders in all countries.[15]

The Answer of Scripture

If human sentiment had the final say about the doctrine of eternal punishment, it would certainly be hard to maintain and even today find few defenders. First, it needs to be gratefully acknowledged that since the eighteenth century the idea of humaneness and the sense of human sympathy have had a powerful awakening and have put an end to the cruelty that used to prevail, especially in the field of criminal justice. No one, however, can be blind to the reality that this humanitarian viewpoint also brings its own imbalances and dangers. The mighty turnabout that has occurred can be described in a single sentence: whereas

before the mentally ill were treated as criminals, now criminals are regarded as mentally ill. Before that time every abnormality was viewed
in terms of sin and guilt; now all ideas of guilt, crime, responsibility,
culpability, and the like, are robbed of their reality.[16] The sense of right
and justice, of the violation of law and of guilt, are seriously weakened
to the extent that the norm of all these things is not found in God but
shifted to the opinions of human beings and society. In the process all
certainty and safety is gradually lost. For when the interest of society
becomes the deciding factor, not only is every boundary between good
and evil wiped out, but justice runs the danger of being sacrificed to
power. "It is better for you to have one man die for the people than to
have the whole nation destroyed" (John 11:50) then becomes the language of the administration of justice. And the same human sentiment
that first pleaded for the humane treatment of a criminal does not
shrink, a moment later, from demanding death by torture of the innocent. Hosannas make way for a cross. The voice of the people *(vox populi)*, which is often wrongly revered as the voice of God *(vox Dei)*, recoils from no horrors whatever. And whereas the righteous person still
takes account of the needs of his animals, even the soft interior, the
heart and mind, of the wicked is still cruel (Prov. 12:10). Human feeling
is no foundation for anything important, therefore, and neither may
nor can it be decisive in the determination of law and justice. All ap-
pearances notwithstanding, it is infinitely better to fall into the hand of
the Lord than into human hands (1 Chron. 21:13). The same applies
with respect to eternal punishment in hell.

It must be noted that this doctrine, though it is often depicted in too
much realistic detail in the church and in theology, is nevertheless
grounded in Scripture. And no one in Scripture speaks of it more often
and at greater length than our Lord Jesus Christ, whose depth of human
feeling and compassion no one can deny and who was the meekest and
most humble of human beings. It is the greatest love that threatens the
most severe punishments. Over against the blessedness of eternal life he
acquired for his own stands the disaster of eternal ruin that he announces to the wicked. In the Old Testament both were veiled in shadows and presented in imagery. But in the New Testament it is Christ
who opens a vista both into the depths of outer darkness and into the
dwellings of eternal light.

That the punishment in this place of outer darkness is eternal is not
something one can doubt on the basis of Scripture. It is indeed true that
the adjective *(aiōnios)* (from *aiōn*, Heb. ʿwlm, i.e., duration of time, the
course of a life, the length of a human life, a long, indefinite period of
time in the past or future; the present world age, *aiōn outos;* the age to
come, *aiōn mellōn)* very often refers to a period of time that is beyond

human calculation but certainly not endless or everlasting. In the New Testament it is also used frequently to describe the entire world-dispensation that passed until the appearance of Christ, the period in which the counsel of God was announced by the prophets but not fully revealed (Luke 1:70; Acts 3:21; Rom. 16:25; Col. 1:26; 2 Tim. 1:9; Titus 1:2). But in the New Testament the word *aiōnios* functions especially to describe the imperishable nature—a nature not subject to any corruption or decay—of the salvific benefits gained by Christ, and is very often linked with the word "life" *(zōe)*—the eternal life that Christ imparts to everyone who believes. It has its beginning here on earth but will only be fully revealed in the future. It essentially belongs to the age to come *(aiōn mellōn,* Luke 18:30), is indestructible (John 11:25, 26), and is called "eternal," like the building from God *(oikodomē ek theou,* 2 Cor. 5:1), salvation *(sōtēria,* Heb. 5:9), redemption *(lytrōsis,* 9:12), the inheritance *(klēronomia,* 9:15), the glory *(doxa,* 2 Tim. 2:10), the kingdom *(basileia,* 2 Peter 1:11), just as God, Christ, and the Holy Spirit are also called "eternal" (Rom. 16:26; Heb. 9:14; 13:8, etc.). Over against this it is stated that the punishment of the wicked will consist in eternal fire *(to pyr to aiōnion,* Matt. 18:8; 25:41; Jude 7), eternal punishment *(kolasis aiōnios,* Matt. 25:46), eternal destruction *(olethros aiōnios,* 2 Thess. 1:9), eternal judgment *(krisis aiōnios,* Mark 3:29). Like eternal life, so by this description also eternal punishment is presented as belonging to the coming age *(aiōn mellōn)* in which a change of state is no longer possible. Scripture nowhere with a single word indicates or even leaves open the possibility that the state that begins there can still come to an end. And positively it says that the fire there is unquenchable (Matt. 3:12), that the worm does not die (Mark 9:48), that the smoke of torment goes up forever (Rev. 14:11) and continues day and night for all eternity (20:10), and that as eternal pain it contrasts with the eternal life of the righteous (Matt. 25:46). Unbiased exegesis will not find anything here other than eternal, never-ending punishment.

The state of the lost is described as destruction *(apōleia,* Matt. 7:13), corruption *(phthora,* Gal. 6:8), ruin *(olethros,* 2 Thess. 1:9), and death *(thanatos,* Rev. 2:11, etc.), which agrees with the fact that, according to the Old and New Testaments, the wicked will be destroyed, eradicated, ruined, put away, cast out, cut off, burnt as chaff, and so on. All these expressions are understood by the proponents of conditional immortality in terms of complete annihilation.[17] But this view is totally unfounded. Life, in Scripture, is never mere existence, and death is never the same as annihilation. Conditionalists cannot deny this fact with respect to temporal physical death of humans. Like the Socinians they usually assume that the wicked will continue to exist also after death, either to be annihilated by God after the resurrection and the final judgment, or gradually to wither away and finally to perish physically as well. The latter idea is impossible, both philosophically and scripturally. For sin is not a substance, no material thing *(materia)*, but a form *(forma)* that presupposes existence, and does not destroy the existent but steers it in a wrong direction, a direction away from God. And physical death is not merely a natural consequence, but a positive—divinely threatened and executed—punishment of sin. In the event of that death God does not annihilate human beings but temporarily separates soul and body in order to maintain both and to reunite them at the resurrection.

Scripture clearly and irrefutably teaches human immortality. When conditionalism views the destruction *(apōleia)* that is the punishment of sin as an annihilation of the human substance, it is confusing the ethical with the physical. And just as God does not annihilate human beings in the first death, so neither does he annihilate them in the second. For in Scripture the latter, too, is described as punishment (Matt. 25:46), weeping and gnashing of teeth (Matt. 8:12), anguish and distress (Rom. 2:9), never-ending fire (Matt. 18:8), the undying worm (Mark 9:44), and so on, expressions that all assume the existence of the lost. Still their state can be called destruction *(apōleia)*, corruption *(phthora)*, ruin *(olethros)*, and death *(thanatos)* because in a moral and spiritual sense they have become total wrecks and in an absolute sense lack the fullness of life granted by Christ to believers. Thus the prodigal son is called "dead" *(nekros)* and "lost" *(apolōlos,* Luke 15:24, 32); the Ephesians in their earlier state are described as "dead" *(nekroi)* through their trespasses and sins (Eph. 2:1; 4:18), and the people of the church of Sardis are called "dead" *(nekroi,* Rev. 3:1, etc.), but no one ever thinks of these three parties as being nonexistent.

The same failure to recognize the ethical character of sin marks the proponents of *apokatastasis* [restoration of all things]. The word derives from Acts 3:21 but there, as is universally acknowledged today, it does not at all mean what is now meant by it. Scripture nowhere teaches that one day all humans and even all devils will be saved. Often it indeed uses very universalistic language but that is because, intensively, Christ's work is of infinite value and benefits the whole world and all of humanity in its organic form of existence. But it unambiguously excludes the idea that all human individuals or even the devils will at some time become citizens in the kingdom of God. The doctrine of the restoration of all things, accordingly, has at all times been taught by only a handful of persons. Even today the theory of conditional immortality has more support among theologians than that of the *apokatastasis*. Actually, and in any case, this doctrine is of pagan—not of Christian—origin and is philosophical, not scriptural, in character.

Underlying the theory is pantheism, which views all things as proceeding from God and, similarly, of successively returning to him. In this view God is not the Lawgiver and Judge who will one day judge the world with equity [Ps. 9:8] but an unconscious immanent force that propels all things to the end and will one day recapture all things into himself. Sin, on this view, is not lawlessness *(anomia)* but a necessary moment in the evolution of the world. And redemption in Christ is not juridical restoration and ethical renewal but a physical process that controls everything.

In order to appreciate the fact of eternal punishment it is above all necessary, therefore, to recognize along with Scripture the integrity of the justice of God and the deeply sinful character of sin. Sin is not a weakness, a lack, a temporary and gradually vanishing imperfection, but in origin and essence it is lawlessness *(anomia)*, a violation of the law, rebellion and hostility against God, the negation of his justice, his authority, even his existence. Granted, sin is finite in the sense that it is committed by a finite creature in a finite period of time but, as Augustine already correctly noted, not the duration of time over which the sin was committed but its own intrinsic nature is the standard for its punishment. "A momentary lapse into carelessness," as the saying goes, "can lead to a lifetime of weeping." The sins of a moment can result in a life of shame and punishment. A person who commits a crime is sometimes given the death penalty, and thereby transferred into an irremediable state by an earthly government. God acts the same way: what the death penalty is on earth, the punishment of hell is in the final judgment. He judges and punishes sin in accordance with its intrinsic quality. And that sin is infinite in the sense that it is committed against the Highest Majesty, who is absolutely entitled to our love and worship. God is absolutely and infinitely worthy of our obedience and dedication. The law in which he requires this of us is therefore absolutely binding and its binding nature infinitely great. The violation of that law, viewed intensively, is therefore an absolute and infinite evil. Furthermore, the thing to be considered here is not so much the "duration of the sinning" as "the will of the sinner which is such that it would always wish to sin if it could."[18] He who commits the sin is a slave to sin: he will not and cannot do otherwise than sin. It is truly not his own doing when he is denied the opportunity to continue his sinful life. In terms of his interior desire he would not want anything other than to live forever so that he could sin forever. Who then, looking at the sinful nature of sin, would have the nerve to say that God is unjust if he visits the sin not only with temporal but also with eternal punishments?

As a rule this argument [against eternal punishment] derived from the justice of God is for that reason advanced somewhat tentatively and hesitantly, but is all the more passionately regarded as inconsistent with the goodness and love of God. However, if it is not inconsistent with the justice of God, it is not and cannot be inconsistent with his goodness either. We have no choice at this point. If eternal punishment is unjust, then that condemns it and one need no longer appeal to God's goodness. If, however, it is consistent with God's justice, then God's goodness remains unscathed: if a thing is just it is also good. The argument against eternal punishment derived from God's goodness therefore secretly, in the manner of Marcion, introduces a conflict between God's justice and his goodness and offers up the former to the latter. But goodness that nullifies justice is no longer true and real goodness. It is mere human weakness and wimpiness and, when projected onto God, an invention of the human brain, one that in no way corresponds to the true and living God who has revealed himself in Scripture as well as in nature. For if eternal punishment is inconsistent with God's goodness, then temporal punishment is inconsistent with it as well. But the latter is a fact no one can deny. Humankind is consumed by God's anger and terrified by his wrath [cf. Ps. 90:7]. Who can square this world's suffering with God's goodness and love? Still it must be possible, for it exists. Now if the existence of immense suffering in this world may not lead us to question God's goodness, then neither may eternal punishment prompt us to deny it. If this world is consistent with God's love, as it is and has to be, then hell is too. For aside from Scripture there is no stronger proof for the existence of hell than the existence of this world, the world from whose misery the features of the [biblical] picture of hell are derived.[19]

Furthermore, for the person who disputes [the reality of] eternal punishment, there is enormous danger of playing the hypocrite before God. Such a person presents himself as extremely loving, one who in goodness and compassion far outstrips our Lord Jesus Christ. This does not stop this same person, the moment his or her own honor is violated, from erupting in fury and calling down on the violator every evil in this life and the life to come. Resentment, hatred, wrath, vindictiveness arise in the heart of all human beings against anyone standing in their way. We promote our own honor but the honor of God is of no concern to us. We stand up for our own rights but let others trample the rights of God into the dirt. Surely this is sufficient evidence that we humans are not suitable judges of the words and actions of God. Still, in that act of standing up for our own rights and reputation there is something good. However wrongly applied, there is implicit in it the fact that our rights and reputation are more precious than our goods and life. Slumbering even in the sinner, there is still a deep sense of justice and honor. And when that sense is violated, it is aroused and suppresses all pity.

When in a given conflict between two people or two nations the issue is one of justice, each party passionately prays that God may bring about the triumph of the right and strike its violators with his judgment. All human beings still have an innate feeling for the saying "Let justice be done though the world perish" *(fiat justitia pereat mundus)* and think it reasonable that justice should triumph at the expense of thousands of human lives. In the day of judgment, too, the issue is one of justice, not some private right or other, but *justice* par excellence, justice in its full import and scope, the justice of God—that God himself may be honored as God in all eternity.

There is, therefore, no doubt that in the day of judgment God will fully vindicate himself in the presence of all his creatures even when he pronounces eternal punishment upon sinners. Now we who know in part also know the horror of sin only in part. But if here already, upon hearing of certain horrors, we consider no punishment severe enough, what then will we think when at the end of time we gain insight into the depths of injustice? And on earth, furthermore, we are always onesided. Over and over our sense of justice and our compassion clash. We are either too soft or much too severe in our judgment. But in the case of the Lord our God this is not, and cannot be, so. In Christ he has fully revealed his love, a love that is so great precisely because it saves us from the wrath to come and from eternal destruction. Critics of eternal punishment not only fail to do justice to the doom-worthiness of sin, the rigorousness of divine justice; they also infringe on the greatness of God's love and the salvation that is in Christ. If the object had not been salvation from eternal destruction, the price of the blood of God's own Son would have been much too high. The heaven that he won for us by his atoning death presupposes a hell from which he delivered us. The eternal life he imparted to us presupposes an eternal death from which he saved us. The grace and good pleasure of God in which he makes us participants forever presuppose a wrath into which we would otherwise have had to be plunged forever. And for that reason it is this Christ who will one day execute judgment and pronounce his sentence. A human being, a true and complete human being who knows what is in human beings, who is the meekest of human beings, will be the judge of human beings, a judge so just that all will acknowledge his justice and very knee will bow before him and every tongue confess that Christ is Lord to the glory of God the Father. In the end God will be recognized as God by all creatures, if not willingly then unwillingly.

This should be enough for us. Inquiries into the location and size of hell, the nature of the fire and the worm, the psychic and physical state of the lost, lead nowhere because Scripture is silent on these topics. All we know besides the things we have discussed so far is that the punishment of hell does not begin until after the day of judgment; that it is consistently threatened against those who stubbornly resist the truth of God—the cowardly, the faithless, the polluted, the murderers, the fornicators, the sorcerers, the idolaters, and the liars (Rev. 21:8)—and that even at that it differs in the measure of each person's unrighteousness. Scripture nowhere teaches that there will still be room there for repentance and forgiveness. The addition in Matthew 12:32 ("either in this age or in the age to come") is not intended to bring out the pardonability of the sin against the Son of Man in the age to come but to underline the absolute unpardonability of the sin against the Holy Spirit. In its essence punishment consists in the maintenance of justice and, after the judgment, serves specifically to requite all persons according to their work, not to purify them. Scripture nevertheless teaches very clearly that there are degrees of punishment. The penalty of damnation *(poena damni)* is the same, but the penalty of sensation *(poena sensus)* differs. All will receive according to their works (Matt. 10:15; 11:24; 23:14; 24:51; Luke 10:12, 14; 12:46, 47; 2 Cor. 5:10, etc.). And this fact as such still demonstrates something of God's mercy.[20] All sin is absolutely opposed to the justice of God, but in punishing it God nevertheless takes account of the relative difference existing between sins. There is infinite diversity also on the other side of the grave.[21] For in eternal punishment God's justice always manifests itself in such a way that his goodness and love remain inviolate and can never be justly faulted. The saying that he does not willingly afflict or grieve anyone (Lam. 3:33) applies also in hell. The pain he inflicts is not an object of pleasure, either for him or for the blessed in heaven, but a means of glorifying his virtues and hence determined in severity and measure by this ultimate goal.[22]

The Renewal of Creation   7

The renewal of creation follows the final judgment. According to Scripture the present world will neither continue forever nor will it be destroyed and replaced by a totally new one. Instead it will be cleansed of sin and re-created, reborn, renewed, made whole. While the kingdom of God is first planted spiritually in human hearts, the future blessedness is not to be spiritualized. Biblical hope, rooted in incarnation and resurrection, is creational, this-worldly, visible, physical, bodily hope. The rebirth of human beings is completed in the glorious rebirth of all creation, the New Jerusalem whose architect and builder is God himself. The salvation of the kingdom of God, including communion with God as well as the communion of the saints, is both a present blessing and a future consummated rich glory. The kingdom of God has come and is coming. The scope of God's mercy is wide. While we should abstain from a firm judgment concerning the salvation of pagans or children who die in infancy, the Reformed Confessions are magnanimous in their outlook. Though many fall away, in Christ the human race, the world, is saved. The final rest of God's children is not to be conceived as inaction; his children remain his servants who joyfully and in diverse ways serve him night and day. What we sow on earth is harvested in eternity; diversity is not destroyed in eternity but cleansed from sin and made serviceable to fellowship with God and others. Scripture even teaches degrees of glory in the future kingdom, commensurate with one's works. The blessedness of salvation is the same for all but there are distinctions in glory. This distinction is not merited by good works but a sovereign, free, and gracious covenantal disposition of God—a given right to believers merited by Christ. God thus crowns his own work in order that in such active diversity the glory of his own attributes shines out. All creatures will then live and move and have their being in God who is all in all, who reflects all his attributes in the mirror of his works and glorifies himself in them.

Following the final judgment comes the renewal of the world. Some indeed, along with Thomas,[1] have put it before the final judgment but the common view is that it will follow upon it and be inaugurated only after the wicked have been banished from the earth. This order undoubtedly best harmonizes with that in Holy Scripture. In the Old Testament the day of the Lord is indeed preceded by a range of fearful signs, and judgment on the nations takes place amid appalling events of different kinds. However, the new earth, with its extraordinary fruitfulness, only comes into being when victory over Israel's enemies has been achieved and the people have returned to, and been restored in, its land. According to the New Testament as well, the day of judgment is preceded by many signs, like the darkening of sun and moon and stars, the shaking of the powers of heaven, and so on (Matt. 24:29). The burning of the earth, though, does not occur until the day of the Lord (2 Peter 3:10) and then follows the coming of the new heaven and new earth in which righteousness dwells (2 Peter 3:13). Once judgment has been executed, John sees the new Jerusalem coming down out of heaven from God (Rev. 21:1f.).

In this expectation of world renewal Scripture assumes a position between two extremes. On the one hand, many thinkers, Plato, Aristotle, Xenophanes, Philo, Maimonides, Averroes, Wolanus, Peyrère, Edelmann, and Czolbe, among them, have asserted that this world is destined to continue in its present form forever. On the other hand, Origen, the Lutherans, the Mennonites, the Socinians, Vorstius, the Remonstrants, and a number of Reformed theologians like Beza, Rivet, Junius, Wollebius, and Prideaux, believed that the world would not only be changed in form but destroyed in substance and replaced by a totally new world.[2]

The Transformation of Creation

Neither of these two views, however, finds support in Scripture. Old Testament prophecy, while it looks for an extraordinary transformation in all of nature, refrains from teaching the destruction of the present world. The passages that are assumed to teach the latter (Ps. 102:26; Isa. 34:4; 51:6, 16; 65:17; 66:22) do indeed describe in very graphic terms the change that will set in after the day of the Lord, but do not imply the destruction of the substance of the world. In the first place, the description given in these passages is much too rich in imagery for us to infer from them a reduction to nothing *(reductio ad nihilum)* of the entire world. Further, the perishing *(ʾbd)* of heaven and earth (Ps. 102:26), which for one thing by itself never conveys an absolute destruction of substance, is explained by the fact that they will wear out like a garment, be changed like clothing, wither like a leaf on a vine, or vanish like smoke (Ps. 102:26; Isa. 34:4; 51:6). And finally the word "create" *(brʾ)* used with reference to the new heaven and the new earth (Isa. 65:17) certainly does not always mean making something out of nothing but frequently denotes a divine activity by which God brings forth something new from the old (Isa. 41:20; 43:7; 54:16; 57:18). For that reason it also frequently alternates with planting, laying the foundations of, and making (Isa. 51:16; 66:22). The Lord can say (Isa. 51:16) that he begins the new creation by putting his word in Israel's mouth and hiding them in the shadow of his hand.

In the same way the New Testament proclaims that heaven and earth will pass away (Matt. 5:18; 24:35; 2 Peter 3:10; 1 John 2:17; Rev. 21:1), that they will perish and wear out like clothing (Heb. 1:11), dissolve (2 Peter 3:10), be burned with fire (2 Peter 3:10), and be changed (Heb. 1:12). But none of these expressions implies a destruction of substance. Peter, for example, expressly teaches that the old earth, which originated as a result of the separation of waters, was deluged with water and so perished (2 Peter 3:6) and that the present world would also perish, not—thanks to the divine promise—by water but by fire. Accordingly, with reference to the passing of the present world we must no more think of a destruction of substance than with regard to the passing of the earlier world in the flood. Fire burns, cleanses, purifies, but does not destroy. The contrast in 1 John 2:17 ("the world and its desire are passing away but those who do the will of God live forever") teaches us that the first statement does not imply a destruction of the substance of the world but a vanishing of the world in its present sin-damaged form. Paul, accordingly, also states very clearly that the present form *(to schēma)* of this world passes away (1 Cor. 7:31). Only such a renewal of the world, for that matter, accords with what Scripture teaches about redemption. For the latter is never a second, brand-new creation but a re-creation of the existing world. God's honor consists precisely in the fact that he redeems and renews the same humanity, the same world, the same heaven, and the same earth that have been corrupted and polluted by sin. Just as anyone in Christ is a new creation in whom the old has passed away and everything has become new (2 Cor. 5:17), so this world passes away in its present form as well, in order out of its womb, at God's word of power, to give birth and being to a new world. Just as in the case of an individual human being, so at the end of time a rebirth of the world will take place as well (Matt. 19:28). This constitutes a spiritual renewal, not a physical creation.[3]

This renewal of the visible world highlights the onesidedness of the spiritualism that limits future blessedness to heaven. In the case of Old Testament prophecy one cannot doubt that it describes earthly blessedness. Its expectation is that following the great day the people of God will live in security and peace in Palestine under the anointed king of the dynasty of David, surrounded and served by the Gentile nations. There is truth in Delitzsch's comments on Isaiah 66:24:

This is just the distinction between the Old Testament and the New; that the Old Testament brings down the life to come to the level of this life, whilst the New Testament lifts up this life to the level of the life to come; that the Old Testament depicts both this life and the life to come as an endless extension of this life, whilst the New Testament depicts it as a continuous line in two halves, the last point in this finite state being the first point of the infinite state beyond; that the Old Testament preserves the continuity of this life and the life to come by transferring the outer side, the form, the appearance of this life to the life to come, the New Testament by making the inner side, the nature, the reality of the life to come, the δυνάμεις μέλλοντος αἰῶνος, immanent in this life.[4]

Still these comments do not do complete justice to the New Testament hope of future blessedness. Present in the New Testament there is undoubtedly some spiritualization of Old Testament prophecy. Since Jesus' advent breaks up into a first and a second coming, the kingdom of God is first planted in human hearts spiritually, and the benefits of that kingdom are all internal and invisible: forgiveness, peace, righteousness, eternal life. The essence of future blessedness, accordingly, is also construed more spiritually, especially by Paul and John, as a being always with the Lord (John 12:26; 14:3; 17:24; 2 Cor. 5:8; Phil. 1:23; 1 Thess. 4:17; 5:10; 1 John 3:2). But this does not confine this blessedness to heaven.[5] This cannot be the case as is basically evident from the fact that the New Testament teaches the incarnation of the Word and the physical resurrection of Christ; it further expects his physical return at the end of time and immediately thereafter has in view the physical resurrection of all human beings, especially that of believers. All this spells the collapse of spiritualism which, if it remains true to its principle—as in Origen—has nothing left after the day of judgment other than spirits in an uncreated heaven.

But the teaching of Scripture is very different. The world, according to it, consists of heaven and earth; humans consist of soul and body; and the kingdom of God, accordingly, has a hidden spiritual dimension and an external, visible side. Whereas Jesus came the first time to establish that kingdom in a spiritual sense, he returns at the end of history to give visible shape to it. Reformation proceeds from the inside to the outside. The rebirth of humans is completed in the rebirth of creation. The kingdom of God is fully realized only when it is visibly extended over the earth as well. This is how also the disciples understood it when, after Jesus' resurrection, they asked him whether this was the time he would restore the kingdom to Israel. In his reply Jesus does not deny that one day he will establish such a kingdom, but only says that the times for it have been set by the Father and that now his disciples are called, in the power of the Holy Spirit, to be his witnesses to the ends of the earth (Acts 1:6–8). Elsewhere he expressly states that the meek will inherit the earth (Matt. 5:5). He pictures future blessedness as a meal at which the guests sit down with Abraham, Isaac, and Jacob (Matt. 8:11), enjoy food and drink (Luke 22:30), eat of the new and perfect Passover (Luke 22:16), and drink of the fruit of the new vine (Matt. 26:29). True, in this dispensation and right up until the parousia, the eyes of believers are directed upward toward heaven. That is where their treasure is (Matt. 6:20; 19:21); there Jesus, who is their life, sits at the right hand of God (John 14:3; 17:24; Col. 3:1–3); their citizenship is there while they are aliens here (Phil. 3:20; Heb. 11:13–16).

But this inheritance is destined to be revealed. Someday Christ will return visibly and then cause the whole believing community—indeed, the whole world—to participate in his glory. Not only are believers changed after his likeness (John 17:24; Rom. 8:17, 18, 28; Phil. 3:21; Col. 3:4; 1 John 3:2), but the whole creation will be set free from its bondage to decay and obtain the freedom of the glory of the children of God (Rom. 8:21). Earth and heaven will be renewed so that justice will be at home in them (2 Peter 3:13; Rev. 21:1). The heavenly Jerusalem, which is now above and was the model for the earthly Jerusalem, then comes down to earth (Gal. 4:26; Heb. 11:10, 13–16; 12:22; 13:14; Rev. 3:12; 21:2f.). This new Jerusalem is not identical with the believing community, even though it is figuratively called the bride of the Lamb (Rev. 21:2, 9), for Hebrews 12:22, 23 clearly distinguishes between the heavenly Jerusalem and the assembly of the firstborn (the Old Testament faithful) and the spirits of the righteous made perfect (deceased Christians). The heavenly Jerusalem is a city built by God himself (Heb. 11:10). It is the city of the living God, inasmuch as God is not just its architect but also makes it his home (Rev. 21:3). In it the angels are the servants and constitute the royal entourage of the great king (Heb. 12:22), while the blessed are its citizens (Rev. 21:27; 22:3, 4).

The description John gives of that Jerusalem (Rev. 21–22) should certainly not be taken literally any more than his preceding visions. This option is excluded by the mere fact that John depicts it as a cube whose length, width, and height are equal, that is, 12,000 stadia or 1,500 miles; still the height of the wall is only 144 cubits, just under 75 yards (Rev. 21:15–17). By this depiction John does not intend to give a sketch of the city; rather, since he cannot bring the glory of the divine kingdom home to us in any other way, he offers his ideas, interpreting them in images. And he derives these images from Paradise, with its river and tree of life (Rev. 21:6; 22:1, 2); from the earthly Jerusalem with its gates and streets (Rev. 21:12f.); from the temple with its Holy of Holies in which God himself dwelt (Rev. 21:3, 22); and from the entire realm of nature with all its treasures of gold and precious stones (Rev.

21:11, 18–21). But although these are ideas interpreted thus by images, these ideas are not illusions or fabrications, but this-worldly depictions of other-worldly realities. All that is true, honorable, just, pure, pleasing, and commendable in the whole of creation, in heaven and on earth, is gathered up in the future city of God—renewed, re-created, boosted to its highest glory.

The substance [of the city of God] is present in this creation. Just as the caterpillar becomes a butterfly, as carbon is converted into diamond, as the grain of wheat, upon dying in the ground, produces other grains of wheat, as all of nature revives in the spring and dresses up in celebrative clothing, as the believing community is formed out of Adam's fallen race, as the resurrection body is raised from the body that is dead and buried in the earth, so, too, by the re-creating power of Christ, the new heaven and the new earth will one day emerge from the fire-purged elements of this world, radiant in enduring glory and forever set free from the bondage of decay *(douleias tēs phthoras).* More glorious than this beautiful earth, more glorious than the earthly Jerusalem, more glorious even than Paradise will be the glory of the new Jerusalem whose architect and builder is God himself. The state of glory *(status gloriae)* will be no mere restoration *(restauratie)* of the state of nature *(status naturae),* but a reformation[6] which, thanks to the power of Christ, transforms all matter *(hylē)* into form *(eidos),* all potency into actuality *(potentia, actus),* and presents the entire creation before the face of God, brilliant in unfading splendor and blossoming in a springtime of eternal youth. *Substantially* nothing is lost. Outside, indeed, are the dogs and sorcerers and fornicators and murderers and idolaters and everyone who loves and practices falsehood (Rev. 22:15). But in the new heaven and new earth the world as such is restored; in the believing community the human race is saved. In that community, which Christ has purchased and gathered from all nations, languages, and tongues (Rev. 5:9, etc.), all the nations, Israel included, maintain their distinct place and calling (Matt. 8:11; Rom. 11:25; Rev. 21:24; 22:2). And all those nations—each in accordance with its own distinct national character—bring into the new Jerusalem all they have received from God in the way of glory and honor (Rev. 21:24, 26).

The Blessings of the Redeemed

The blessings in which the blessed participate are not only spiritual, therefore, but also material and physical in nature. As misguided as it is—along with pagan peoples and some chiliasts—to make the material into the chief component of future blessedness, so it is also onesided and stoical to regard the physical indifferently or to exclude it totally from the state of blessedness. Scripture consistently maintains the intimate connectedness of the spiritual and the natural. Inasmuch as the world consists of heaven and earth and humans consist of soul and body, so sanctity and glory, virtue and happiness, the moral and the natural world order ought finally to be harmoniously united. The blessed will therefore not only be free from sin but also from all the consequences of sin, from ignorance and error (John 6:45), from death (Luke 20:36; 1 Cor. 15:26; Rev. 2:11; 20:6, 14), from poverty and disease, from pain and fear, hunger and thirst, cold and heat (Matt. 5:4; Luke 6:21; Rev. 7:16, 17; 21:4), from all weakness, dishonor, and corruption (1 Cor. 15:42, etc.).

Still the spiritual blessings are the more important and innumerably abundant: holiness (Rev. 3:4, 5; 7:14; 19:8; 21:27); salvation (Rom. 13:11; 1 Thess. 5:9; Heb. 1:14; 5:9); glory (Luke 24:36; Rom. 2:10; 8:18, 21); adoption (Rom. 8:23); eternal life (Matt. 19:16, 29, etc.); the vision of and conformity to God and Christ (Matt. 5:18; John 17:24; Rom. 8:29; 1 Cor. 13:12; 2 Cor. 3:18; Phil. 3:21; 1 John 3:2; Rev. 22:4); fellowship with, and the service and praise of, God and Christ (John 17:24; 2 Cor. 5:8; Phil. 1:23; Rev. 4:10; 5:9, 13; 7:10, 15; 21:3; 22:3, etc.). Since in principle all these benefits have been given to believers on earth already—such as, for example, adoption (Rom. 8:15; 9:4; Gal. 4:5; Eph. 1:5) and eternal life (John 3:15, 16, 36, etc.)—many people have construed Christian salvation exclusively as a present salvation that is increasingly realized solely in the way of an ethical process.[7] Ritschl and many of his followers also onesidedly stressed the present-world orientation of people ("diesseitige Weltstellung des Menschen"). They consider the moral freedom relative to the world, which the Christian receives in faith, as the most significant benefit and say little or nothing about the eternal salvation that Christ prepares for his own in the future.[8]

Against the abstract supernaturalism of the Greek Orthodox and Roman Catholic Church—which sees salvation as exclusively transcendent and therefore, as it concerns the earth, considers the Christian life embodied ideally in monasticism—this [present-worldly] view stands for an important truth. The Reformation, going back to Scripture, in principle overcame this supernaturalistic and ascetic view of life. Those who believe, at the very moment of believing, receive the forgiveness of sins and eternal life. They are children of God who serve the Father, not as hired employees in hope of compensation, but as children who do the will of the Father out of love and gratitude. They carry out this will not by fleeing from the world, but by being faithful in the calling entrusted to them on earth. Living for heaven, therefore, does not compete with life in the midst of the world: it is precisely in that world that Christ keeps his disciples from the Evil One.

The new heaven and earth, as we indicated earlier, is composed of the elements of the world that exists now, and the believing community is humanity restored under Christ as head. However much believers on earth in a sense already enjoy salvation, that is the case only in principle and not in full. For in hope we believers are saved (Rom. 8:24). Jesus pronounces his blessing on the poor in spirit (etc.), for theirs is the kingdom of heaven that in the future will be established on earth (Matt. 5:3–10). Believers are children of God but still await the full realization of their "sonship" (Matt. 5:9; Rom. 8:23). They have eternal life but must still receive it at the resurrection—as even John points out (5:20–29; 6:40, 44, 45). Both are therefore true: the kingdom of heaven has come and it is still coming. And this twofold truth conditions the entire character of the state of glory. As the new heaven and earth are formed out of the elements of this world, and the believing community is a re-creation of the human race that fell in Adam, so the life of the redeemed in the hereafter is to be conceived as analogous with the life of believers here on earth. On the one hand, it does not consist in the contemplation of God *(visio Dei)* in a Catholic sense, a contemplation to which human nature can only be elevated by a superadded gift *(donum superadditum)*. On the other hand, neither is it a slow and gradual development of the Christian life as led by believers already on earth. It is a genuinely natural life but unfolded by grace to its highest splendor and its most bountiful beauty. The matter *(materia)* remains but the form *(forma)* differs. In that life religion—fellowship with God—is primary and central. But that fellowship will be richer, deeper, and more blessed than it ever was or could be on earth, since it will not be disturbed by any sin, or interrupted by any distance, or mediated by either Scripture or nature.

Now, as we look into the mirror of God's revelation, we only see his image; then we will see him face to face and know as we are known. Contemplation *(visio)*, understanding *(comprehensio)*, and enjoyment of God *(fruitio Dei)* make up the essence of our future blessedness. The redeemed see God, not—to be sure—with physical eyes but still in a way that far outstrips all revelation in this dispensation via nature and Scripture. And thus they will all know him, each in the measure of his mental capacity, with a knowledge that has its image and likeness in God's knowledge—directly, immediately, unambiguously, and purely. Then they will receive and possess everything they expected here only in hope. Thus contemplating and possessing God, they enjoy him, and are blessed in his fellowship: blessed in soul and body, in intellect and will. In theology men have disputed whether this blessedness in the hereafter formally had its seat in the intellect or in the will and hence consisted in knowledge or love. Thomas claimed the former,[9] Duns Scotus the latter,[10] but Bonaventure combined the two, observing that the enjoyment of God *(fruitio Dei)* was the fruit not only of the knowledge of God *(cognitio Dei)* but also of the love of God *(amor Dei)* and resulted from the union and cooperation between the two.[11]

The blessedness of communion with God is enjoyed in and heightened by the communion of saints. On earth already this communion is a wonderful benefit of faith. Those who for Jesus' sake have left behind house or brothers or sisters or father or mother or wife or children or fields already in this life receive houses, brothers, sisters, mothers, children and fields—along with persecutions—(Mark 10:29, 30), for all who do the will of the Father are Jesus' brother and sister and mother (Matt. 12:50). Through the Mediator of the New Testament believers enter into fellowship, not only with the militant church on earth, but also with the triumphant church in heaven, the assembly of the firstborn, the spirits of the righteous made perfect, even with innumerable angels (Heb. 12:22–24). But this fellowship, though in principle it already exists on earth, will nevertheless be incomparably richer and more glorious when all dividing walls of descent and language, of time and space, have been leveled, all sin and error have been banished, and all the elect have been assembled in the new Jerusalem. Then will be fully answered the prayer of Jesus that all his sheep may be one flock under one Shepherd (John 10:16; 17:21).

All the saints together will then fully comprehend the breadth and length and height and depth of the love of Christ (Eph. 3:18). They will together be filled with all the fullness of God (Eph. 3:19; Col. 2:2, 10), inasmuch as Christ, himself filled with the fullness of God (Col. 1:19), will in turn fill the believing community with himself and make it his fullness *(plērōma;* Eph. 1:23; 4:10). And sitting down at one table with Abraham, Isaac, and Jacob (Matt. 8:11), they will unitedly lift up a song of praise to the glory of God and of the Lamb (Rev. 4:11; 5:12, etc.). Speaking of the believing community on earth Scripture frequently says that it is a "little flock" (Matt. 7:14; 22:14; Luke 12:32; 13:23), a statement confirmed by history right up until the present. And even toward the end of history, when the gospel will have been preached among all nations, apostasy will increase and the faithful will be few. Old Testament prophecy already announced that only a remnant of Israel would repent and be saved. The New Testament likewise expects that those who persevere to the end will be few (Matt. 24:13; 25:1f.; Luke 18:8).

On the other hand, however, Scripture often uses very universalistic language. In Adam the covenant of grace is made known to humanity as a whole (Gen. 3:15). The covenant of nature concluded after the flood embraces all creatures (Gen. 9:9, 10). In Abraham all generations of the earth are blessed (Gen. 12:3). The salvation that will one day be granted to Israel profits all the Gentiles. Jesus says that he will give his life as a ransom for *many* (Matt. 20:28) and that *many* will come from east and west to sit down with Abraham, Isaac, and Jacob in the kingdom of heaven (Matt. 8:11). The grace that appeared in Christ is much more abundant than the trespass of Adam: it comes to all people for justification and life (Rom. 5:12–20; 1 Cor. 15:22). In this dispensation all things in heaven and on earth will be gathered up under Christ (Eph. 1:10). And one day at the end every knee will bow before Christ and every tongue will confess him as Lord (Phil. 2:10, 11). Then a great multitude that no one can number will stand before the throne and the Lamb (Rev. 7:9; 19:1, 6). *Nations* will be saved and walk in the light of the new Jerusalem (Rev. 21:24, 26; 22:2). And God will then be all in all (1 Cor. 15:28).

The Wideness of God's Mercy

Because of this last series of texts many people have cherished the hope that in the end, if not all creatures, then surely all humans, or if this should fail, then far and away the majority of humans will be saved. Hell will either be totally nonexistent or only a small and remote corner of the universe. They based this expectation either on the possibility of salvation by the works of the law (Pelagians, Socinians, deists, etc.), or on the opportunity of hearing and accepting the gospel either after death in the intermediate state or even after the day of judgment (universalists). I have discussed these sentiments in the previous chapter[12] and therefore do not need to examine them in light of Scripture again here.

But even among those who adhere to the confession that no one comes to the Father except by Christ, and that only one name has been given under heaven for salvation (John 14:6; Acts 4:12), there have always been a few people who believed in the possibility of salvation in this life aside from the preaching of the gospel. They taught this view with respect to children of the covenant, to all children who die in infancy within or outside the bounds of Christianity, to the developmentally or emotionally handicapped, and to the hearing-and-speech-impaired who are practically shut off from the preaching of the gospel. The same applies to some or many pagans who in terms of their clear insights and virtuous life gave evidence of true piety. Some of the Church Fathers assumed that the Logos was active in the pagan world.[13] Augustine believed that from the beginning there have always been a few persons, in Israel but in other nations as well, who believed in the Logos and lived faithfully and righteously in accordance with his commandments.[14] Abelard asserted that pagans, too, could inherit salvation.[15] According to Strauss, Luther once expressed the wish that God would be gracious also to men like Cicero and Seneca, while Melanchthon left open the possibility that, in some cases and by a special method, God had communicated some knowledge of forgiveness in Christ to Solon, Themistocles, and others.[16] Zwingli was more definite and believed that God had his elect also among pagans.[17] But others left open only the possibility and did not venture to go beyond hoping and wishing.[18] This opinion, however, was never held by more than a handful.

The churches, in their confessions, made no pronouncements on this issue and most theologians opposed the idea.[19] Somewhat more favorable were their views on the salvation of children who died in infancy. Catholics teach that all children of Christian parents who died, having been baptized through express intention *(voto)* or in reality *(re)*, were saved and that all other children who died young suffered a penalty of damnation but not of sensation *(poene damni,* not *sensus)* in the limbo of children *(limbus infantum).*[20] With respect to children of Christian parents Lutherans hold the same view as Catholics and leave the others to the judgment of God.[21] The Reformed were inclined to believe that all children who were born in the covenant of grace and died before reaching the age of discretion attained to blessedness in heaven,[22] though in this connection as well many of them made a distinction between elect and reprobate children and did not dare to attribute salvation with certainty to each of these children individually.[23] As for children outside the covenant who died in infancy, the judgment of some was quite magnanimous. Junius, for example, would rather surmise out of love that they were saved than that they were lost.[24] Voetius said: as to whether they are lost or some among them are elect and were regenerated before they died, "I would not wish to deny, nor am I able to affirm" *(nolim negare, affirmare non possum).*[25]

In light of Scripture, both with regard to the salvation of pagans and that of children who die in infancy, we cannot get beyond abstaining from a firm judgment, in either a positive or a negative sense. Deserving of note, however, is that in the face of these serious questions Reformed theology is in a much more favorable position than any other. For in this connection all other churches can only entertain a more temperate judgment if they reconsider their doctrine of the absolute necessity of the means of grace or infringe upon that of the accursedness of sin. But the Reformed refused to establish the measure of grace needed for a human being still to be united with God, though subject to many errors and sins, or to determine the extent of the knowledge indispensably necessary to salvation.[26] Furthermore, they maintained that the means of grace are not absolutely necessary for salvation and that, also aside from the Word and sacraments, God can regenerate persons for eternal life.[27]

Thus, in the Second Helvetic Confession, Article 1, we read: "At the same time we recognize that God can illuminate whom and when he will, even without the external ministry, for that is in his power" (*agnoscimus Deum illuminare posse homines, etiam sine externo ministerio, quos et quando velit; id quod ejus potentiae est*). And the Westminster Confession states (in ch. X, §3) that "Elect infants, dying in infancy, are regenerated and saved by Christ through the Spirit, who works when, and where, and how he pleases" (*Christus, qui quando et ubi et quo sibi placuerit modo operatur*) and that this applies also to "all other elect persons who are incapable of being outwardly called by the ministry of the Word" (*quotquot externae vocationis per ministerium verbi sunt incapaces*). Reuter, accordingly, after explaining Augustine's teaching on this point, correctly states: "One could in fact defend the paradox that it is precisely the *particularistic* doctrine of predestination that makes possible those *universalistic*-sounding phrases."[28] In fact, even the universalistic passages of Scripture cited above come most nearly and most beautifully into their own in Reformed theology. For these texts are certainly not intended universalistically in the sense that all humans or even all creatures are saved, nor are they so understood by any Christian church. All churches without exception confess that there is not only a heaven but also a hell. At most, therefore, there is a difference of opinion about the number of those who are saved and of those who are lost. But that is not something one can argue about inasmuch as that number is known only to God. When Jesus was asked: "Lord, will only a few be saved?" he only replied: "Strive to enter through the narrow door, for many will try to enter but will not be able" (Luke 13:24).

Directly important to us is only that we have no need to know the number of the elect. In any case, it is a fact that in Reformed theology the number of the elect need not, for any reason or in any respect, be deemed smaller than in any other theology. In fact, at bottom the Reformed confessions are more magnanimous and broader in outlook than any other Christian confession. It locates the ultimate and most profound source of salvation solely in God's good pleasure, in his eternal compassion, in his unfathomable mercy, in the unsearchable riches of his grace, grace that is both omnipotent and free. Aside from it, where could we find a firmer and broader foundation for the salvation of a sinful and lost human race? However troubling it may be that many fall away, still in Christ the believing community, the human race, the world, is saved. The organism of creation is restored. The wicked perish from the earth (Ps. 104:35); they are cast out (John 12:31; 15:6; Rev. 22:15). Still, all things in heaven and earth are gathered up in Christ (Eph. 1:10). All things are created through him and for him (Col. 1:16).

Service in the Eternal Sabbath

The communion with God that is enjoyed in the communion of saints no more excludes all action and activity in the age to come than it does in the present dispensation. Christian theology indeed as a rule paid little attention to this fact and primarily spoke of heavenly blessedness as a matter of knowing and enjoying God. And this, undoubtedly, is the core and center, the source and power, of eternal life. Also, Scripture offers but little information enabling us to form a clear picture of the activity of the blessed. It describes this blessedness more in terms of resting from our earthly labors than of engaging in new activities (Heb. 4:9; Rev. 14:13). Still the rest enjoyed in the new Jerusalem is not to be conceived, either in the case of God (John 5:17) or in the case of his children, as blessed inaction. Scripture itself tells us that eternal life consists in knowing and serving God, in glorifying and praising him (John 17:3; Rev. 4:11; 5:8, etc.). His children remain his servants, who serve him night and day (Rev. 22:3). They are prophets, priests, and kings who reign on earth forever (Rev. 1:6; 5:10; 22:5). Inasmuch as they have been faithful over little on earth, they will be put in charge of many things in the kingdom of God (Matt. 24:47; 25:21, 23). All will retain their own personalities, for the names of all who enter the new Jerusalem have been written in the Lamb's book of life (Rev. 20:15; 21:27) and all will receive a new name of their own (Isa. 62:2; 65:15; Rev. 2:17; 3:12; cf. 21:12, 14). The dead who die in the Lord rest from their labors but each is followed by his or her own works (Rev. 14:13). Tribes, peoples, nations all make their own particular contribution to the enrichment of life in the new Jerusalem (Rev. 5:9; 7:9; 21:24, 26). What we have sown here is harvested in eternity (Matt. 25:24, 26; 1 Cor. 15:42ff.; 2 Cor. 9:6; Gal. 6:7, 8). The great diversity that exists among people in all sorts of ways is not destroyed in eternity but is cleansed from all that is sinful and made serviceable to fellowship with God and each other. And just as the natural diversity present in the believing community on earth is augmented with spiritual diversity (1 Cor. 12:7ff.), so this natural and spiritual diversity is in turn augmented in heaven by the diversity of degrees of glory present there.

Moved by their opposition to the meritoriousness of good works, some Reformed scholars[29] have denied—as did Jovian in the fourth century, and later certain Socinians, and Gerlach even today—there is any distinction in glory. And it is in fact true that all believers have been promised the same benefits in Christ's future: they all receive the same eternal life, the same abode in the new Jerusalem, the same fellowship with God, the same blessedness, and so on. Nevertheless, Scripture leaves no doubt whatever that in all that oneness and sameness there is enormous variation and diversity. Even the parable frequently cited to prove the opposite (Matt. 20:1–16) argues for such distinction. By this parable Jesus makes the point that many who in their own opinion and that of others have worked long and hard will certainly not be behind in the messianic kingdom of the future by comparison with those who worked in the vineyard a much shorter period. The latter catch up with the former for, though many have been called and labor in the service of the kingdom of God, in the hereafter few will on that account enjoy special status and receive a position of distinction.

Such degrees of distinction in glory are taught much more clearly in other passages in Scripture, especially in those which state that all will receive a reward commensurate with their works. That reward is now kept in heaven (Matt. 5:12; 6:1ff.; Luke 6:23; 1 Tim. 6:19; Heb. 10:34–37) and will be publicly distributed only at the parousia (Matt. 6:4, 6, 18; 24:47; 2 Thess. 1:7; 1 Peter 4:13). It is then given as compensation for that which the disciples of Jesus have given up and suffered on his account on earth (Matt. 5:10ff.; 19:29; Luke 6:21f.; Rom. 8:17, 18; 2 Cor. 4:17; 2 Thess. 1:7; Heb. 10:34; 1 Peter 4:13) and also as a reward for the good works they have done, for example, the good use they made of their talents (Matt. 25:15ff.; Luke 19:13ff.), the love of one's enemies and the practice of selfless generosity (Luke 6:35), the care of the poor (Matt. 6:1), prayer and fasting (Matt. 6:6, 18), ministering to the saints (Matt. 10:40–42), faithful service in the kingdom of God (Matt. 24:44–47; 1 Cor. 3:8, etc.). That reward will be linked with and proportionate to the works performed (Matt. 16:27; 19:29; 25:21, 23; Luke 6:38; 19:17, 19; Rom. 2:6; 1 Cor. 3:8; 2 Cor. 4:17; 5:10; 9:6; Gal. 6:8–9; Heb. 11:26; Rev. 2:23; 11:18; 20:12; 22:12). Blessedness is indeed the same for all but there are distinctions in "brightness" and glory (Dan. 12:3; 1 Cor. 15:41). In the Father's house, in which all God's children are welcomed, there are many dwellingplaces (John 14:2); the churches all receive from the King of the church a precious token and crown of their own in accordance with their faithfulness and dedication (Rev. 1–3).

On these statements of Scripture Catholic theologians have built the doctrine of the meritoriousness of good works and ascribed especially to martyrs, celibates, and teachers the right to special rewards in heaven. These (following Exod. 25:25) are called aureoles *(aureolae)* and are added to the crown of gold *(corona aurea)* everyone receives.[30] This misuse, however, does not alter the truth that there is disparity in glory depending on the works done by believers on earth. There is no reward to which humans are by nature entitled, inasmuch as the law of God is absolutely binding and does not let the demand of fulfillment depend on the free choice of people. Therefore, even if they have fulfilled the whole law, it only behooves them to say: "We are worthless slaves;

we have done only what we ought to have done!" (Luke 17:10). All claims to reward can therefore flow only from a covenant, a sovereignly free and gracious disposition of God, and hence is a *given* right. That is how it was in the covenant of works and is even much more so in the covenant of grace.[31] For Christ has fulfilled all the requirements; he not only suffered the penalty but also, by fulfilling the law, won eternal life. The eternal blessedness and glory he received was, for him, the reward for his perfect obedience. But when he confers this righteousness of his on his own through faith and unites eternal life with it, then the two, both the righteousness conferred and future blessedness, are the gifts of his grace, a reality that utterly excludes all merit on the part of believers. For believers are what God has made them, created in Christ Jesus for good works, which God prepared beforehand to be their way of life (Eph. 2:10). In the cause of Christ it is graciously given them, not only to believe in him but also to suffer for him (Acts 5:41; Phil. 1:29). God crowns his own work, not only in conferring eternal life on everyone who believes but also in distributing different degrees of glory to those who, motivated by that faith, have produced good works.

His purpose in doing this, however, is that, on earth as in heaven, there would be profuse diversity in the believing community and that in that diversity the glory of his attributes would be manifest. Indeed, as a result of this diversity the life of fellowship with God and with the angels, and of the blessed among themselves, gains in depth and intimacy. In that fellowship everyone has a place and task of his or her own, based on personality and character, just as this is the case in the believing community on earth (Rom. 12:4–8; 1 Cor. 12). While we may not be able to form a clear picture of the activity of the blessed, Scripture does teach that the prophetic, priestly, and royal office, which was humanity's original possession, is fully restored in them by Christ. The service of God, mutual communion, and inhabiting the new heaven and the new earth undoubtedly offer abundant opportunity for the exercise of these offices, even though the form and manner of this exercise are unknown to us. That activity, however, coincides with resting and enjoying. The difference between day and night, between the Sabbath and the work days, has been suspended. Time is charged with the eternity of God. Space is full of his presence. Eternal becoming is wedded to immutable being. Even the contrast between heaven and earth is gone. For all the things that are in heaven and on earth have been gathered up in Christ as head (Eph. 1:10). All creatures will then live and move and have their being in God who is all in all, who reflects all his attributes in the mirror of his works and glorifies himself in them.[32]

Appendix

Cross-Reference with *Gereformeerde Dogmatiek*

This appendix cross-references the paragraph and subparagraph sections in the eleventh chapter of Bavinck's *Gereformeerde Dogmatiek* ("Over de Laatste Dingen") with the pages of this separate volume on eschatology. Bavinck divided this material into three major sections (paragraphs 60–62), which constitute the three sections of this volume, and subdivided those sections into thirty-two additional sections (#s 548–80). This method of cross-referencing was chosen rather than using the pagination of any particular edition since it is consistent from the second, revised edition through the fifth edition though the pagination is not the same in all editions. In the list that follows the first number under *G.D.* (60–62) is the paragraph number and the second (548–580) the subparagraph number.

G.D.[a]	L.T.[b]	G.D.	L.T.	G.D.	L.T.
60 #548	p. 21	61 #562	p. 79	62 #572	p. 131
#549	p. 25	#563	p. 82	#573	p. 136
#550	p. 28	#564	p. 89	#574	p. 138
#551	p. 34	#565	p. 94	#575	p. 142
#552	p. 39	#566	p. 99	#576	p. 147
#553	p. 43	#567	p. 102	#577	p. 155
#554	p. 44	#568	p. 107	#578	p. 160
#555	p. 47	#569	p. 112	#579	p. 163
#556	p. 49	#570	p. 118	#580	p. 167
#557	p. 51	#571	p. 122		
#558	p. 54				
#559	p. 59				
#560	p. 64				
#561	p. 71				

a. *Gereformeerde Dogmatiek* (Vol. 4)
b. *The Last Things*

Bibliography

This bibliography[1] includes the items Bavinck listed at the head of sections 61 and 62 in the *Gereformeerde Dogmatiek* as well as the additional works cited in his footnotes. Particularly with respect to the footnote references, where Bavinck's own citations were quite incomplete by contemporary standards with titles often significantly abbreviated, this bibliography provides fuller information. In some cases full bibliographic information was available only for an edition other than the one Bavinck cited. Where English translations of Dutch or German works are available they have been cited rather than the original. In a few instances where Bavinck cited Dutch translations of English originals, the original work is listed. In cases where multiple versions or editions are available in English (e.g., Calvin's *Institutes*) the most recent, most frequently cited, or most accessible edition was chosen. Not included here is the literature Bavinck refers to at the beginning of his bibliography heading section 62 of the *Gereforemeerde Dogmatiek*, literature dealing with Old Testament and Jewish messianic expectation and listed in the *Gereformeerde Dogmatiek*, III, 214–24. These items will be included in the bibliography of the DRTS's projected third volume of the translated *Reformed Dogmatics*. In spite of best efforts to track down each reference to confirm or complete bibliographic information, some of Bavinck's abbreviated and cryptic notations remain unconfirmed or incomplete. Where information is unconfirmed, incomplete, and/or titles have been reconstructed, the work is marked with an asterisk.

Abbreviations

ANF *The Ante-Nicene Fathers*. Edited by Alexander Roberts and James Donaldson. 10 vols. New York: Christian Literature Co., 1885–96. Reprint ed., Grand Rapids: Eerdmans, 1950–51.
NPNF (1) *A Select Library of Nicene and Post-Nicene Fathers of the Christian Church*, First Series, 14 vols. Edited by Philip Schaff. New York: Christian Literature Co., 1887–1900. Reprint ed., Grand Rapids: Eerdmans, 1956.

NPNF (2) A Select Library of Nicene and Post-Nicene Fathers of the Christian Church, Second Series, 14 vols. Edited by Philip Schaff and Henry Wace. New York: Christian Literature Co., 1890–1900. Reprint ed., Grand Rapids: Eerdmans, 1952.

PRE Realencyklopädie für protestantische Theologie und Kirche. 24 vols. Edited by Albert Hauck. 3rd ed. Leipzig: J. C. Hinrichs, 1896–1913.

Books

Ames, William. *Bellarminus enervatus, sive disputationes anti-Bellarminianae*. 3rd ed. London, 1629.

Amyraut, Moise. *Verhandeling van den Staet der Gelooven na de Doodt*. Utrecht: F. Halma, 1680.

Andersen, Carl. *Die Lehre von der Wiedegeburt auf theistischen Grundlage*. 2nd ed. Hamburg: Grafe, 1899.

Aquinas, Thomas. *Summa Theologiae*. Translated by Thomas Gilby et al. 61 vols. New York: McGraw-Hill, 1964–81.

Atzberger, Leonhard. *Die christliche Eschatologie in den Stadien ihrer Offenbarung im Alten und Neuen Testamente. Mit besonderer Berücksichtigung der jüdischen Eschatologie im Zeitalter Christi*. Freiburg i.B.: Herder, 1890.

———. *Geschichte der christlichen Eschatologie innerhalb der vornicänischen Zeit mit theilweiser Einbeziehung der Lehre vom christlichen Heile uberhaupt*. Freiburg i.B: St. Louis, Mo.: Herder, 1896.

Augustine, Aurelius. *The City of God*. NPNF (1), II, 1–511.

———. *The Enchiridion*. NPNF (1), III, 229–76.

Baumann, Julius. *Unsterblichkeit und Seelenwanderung: Ein Vereinigungspunkt morgenlandischen und abendlandischen Weltansicht*. Leipzig: S. Hirzel, 1909.

Bautz, Joseph. *Die Hölle in Anschluss an die Scholastiek dargestellt*. Mainz: Kirchheim & Co., 1905.

Bavinck, Herman. *De Theologie van Daniel Chantepie de la Saussaye*. Leiden: Donner, 1884.

———. *The Philosophy of Revelation*. New York: Longman, Green and Co., 1909.

Bellarmine, Robert. *De Controversiis Christianae fidei adversus huius temporis haereticos*. Cologne: G. Gualtheri, 1617–20.

Bertholet, Alfred. *Die israelitischen Vorstellungen vom Zustand nach dem Tode, ein offentlicher Vortrag*. Freiburg i.B.: J. C. B. Mohr (Paul Siebeck), 1899.

———. *Seelenwanderung*. Tübingen: J. C. B. Mohr (Paul Siebeck), 1906.

*Beuningen, F. von. *Dein Reich komme*. Riga, 1901.

Beyschlag, Willibald. *Neutestamentliche Theologie, oder geschichtliche Darstellung der Lehren Jesu und des Urchristenthums nach den neutestamentlichen Quellen*. 2nd ed. Halle: E. Strien, 1896.

Bie, Jan Pieter de. *Het Leven en Werken van Petrus Hofstede*. Rotterdam: Daamen, 1899.

Biedermann, Aloys Emmanuel. *Christliche Dogmatik*. Zurich: Orell, Fussli, 1869.

Bilderdijk, W. *Brieven*. Vol. 5. Amsterdam: W. Messchert, 1836–37.

Bogue, David. *Discourses on the Millennium*. London: T. Hamilton, 1818.

Bonaventure. *The Breviloquium*, vol. 2, *The Works of Bonaventure*. Translated by Jose DeVinck. Paterson, N.J.: St. Anthony Guild Press, 1963.

Bretschneider, Karl Gottlieb. *Handbuch der Dogmatik der Evangelischluther-ischen Kirche, oder Versuch einer beurtheilenden Darstellung der Grundstze, welche diese Kirche in ihren symbolischen Schriften bei die Christliche Glaubenslehre ausgesprochen hat, mit vergleichung der Glaubenslehre in der Bekenntnisschriften der reformirten Kirche*. Leipzig: n.p., 1838.

————. *Systematische Entwickelung aller in der Dogmatik verkommenden Be-griffe nach den symbolischen Schriften der evangelisch-lutherischen und re-formirten Kirche und den wichtigsten dogmatischen Lehrbüchern ihrer Theol-ogen*. Leipzig: J. A. Barth, 1841.

Briet, J. P. *De Eschatologie of Leer der Toekomende Dingen*. Tiel, 1857–58.

Brinck, Hendrik. *Toetsteen der Waarheid en der Dwalingen*. Amsterdam: G. Borstius, 1685.

Bruining, Albert. *Het Voortbestaan der Menschelijke Persoonlijkheid na den Dood*. Assen, 1904.

Büchner, Ludwig. *Force and Matter; or Principles of the Natural Order of the Uni-verse*. 4th ed. translated from the 15th German ed. New York: P. Eckler, 1891.

Buddeus, Joannes Franciscus. *Institutiones theologiae dogmaticae variis obser-vationibus illustratae*. Frankfurt and Leipzig, 1741.

*Burger. *De Platonische Leer der Zielsverhuizing*. Amersfoort, 1877.

Burnet, Thomas. *De Statu mortuorum et resurgentium*. London, 1726.

*Byse, Charles. *L'immortalité conditionelle ou la vie en Christ*. Translation of Edward White, Life in Christ, 1878. Paris, 1880.

Calvin, John. *Institutes of the Christian Religion* (1559). Edited by John T. Mc-Neill, translated by F. L. Battles. 2 vols. Philadelphia: Westminster, 1960.

————. "Psychopannychia; Or, the Soul's Imaginary Sleep Between Death and Judgment." In *Selected Works of John Calvin*. Edited by Henry Beveridge and Jules Bonnet. Vol. 3. Grand Rapids: Baker, 1983 [1851].

Canons and Decrees of the Sacred and Oecumenical Council of Trent. Translated by J. Waterforth. Chicago: The Christian Symbolic Publication Society, 1848.

Chamier, Daniel. *Panstratiae Catholicae, sive controversiarum de religione ad-versus Pontificios corpus*. Geneva, 1626.

Chantepie de la Saussaye, Pierre Daniel. *Lehrbuch der Religionsgeschichte*. 2 vols. Freiburg i.B.: Mohr (Siebeck), 1887–89.

Cicero, Marcus Tullius. *Tusculan Disputations*. London and New York: W. Hei-neman and G. P. Putnam's Sons, 1927.

Cremer, Hermann. *Ueber den Zustand nach dem Tode. Nebst einigen Andeutun-gen über das Kindersterben und über den Spiritismus*. Gütersloh: Bertels-mann, 1883.

Cumming, John. *Beschouwingen over het Duizendjarige Rijk*. 1866.

————. *De Duizendjarige Rust*. Translated by G. Jasperus. Amsterdam: H. de Hoogh, 1863.

———. *De Groote Verdrukking*. Amsterdam, 1861.

———. *De Verlossing Nabij*. 1862.

Davidson, Andrew Bruce. *The Theology of the Old Testament*. Edited from the author's manuscripts by S. D. F. Salmond. New York: Charles Scribner's, 1904.

Decoppet, Auguste. *Les grands problèmes de l'au delà*. 8th ed. Paris: Fischbacher, 1906.

Delitzsch, Franz. *Biblical Commentary on the Prophecies of Isaiah*. Translated by James Martin. Grand Rapids: Eerdmans, 1954 [1887].

———. *Das Land ohne Heimkehr, die Gedanken der Babylonier-Assyrer über Tod und Jenseits: nebst Schlussfolgerungen*. Stuttgart: Deutsche Verlags-Anstalt, 1911.

———. *A System of Biblical Psychology*. Translated by Robert E. Wallis. 2nd ed. Edinburgh: T. & T. Clark, 1875.

Denzinger, Heinrich. *The Sources of Catholic Dogma (Enchiridion Symbolorum)*. Translated from the 30th ed. by Roy J. Deferrari. London and St. Louis: Herder, 1955.

Doedes, J. I. *Inleiding tot de Leer van God*. Utrecht: Kemink, 1870.

Dorner, I. A. *A System of Christian Doctrine*. 4 vols. Translated by A. Cave and J. S. Banks. Edinburgh: T. & T. Clark, 1882.

Drummond, Henry. *Natural Law in the Spiritual World*. New York: J. Pott, 1887.

Eberhard, Johann August. *Neue Apologie des Sokrates, oder Untersuchung der Lehre von der Seligkeit der Heiden*. Berlin: F. Nicolai, 1772.

Ebrard, A. *Das Dogma vom heiligen Abendmahl und seine Geschichte*. 2 vols. Frankfurt a.M.: Heinrich Zimmer, 1845–46.

Ebrard, Johannes Heinrich August. *Christliche Dogmatik*. 2 vols. 2nd ed. Konigsberg: A. W. Unser, 1862–63.

Episcopius, Simon. *Opera theologica*. 2 vols. Amsterdam, 1650.

Falke, Robert. *Gibt es eine Seelenwanderung?* Halle: S. E. Strein, 1904.

Farrar, Frederick W. *Eternal Hope*. London: Macmillan, 1883.

———. *Mercy and Judgment: Last Words on Christian Eschatology*. New York: E. P. Dutton & Co., 1881.

Faure. H. *De Troostingen des Vagevuurs, volgens de Leeraren der Kerk en de Openbaring der Heiligen*. Translated by Br. Modestus. Amsterdam: Bekker, 1901.

Fichte, Immanuel Herman. *Die Idee der Personlichkeit und der individuellen Fortdauer*. Leipzig: Dyk, 1855.

Flink, Carl Otto. *Schopenhauers Seelenwanderungslehre und ihre Quellen*. Ph.D. diss., University of Bern, 1906.

Fock, Otto. *Der Socianianismus nach seiner stellung in der desammtentwicklung des christlichen Geistes, nach seinem historischen Verlauf und nach seinem Lehrbegriff*. Kiel: C. Schröder, 1847.

Frank, Franz Herman Reinhold. *System der christlichen Wahrheit*. 2 vols. 3rd rev. ed. Erlangen and Leipzig: Deichert, 1894.

Frank, Henry. *Modern Light on Immortality*. Boston: Sherman, French & Co., 1909.

Franz. Das Gebet für die Todten in Seinem Zusammenhange mit Kultus und Lehre nach den Schriften des heiligen Augustinus. Nordhausen, 1857.

Fremery, H. N de. *Wat Gebeurt er met Ons als Wij Sterven.* Bussum: Van Dishoeck, 1910.

Frey, Johannes. *Tod, Seelenglaube und Seelenkult im alten Israel.* Leipzig: A. Deichert, 1898.

Furer. Weltende und Endgericht. Gütersloh, 1896.

Gennrich, Paul. *Die Lehre von der Wiedergeburt; die christliche Zentrallehre in dogmengeschichtlicher und religionsgeschichlicher Beleuchtung.* Leipzig: Deichert, 1907.

Gerhard, Johann. *Loci Theologici.* Edited by E. Preuss. 9 vols. Berlin: G. Schlawitz, 1863–75.

Girgenshohn, Karl. *Zwölf Reden über die Christliche Religion.* 4th ed. München: C. H. Beck, 1921.

Gomarus, Franciscus. *Opera Theologica Omnia.* Amsterdam, 1644.

Göschel. Von den Beweisen für die Unsterblichkeit der Menschliche Seele. 1835.

Groenen, Petrus Gerardus. *Lijkverbranding.* 's-Hertogenbosch: Teulings, 1909.

Grosheide, F. W. *De Verwachting der Toekomst van Jezus Christus.* Amsterdam: Bottenburg, 907.

Grüneissen, Carl. *Der Ahnenkultus und die Urreligion Israels.* Halle: Niemeyer, 1900.

Guers, E. *Israel in the Last Days of the Present Economy.* Translated by Aubrey Price. London: Wertheim, MacIntosh, and Hunt, 1862.

Haeckel, Ernst. *The Riddle of the Universe at the Close of the Nineteenth Century.* Translated by Joseph McCabe. New York: Harper & Brothers, 1900.

Harnack, Adolf von. *History of Dogma.* 7 vols. Translated by N. Buchanan, J. Millar, E. B. Speirs, W. McGilchrist, edited by A. B. Bruce. London: Williams & Norgate, 1896–99.

———. *The Mission and Expansion of Christianity.* Translated by James Moffat. New York: Harper, 1908.

Hartmann, Eduard von. *Die Geisterhypothese des Spiritismus und seine Phantome.* Leipzig: Friedrich, 1891.

———. *Religionsphilosophie.* Leipzig: Friedrich, 1888.

———. *Der Spiritismus.* Leipzig: Friedrich, 1885.

Hastie, William. *The Theology of the Reformed Churches in its Fundamental Principles.* Edinburgh: T. & T. Clark, 1904.

Haupt, Erich. *Die eschatologischen Aussagen Jesu in den synoptischen Evangelien.* Berlin: Reuther & Reichard, 1895.

Heidegger, Johann Heinrich. *Corpus theologiae.* Zurich, 1700.

Heinrich, Johann Baptist, and Gutberlet, Konstantine. *Dogmatische Theologie.* 10 vols. 2nd ed. Mainz: Kircheim, 1881–1900.

Heinzelmann, Gerhard. *Der Begriff der Seele und die Idee der Unsterblichkeit bei Wilhelm. Wundt.* Ph.D. diss., University of Göttingen, 1910.

Hellwald, Friedrich von. *Die Erde und Ihre Volker: Ein Geographischer Hausbuch.* Stuttgart: Spemann, 1877–78.

Hengstenberg, E. W. *Openbaring van Johannes.* 's Hertogenbosch: Muller, 1852.

Hesselink. Wetenschap en Onsterfelijkheid. Middelburg, 1904.

Hettinger, Franz. *Apologie des Christenthums.* 5 vols. 7th ed., prepared by Eugen Muller. Freiburg i.B.: Herder, 1895–98.

Hodge, Charles. *Systematic Theology.* 3 vols. New York: Charles Scribner's Sons, 1888.

Hoekstra, H. *Bijdrage tot de Kennis en de Beoordeling van het Chiliasme.* Kampen: Kok, 1903.

Hoekstra, Sytse. *De Hoop der Onsterfelijkheid.* Amsterdam: P. N. van Kampen, 1867.

Hofmann, Johann Christian Conrad von. *Der Schriftbeweis.* 3 vols. Nördlingen: Beck, 1857–60.

Hollaz, David. *Examen theologicum acroamaticum.* Rostock and Leipzig, 1718.

Holmes, E. E. *Immortality.* London: Longman, Green & Co., 1908.

Holtzmann, Heinrich Julius. *Lehrbuch der neutestamentlichen Theologie.* Freiburg i.B. and Leipzig: Mohr, 1897.

*Hurgronje, C. Snouck. *Der Mahdi.* Published by the Revue Coloniale Internationale, 1885.

Irenaeus. *Against Heresies. ANF,* I, 309–567.

Isenkrahe, Kaspar. *Energie, Entropie, Weltanfang, Weltende.* Trier: Lintz, 1910.

Jeremias, Alfred. *Hölle und Paradies bei den Babyloniern.* Leipzig: J. C. Hinrichs, 1900.

John of Damascus. *Exposition of the Orthodox Faith. NPNF* (2), IX, 259–360.

Josephus, Flavius. *The Works of Josephus.* Translated by William Whiston. New updated edition. Peabody, Mass.: Hendrickson, 1987.

Jung-Stillung, Johann Heinrich. *Theorie der Geisterkunde: in einer naturvernunft und bibelmüssigen Beantwortung der Frage was von Ahnungen, Geschichten und Geisterscheinungen geglaubt und nicht geglaubt werden musste.* Leipzig: Dieter, ca. 1800.

Junius, Franciscus. *Opuscula theologica selecta.* Edited by Abraham Kyuper. Amsterdam: F. Muller, 1882.

Justin, Martyr. *Dialogue with Trypho. ANF,* I, 194–270.

Kabisch, Richard. *Die Eschatologie des Paulus in ihrem Zusammenhang mit dem Gesammtbegriff des Paulinismus.* Göttingen: Vandenhoek & Ruprecht, 1893.

Kahnis, Friedrich August. *Die Luthersche Dogmatik, historisch-genetisch dargestellt.* Leipzig: Dorffling & Francke, 1861–68.

Kattenbusch, Ferdinand. *Lehrbuch der vergleichenden Confessionskunde.* Freiburg i.B.: J. C. B. Mohr (Paul Siebeck), 1892.

Kayser, August. *Theologie des Alten Testaments.* Prepared by Karl Marti. 2nd ed. Strassburg: Friedrich Bull, 1894.

Keil, C. F. *Biblical Commentary on the Prophecies of Ezekiel.* Translated by James Martin. Grand Rapids: Eerdmans, 1970, reprint.

Keyserling, Herman. *Unsterblichkeit, eine Kritik der Beziehungen zwischen naturgeschehen und menschlichen Vorstellungswelt.* München, 1907.

Kiefl, Franz Xaver. *Herman Schell und die Ewigkeit der Höllenstrafen.* Mainz: Kirchheim, 1907.

Kirchner. *Der Spiritismus, die Narrheit unseres Zeitalters.* Berlin: Habel, 1883.

Klieforth, Theodore F. D. *Christliche Eschatologie*. Leipzig: Dorffling & Franke, 1886.

Kneib, Philipp. *Die Beweise für die Unsterblichkeit der Seele als allgemeinen psychologischen Tatsachen*. Freiburg: Herder, 1903.

Köstlin, Julius. *The Theology of Luther in Its Historical Development and Inner Harmony*. Translated by Charles E. Hay. 2 vols. Philadelphia: Lutheran Publication Society, 1897.

Kuenen, Abraham. *The Prophets and Prophecy in Israel*. Translated by Adam Milroy. Amsterdam: Philo, 1969; reprint London, 1877.

Kuyper, Abraham. *Ons Program*. 5th ed. Hilversum: Hoveker & Wormser, 1907.

———. *Van de Voleinding*. 4 vols. Kampen: Kok, 1928–31.

Landau, Marcus. *Hölle und Fegfeur in Volksglaube, Dichtung, und Kirchenlehre*. Heidelberg: Winter, 1910.

Lange, Friedrich Albert. *Geschichte des Materialismus und Kritik seiner Bedeutung in der Gegenwart*. 8th ed. Leipzig: Baedekker, 1908.

Leibbrand, Karl M. *Das Gebet für die Todten in der evangelischen Kirche*. Stuttgart: Schweizerbart, 1864.

Leibnitz, Gottfried Wilhelm von. *System der Theologie nach dem Manuskripte von Hanover*. Mainz: Müller, 1820.

Lemme, Ludwig. *Endlosigkeit der Verdammnis und allgemeine Wiederbringung*. Berlin: Runge, 1898.

Lessing, G. E. *Erziehung des Menschengeschlechts*. Edited by Louis Ferdinand Helbig. Bern and Las Vegas: Peter Lang, 1980.

Limborch, Phillip van. *Theologia christiana ad praxin pietatis ac promotionem pacis christiana unice directa*. Amsterdam, 1735.

Lodge, Oliver. *The Survival of Man: A Study in an Unrecognized Human Faculty*. New York: Moffat, Yard & Co., 1909.

Lombard, Peter. *Sententiae in IV libris distinctae*. 2 vols. 3rd ed. Grottaferrata: Colleggi S. Bonaventurae ad Claras Aquas, 1971–81.

Lucius, Ernst. *Die Anfänge des Heiligenkults in der Christlichen Kirche*. Tübingen: Mohr, 1904.

Lüken, Heinrich. *Die Traditionen des Menschengeschlechts oder die Uroffenbarung Gottes unter den Heiden*. 2nd rev. ed. Munster: Aschendorff, 1869.

Luthardt, Christoph Ernst. *Die Lehre von den Letzten Dingen*. 3rd ed. Leipzig: Dörffling & Franke, 1885.

Marckius, Johannes, *Expectatio gloriae futurae Jesu Christi*. Leiden: Abraham Kallewier, 1730.

Maresius, Samuel. *Collegium theologicum sive systema breve universae theologiae comprehensum octodecim disputationibus*. Groningen, 1645, 1659.

Martensen, H. *Christian Dogmatics*. Translated by W. Urwick. Edinburgh: T. & T. Clark, 1871.

Marti, Karl. *Die Religion des Alten Testaments unter den Religionen des vorderen Orient*. Tübingen: J. C. B. Mohr, 1906.

Mastricht, Peter van. *Theoretico-practica theologia*. Utrecht, 1714.

McConnell, Samuel David. *The Evolution of Immortality*. New York and London: Macmillan, 1901.

Meyers Konversations-lexikon. 5th ed. Leipzig, Vienna: Bibliographische Institute, 1892–93.

Möhler, J. A. *Symbolik.* Regensburg: G. J. Manz, 1871.

Moor, Bernhard de. *Commentarius perpetuus in Joh. Marckii compendium theologiae christianae didactico-elencticum.* 6 vols. Leiden, 1761–71.

*Mühlhäusser. *Die Zukunft der Menschheit.* Heilbron, 1881.

Muller, Julius. *Die Christliche Lehre von der Sunde.* 2 vols. Bremen: C. Ed. Muller, 1889.

Munscher, Wilhelm. *Lehrbuch des christlichen Dogmengeschichte.* 3rd ed. Edited by Daniel von Coelln. Cassel: J. C. Krieger, 1832–38.

Myers, Frederick William Henry. *Human Personality and Its Survival of Bodily Death.* 2nd ed. London: Longmans, Green, 1903.

Niederhuber, Joh. *Die Eschatologie des heiligen Ambrosius: eine patristische Studie.* Paderborn: Schöningh, 1907.

Nitzsch, Carl Emmanuel. *Lehrbuch der evangelischen Dogmatik.* 3rd ed. prepared by Horst Stephan. Tübingen: J. C. B. Mohr, 1912.

Nowack, W., et al. *Theologische Abhandlung: Eine Festgabe für Heinrich Julius Holtzmann.* Tübingen: J. C. B. Mohr, 1902.

Oehler, Gustav Friedrich. *Theologie des Alten Testament.* 2nd ed. Stuttgart: J. F. Steinkopf, 1882.

Oosterzee, J. J. van. *Christian Dogmatics.* Translated by J. Watson and M. Evans. 2 vols. New York: Scribner, Armstrong, 1874.

Origen. *Against Celsus*, ANF, IV, 395–669.

———. *On First Principles*, ANF, IV, 239–384.

Oswald, Johann Heinrich. *Eschatologie, das ist die letzten Dinge, dargestellt nach der Lehre der katholischen Kirche.* Paderborn: F. Schöningh, 1869.

Paulsen, Peter. *Das Leben nach dem Tode.* 2nd ed. Stuttgart: Chr. Belser, 1905.

Perrone, Giovanni. *Praelectiones Theologicae.* 9 vols. Louvain: Vanlinthout & Vandezande, 1838–43.

Pesch, Tillman. *Die Grosen Welträthsel.* 2 vols. 2nd ed. Freiburg: Herder, 1892.

Peschel, Oscar. *Abhandlungen zur Erd und Völkerkunde.* Leipzig: Duncker & Humboldt, 1878.

Petau, Denis (Dionysius Petavius). *Opus de theologicus dogmatibus.* Antwerp: Gallet, 1700.

Pétavel-Oliff, Emmanuel. *Le problème de l'immortalité.* Paris: Fischbacher, 1891.

Pfanner, Tobias. *Systema theologiae gentilis purioris.* Basel: Joh. Hermann Widerhold, 1679.

Pfister, Friedrich. *Der Reliquienkult im Altertum*, vol. 1, *Das Objekt des Reliquienkultus.* Giessen: A Topelman, 1909.

Pfleiderer, Otto. *Grundriss der Christlichen Glaubens und Sittenlehre.* Berlin: G. Reimer, 1888.

———. *Religionsphilosophie auf geschichtlicher Grundlage.* Berlin: G. Reimer, 1896.

Phillipi, F. A. *Kirchliche Glaubenslehre.* Gütersloh: Bertelsmann, 1902.

Pichler, A. *Die Theologie des Leibnitz.* München: J. G. Cotta, 1869–70.

Pierson, Allard. *Eene Levensbeschouwing.* Haarlem: Kruseman, 1875.

Plitt, Herman. *Evangelische Glaubenslehre.* 2 vols. Gotha: n.p., 1863.

Pohle, Joseph. *Lehrbuch der Dogmatik.* 3 vols. 10th ed. Revised by M. Gierens. Paderborn: Ferdinand Schöningh, 1931.

Polanus, Amandus. *Syntagma theologiae christianae.* Hanover, 1609; Geneva, 1617.

Quenstedt, Johann Andreas. *Theologia didactico-polemica sive systema theologicum.* 1685.

Rauwenhof, Lodewijk, W. E. *Wijsbegeerte van den Godsdienst.* Leiden: Brill & van Doesburgh, 1887.

*Reiff, Franz. *Die Zukunft der Welt.* 2nd ed. Basel, 1875.

Reinhard, Franz Volkmar. *Grundriss der Dogmatik.* Munich: Seidel, 1802.

Reuter, Hermann. *Augustinische Studien.* Aalen: Scientia Verlag, 1967 [1887].

Richter, Friedrich. *Die Lehre von der letzten Dingen.* Breslau: J. Hebenstreit, 1833–44.

*Riemann, Otto. *Die Lehre von den Apokatastasis.* 2nd ed. Magdeburg, 1897.

———. *Was wissen wir über die Unsterblichkeit der Seele?* Magdeburg, 1900.

Rinck, Heinrich Wilhelm. *Vom Zustand nach dem Tode.* 2nd ed. Ludwigsburg and Basel: Balmer & Riehm, 1866.

Ritschl, Albrecht. *Die Christliche Lehre von der Rechfertigung und Versöhnung.* 4th ed. Bonn: A. Marcus, 1895–1903.

Rohde, Erwin. *Psyche; Seelenkult und Unsterblichkeitsglaube der Griechen.* Two volumes in one. 2nd ed. Freiburg: J. C. B. Mohr, 1898.

Rothe, Richard. *Theologische Ethik.* 5 vols. 2nd rev. ed. Wittenberg: Zimmerman, 1867–71.

Row, Charles Adolphus. *Future Retribution Viewed in the Light of Reason and Revelation.* New York: Whittaker, 1887

Russell, Charles. *The Millennial Dawn.* Allegheny, Pa.: Watchtower Bible and Tract Society, 1898–1901.

*Sachs. *Die ewige Dauer der Höllenstrafen.* Paderborn, 1882.

Salmond, S. D. F. *The Christian Doctrine of Immortality.* 4th ed. Edinburgh: T. & T. Clark, 1901.

Sartorius, Karl. *Die Leichenverbrennung innerhalb der christlichen Kirche.* Basel: C. Detloff, 1886.

Schaff, Philip. *Creeds of Christendom.* 3 vols. New York: Harper & Brothers, 1877.

Schell, Herman. *Katholische Dogmatik.*Three volumes in four. Paderborn: F. Schöningh, 1889–93.

Schleiermacher, Friedrich. *The Christian Faith.* Edited by H. R. MacIntosh and J. S. Steward. Edinburgh: T. & T. Clark, 1928.

———. *On Religion: Speeches to Its Cultured Despisers.* Translated by John Oman. Louisville, Ky.: Westminster/John Knox, 1994 [1958].

*Schmid, F. *Der Fegfeur nach katholischen Lehre.* Brixen, 1904.

Schmid, H. *Doctrinal Theology of the Evangelical Churches.* Translated by Charles A. Hay and Henry E. Jacobs. Philadelphia: United Lutheran Publication House, 1899.

Schmidt, Wilhelm. *Christliche Dogmatik.* 4 vols. Bonn: E. Weber, 1895–98.

Schneider, Leonhard. *Die Unsterblichkeitsidee im Glauben und in der Philosophie der Volker.* Regensburg: Verland von Alfred Coppenrath, 1870.

Scholten, Johannes Henricus. *Dogmatices Christianae initia.* 2nd ed. 1858.

Schopenhauer, Arthur. *Die Welt als Wille und Vorstellung,* in *Sammtliche Werke.* Vols. 2 and 3. Leipzig: F. M. Brodhaus, 1919.

Schrader, Otto. *Die Lehre von der Apokatastasis.* Berlin: R. Boll, 1901.

Schultz, Hermann. *Alttestamentliche Theologie. Die offenbarungsreligion auf ihrer vorchristliche, Entwickelungsstufe.* 5th ed. Göttingen: Vandenhoeck & Ruprecht, 1896.

————. *Voraussetzungen der Christlichen Lehre von der Unsterblichkeit.* Göttingen: Vandenhoeck & Ruprecht, 1861.

Schürer, Emil. *The History of the Jewish People in the Age of Jesus Christ (175 B.C.–A.D. 135).* Vol. 2. Revised and edited by Geza Vermes, Fergus Miller, and Matthew Black. Edinburgh: T. & T. Clark, 1979 (1885).

Schwally, Friedrich. *Das Leben nach dem Tode nach dem Vorstellungen des alten Israel und das Judentums einschliesslich des Volksglaubens im Zeitalter Christi, eine biblische-theologischen Untersuchung.* Giessen: J. Ricker, 1892.

Schwane, Joseph. *Dogmengeschichte.* 4 vols. Freiburg i.B.: Herder, 1882–95.

Schweizer, Alexander. *Die Glaubenslehre der evangelisch–reformirten Kirche.* Zurich: Orell, Fussli [1847].

Seeberg, Reinhold. *Textbook of the History of Doctrine.* Translated by Charles A. Hay. Two volumes in one. Philadelphia: Lutheran Publication Society, 1905.

Seiss, J. A. *The Apocalypse.* New York: Charles C. Cook, 1909.

Shedd, William Greenough Thayer. *Dogmatic Theology.* 2 vols. New York: Charles Scribner's Sons, 1888–89.

Siebeck, Herman. *Der Religionsphilosophie.* Tübingen: J. C. B. Mohr, 1893.

Simar, H. Th. *Lehrbuch der Dogmatik,* 2 vols. Freiburg i.B.: Herder, 1879–80.

Smend, Rudolf. *Lehrbuch der alttestamentlichen Religionsgeschichte,* Freiburg: J. C. B. Mohr, 1893.

Smyth, John Paterson. *The Gospel of the Hereafter.* London: Hodder and Stoughton, 1910.

Spanheim, Friedrich. *Dubia evangelica in tres partes distributa.* Genevae: Petri Chovet, 1655–58.

Speyer, Jacobus Samuel. *De Indische Theosophie en hare Beteekenis voor Ons.* Leiden: Van Doesburgh, 1910.

Spiess, Edmund. *Entwicklungsgeschichte der Vorstellungen vom Zustande nach dem Tode: auf Grund vergleichender Religionsforschung.* Jena: Hermann Costenoble, 1877.

Spinoza, Baruch. *The Ethics.* Malibu, Calif.: J. Simon, 1981.

Splittgerber, Franz Joseph. *Tod, Fortleben und Auferstehung.* 3rd ed. Halle: Fricke, 1879.

Stade, Bernhard. *Geschichte des Volkes Israel.* 2 vols. Berlin: Baumgärtel, 1887.

Stapfer, Paul. *Questions esthétiques et religieuses.* Paris: F. Alcan, 1906.

Steinmann, Theophil. *Der religiose Unsterblichkeitsglaube.* Göttingen: Vandenhoeck & Ruprecht, 1912.

Stern, A. *Das Jenseits. Der Zustand der Verstorbenen bis zur Auferstehung nach der Lehre der Bible und den Ergebnissen der Erfahrung.* 3rd ed. Gotha, 1907.

Stevens, George Barker. *The Theology of the New Testament.* New York: Charles Scribner's Sons, 1899.

Strauss, David Friedrich. *Der alte und der neue Glaube.* Leipzig: Hirzel, 1872.

———. *Die Christliche Glaubenslehre in ihrer geschichtlichen Entwicklung und im Kampfe mit der moderne Wissenschaft.* 2 vols. Tübingen: Osiander, 1840–41.

Strindberg, August. *The Dance of Death.* Translated by Arvid Paulsen. New York: Norton, 1976.

*Stufler. *Die Heiligkeit Gottes und die ewige Tod.*

———. *Die Verteidigung Schells durch Prof. Kiefl.* Innsbrück: Rauch, 1905. *Synopsis purioris theologiae, disputationibus quinquaginta duabus comprehensa ac conscripta per Johannem Polyandrum, Andream Rivetum, Antonium Walaeum, Antonius Thysium.* Leiden, 1625; editio sexta, curavit et praefatus est Dr. H. Bavinck. Leiden: Donner, 1881.

Teichmann, Ernst. *Die paulinischen Vorstellung von Auferstehung und Gericht und ihre Beziehung zur Jüdischen Apokalyptic.* Freiburg i.B.: J. C. B. Mohr, 1896.

Tertullian. *The Chaplet, or De Corona. ANF,* III, 93–104.

———. *On Exhortation to Chastity. ANF,* IV, 50–58.

———. *On Monogamy. ANF,* IV, 59–73.

———. *On the Resurrection of the Flesh. ANF,* III, 545–95.

———. *A Treatise on the Soul. ANF,* III, 181–235.

Theophilus. *To Autolycus, ANF,* II, 85–121.

Thompson, Robert J., ed. *The Proofs of Life After Death: A Collection of Opinions as to a Future Life by Some of the World's Most Eminent Scientists and Thinkers.* Boston: Small, Maynard & Co., 1906.

Tiele, C. P. *Elements of the Science of Religion,* 2 vols. Edinburgh and London: W. Blackwood and Sons, 1897–99.

Tillmann, Fritz. *Die Wiederkunft Christi nach den Paulinischen Breifen.* Freiburg i.B.: Herder, 1909.

Titius, Arthur. *Die Neutestamentliche Lehre von der Seligkeit und ihre Bedeutung für die Gegenwart.* Freiburg i.B.: J. C. B. Mohr (Paul Siebeck), 1895–1900.

Torge, Paul. *Seelenglaube und Unsterblichkeitshoffnung im Alten Testament.* Leipzig: J. C. Hinrichs, 1909.

Turretin, Francis. *Institutes of Elenctic Theology.* 3 vols. Translated by George Musgrove Giger, edited by James T. Dennison. Phillipsburg, N.J.: Presbyterian and Reformed, 1992–.

Vallotton, Paul. *La vie après la mort.* Laussane: Rouge & Co., 1906.

Vermigli, Peter Martyr. *The Common Places of Peter Martyr.* Translated by Antony Marten. London, 1583.

———. *Loci Communes.* Edited by R. Massonius. London, 1576.

Vilmar, August Friedrich Christian. *Handbuch der evangelischen Dogmatik für studierende de Theologie.* Gütersloh: Bertelsmann, 1895.

Vitringa, Campegius. *Doctrina christianae religionis, per aphorismos summatim descripta.* 8 vols. Arnheim, 1761–86.

Voetius, Gisbert. *Selectae disputationes theologicae.* 5 vols. Utrecht, 1648–69.

Walaeus, Antonius. *Opera Omnia.* Leiden, 1643.

Walch, Johann Georg (1693–1775). *[Io. George Walchii] Miscellanea sacra, sive Commentationum ad historiam ecclesiasticam sanctioresque disciplinas pertinentium collectio.* Amsterdam: Romberg, 1744.

Walsh, Walter. *The Secret History of the Oxford Movement.* 6th ed. London: Church Association, 1899.

Watts, Isaac. *The World to Come.* Chicago: Moody, 1954 [1739, 45].

Weber, Ferdinand Wilhelm. *System der altsynagogalen palastinischen Theologie: aus Targum, Midrasch und Talmud.* Leipzig: Dorffling & Franke, 1880.

Wegschneider, Julius August Ludwig. *Institutiones theologiae christianae dogmaticae.* Halle: Gebauer, 1819.

Weiss, Albert Maria. *Die Religiose Gefahr.* Freiburg i.B.: Herder, 1904.

Weiss, Bernhard. *Die Religion des Neuen Testaments.* Stuttgart: Cotta, 1908.

Weisse, Christian Herman. *Philosophische Dogmatik oder Philosophie des Christentums.* 3 vols. Leipzig: Hirzel, 1855–62.

White, Edward. *Life in Christ, A Study of the Scripture Doctrine on the Nature of Man, the Object of the Divine Incarnation and the Conditions of Human Immortality.* 3rd rev. and enlarged ed. London: Elliott, Stock, 1878.

Wiedemann, Alfred. *Die Toten und ihre Reiche im Glauben der alten Agypter.* 2nd ed. Leipzig: J. C. Hinrichs, 1902.

Wildeboer, Gerrit. *Jahvedienst en Volksreligie in Israel.* Groningen: Wolters, 1898.

Windelband, Wilhelm. *Geschichte und Naturwissenschaft.* 3rd unaltered ed. Strassbourg: Heitz, 1904.

Witsius, Herman. *The Oeconomy of the Covenants between God and Man. Comprehending a Complete Body of Divinity.* 3 vols. London, 1763; 2nd ed, revised and corrected, 1775.

———. *Oeffeningen over de grondstukken van het Algemeyne Christelijke gelloove.* Rotterdam: Jan Daniel Beman, 1743.

———. *Exercitationes sacrae in symbolum quod Apostolorum dicitur.* Amsterdam, 1697.

Wobbermin. Georg. *Theologie und Metaphysik, das Verhältnis der Theologie zur moderne Erkenntnistheorie und Psychologie.* Berlin: Alexander Duncker, 1901.

*Wötzel, J. C. *Meiner Gattin wirkliche Erscheinung nach ihrem Tode.* Chemniz, 1804.

Wright, Charles H. H. *The Intermediate State and Prayers for the Dead Examined in the Light of Scripture and Ancient Jewish and Christian Literature.* London: Nisbet, 1900.

Wulf, M. von. *Ueber Heilige und Heiligenverehrung in den ersten Christlichen Jahrhunderten.* Leipzig: Eckhardt, 1910.

Ypey, A. *Geschiedenis der Christliche kerk in de Achttiende Eeuw.* Utrecht: Van Ijzergorst, 1797–1811.

Ypey, A., and I. J. Dermout. *Geschiedenis der Nederlandsche Kerk.* Breda: F. B. Hollingers Pijpers, 1824.

Ziegler, Theobald. *Sittliche Sein und sittliche Werden.* Strassbourg: K. I. Trübner, 1890.

Zwingli, Ulrich. *Commentary on True and False Religion*. Edited by Samuel Macauley Jackson and Clarence Nevin Heller. Philadelphia, 1929; reprint Durham, N.C.: Labyrinth Press, 1981.

Articles and Essays

Anrich, G. "Clemens und Origenes als Begründer der Lehre vom Fegfeur." In *Theologische Abhandlung: Eine Festgabe für H. J. Holtzmann*. Tübingen, 1902. Pp. 97–120.

Bavinck, B. "Das Entropiegesetz und die Endlichkeit der Welt." *Der Geisteskampf der Gegenwart* 45 (1909): 260–67.

Beer, G. "Der biblische Hades." In *Theologische Abhandlung: Eine Festgabe für H. J. Holtzmann*. Tübingen, 1902. Pp. 3–29.

Benzinger, B. "Gericht, göttliches." *PRE*, VI, 568–85.

*Bois, H. "La terre et le ciel." *Foi et Vie* (15 Aout–1 Oct. 1906).

Bonwetsch, G. Nathanael. "Heiligenverehrung." *PRE*, VII, 554–59.

———. "Kanonization." *PRE*, X, 17–18.

Charles, R. H., A. B. Davidson, and S. D. F. Salmond. "Eschatology." *Hastings Dictionary of the Bible*, I, 734–57.

*Cramer, J. A. "Het Evangelie en de Eeuwige Straf." *Theologische Studiën* 20 (1902): 241–66.

Dalman, Gustaf. "Hades." *PRE*, VII, 295–99.

Darling, T. G. "The Apostle Paul and the Second Advent." *The Princeton Theological Review* 2 (April 1904): 197–214.

Davis, John D. "The Future Life in Hebrew Thought during the Pre-Persian Period." *The Princeton Theological Review* 6 (October 1907): 246–68.

Dobschütz, Ernst. "Zur Eschatologie der Evangelien." *Theologische Studien und Kritiken* 84 (1911): 1–20.

*Dressel, L. "Der Gottesbeweis auf Grund des Entropiesatzes." *Stimmen aus Maria Laach* (1909): 150–60.

*Eyckman, J. C. "Algemeene of Conditioneele Onsterfelijkheid." *Theologische Studiën* 26 (1908): 359–80.

Gröbler, Paul. "Die Ansichten über Unsterblichkeit und Auferstehung in der jüdischen Literatur der beiden letzten Jahrhunderte v. Chr." *Theologische Studien und Kritiken* 52 (1879): 651–700.

Hauck, Albert. "Reliquien." *PRE*, XVI, 630–34.

Hofman, Rudolf. "Fegfeur." *PRE*, V, 788–92.

James, M. R. "Man of Sin and Antichrist." *Hastings Dictionary of the Bible*, III, 226–28.

*Jankelvitch, "La Mort et l'immortalité d 'après les donnees de la Biologie." *Revue Philosophique* (1910), no. 4.

*Jonker. "De Leer der Conditioneele Onsterfelijkheid." *Theologische Studiën* 1 (1882).

Kahler, Martin. " Ewiges Leben." *PRE*, XI, 330–34.

———. "Seligkeit." *PRE*, XVIII, 179–84.

*Knabenhauer, Joseph. "Jesus und die Erwartung des Weltendes," *Stimmen aus Maria Laach* (1908): 487–97.

Köstlin, Julius. "Apokatastasis." *PRE*, I, 616–22.

———. "Ein Beitrag zur Eschatologie der Reformatoren." *Theologische Studien und Kritiken* 51 (1878): 125–35.

Lodge, Oliver. "The Immortality of the Soul." *The Hibbert Journal* 6 (1908): 836–51.

MacKay, D. S. "Personal Immortality in the Light of Recent Science." *The North American Review* 185 (1907): 387–93.

*Matthes. "Twee Israelitische Rouwbedrijven." *T. T. T.* (1910): 145–69.

———. "Rouw en Doodenvereering bij Israel." *T. T. T.* (1905): 1–30.

Maurice, F. D. ""The Word 'Eternal' and the Punishment of the Wicked." In *Theological Essays*. London: James Clarke, 1957 [1857].

*Meusel, "War die vorjahwistische Religion Israels Ahnenkultus?" *Neue Kirchliche Zeitschrift* (1905): 484ff.

Morey, Charles A. "The Beginnings of Saint Worship." *The Princeton Theological Review* 6 (April 1908): 278–90.

Muirhead, Lewis. "Eschatology." *Dictionary of Christ and the Gospels*. Edited by James Hastings. Vol. I, 525–38.

*Oort, H. "De Doodenvereering bij de Israelieten." *Theologisch Tijdschrift* 15 (1881): 359–63.

Post, G. E. "Millennium." *Hastings Dictionary of the Bible*, III, 370–73.

*Ritschl, Otto. "Luthers Seligkeitsvorstellung in ihrer Entstehung und Bedeutung." *Christ. Welt* (1889): 874–80.

Royce, Josiah. "Immortality." *The Hibbert Journal* 5 (1907): 724–44.

Runze, Georg. "Unsterblichkeit." *PRE*, XX, 294–301.

Salmond, S. D. F. "Paradise." *Hastings Dictionary of the Bible*, III, 668–72.

Schaeder, Erich. "Auferstehung der Todten." *PRE*, I, 219–24.

Seiffert, Anton Emil Friedrich. "Antichrist." *PRE*, I, 577–84.

Semisch-Bratke. "Chiliasmus." *PRE*, III, 805–17.

Spitta, Friedrich. "Die grosse eschatologische Rede Jesu." *Theologische Studien und Kritiken* 82 (1909): 348–401.

Steude, "Die Unsterblichkeitsbeweise." *Beweis des Glaubens* 39 (1903); 40 (1904): 73–82, 145–59, 172–83, 201–15.

Stout, G. F. "Mr. F. W. Meyers on 'Human Personality and its Survival of Bodily Death." *The Hibbert Journal* 2 (1903): 44–64.

Suicerus, Johann Casper, "ταφή." In *Thesaurus ecclesiasticus, e patribus graecis ordine alphabetico*. Amsterdam: J. H. Wetsten, 1682.

Traub, Th. "Seelenwanderung." *Der Geisteskampf der Gegenwart* 45 (1909): 285–303.

Vos, Geerhardus. "The Pauline Eschatology and Chiliasm." *The Princeton Theological Review* 9 (January 1911): 26–60.

Warfield, Benjamin. "The Millennium and the Apocalypse." *The Princeton Theological Review* 2 (October 1904): 599–617.

———. "The Development of the Doctrine of Infant Salvation." In *Two Studies in the History of Doctrine*. New York: Christian Literature Co., 1897.

Weisse, Chr. H. "Ueber die philosophische Bedeutung der Christliche Lehre von der letzten Dinge." *Theologische Studien und Kritiken* 9 (1836): 271–340.

*Wünsche. "Die Vorstellung von Zustande nach dem Tode nach Apokrypha, Talmud und Kirchenvätern." *Jahrbuch für Protestantische Theologie* (1880): 355–83, 435–523.

Zandstra, Sidney. "The Theory of Ancestor Worship Among the Hebrews." *The Princeton Theological Review* 5 (1907): 281–87.

———. "Sheol and Pit in the Old Testament." *The Princeton Theological Review* 5 (October 1907): 631–41.

Zöckler, Otto. "Spiritismus." *PRE*, XVIII, 654–66.

Notes

Introduction

1. The Leiden *Synopsis*, first published in 1625, is a large manual of Reformed doctrine as it was defined by the Synod of Dordt. It served as a standard reference textbook for the study of Reformed theology well into the twentieth century (it is even cited by Karl Barth in his *Church Dogmatics*). As an original-source reference work of classic Dutch Reformed theology it is comparable to Heinrich Heppe's nineteenth-century more broadly continental anthology, *Reformed Dogmatics* (London: Allen & Unwin, 1950). While serving as the minister of a Christian Reformed church in Franeker, Friesland, Bavinck edited the sixth and final edition of this handbook, which was published in 1881.

2. For a brief description of the background and character of the Secession church, see James D. Bratt, *Dutch Calvinism in Modern America* (Grand Rapids: Eerdmans, 1984), ch. 1, "Secession and Its Tangents."

3. See Joel R. Beeke, "The Dutch Second Reformation (*Nadere Reformatie*)," *Calvin Theological Journal* 28 (1993): 298–327.

4. The crowning theological achievement of the *Nadere Reformatie* is the devout and theologically rich work of Wilhelmus à Brakel, *Redelijke Godsdienst*, first published in 1700 and frequently thereafter (including twenty Dutch editions in the eighteenth century alone!). This work is now available in English translation: *The Christian's Reasonable Service*, trans. Bartel Elshout, 4 vols. (Ligonier, Pa.: Soli Deo Gloria, 1992–95).

5. The standard work on the *Réveil* is M. Elizabeth Kluit, *Het Protestantse Réveil in Nederland en Daarbuiten, 1815–1865* (Amsterdam: Paris, 1970). Bratt also gives a brief summary in *Dutch Calvinism in America*, 10–13.

6. Bavinck himself called attention to this in his Kampen rectoral oration of 1888 when he complained that the Seceder emigration to America was a spiritual withdrawal and abandonment of "the Fatherland as lost to unbelief" ("The Catholicity of Christianity and the Church," trans. John Bolt, *Calvin Theological Journal* 27 [1992]: 246). Recent historical scholarship, however, suggests that this note of separatism and cultural alienation must not be exaggerated. Though clearly a marginalized community in the Netherlands, the Seceders were not indifferent to educational, social, and political responsibilities. See John Bolt, "Nineteenth- and Twentieth-Century Dutch Reformed Church and Theology: A Review Article," *Calvin Theological Journal* 28 (1993): 434–42.

7. For an overview of the major schools of Dutch Reformed theology in the nineteenth century, see James Hutton MacKay, *Religious Thought in Holland During the Nineteenth Century* (London: Hodder & Stoughton, 1911). For more detailed discussion of the "modernist" school, see K. H. Roessingh, *De Moderne Theologie in Nederland: Hare Voorbereiding en Eerste Periode* (Groningen: Van der Kamp, 1915); Eldred C. Vanderlaan, *Protestant Modernism in Holland* (London and New York: Oxford University Press, 1924).

8. R. H. Bremmer, *Herman Bavinck en Zijn Tijdgenoten* (Kampen: Kok, 1966), 20. Cf. V. Hepp, *Dr. Herman Bavinck* (Amsterdam: W. Ten Have, 1921), 30.

9. R. H. Bremmer, *Tijdgenoten*, 19.

10. V. Hepp, *Dr. Herman Bavinck*, 84.

11. Cited by Jan Veenhof, *Revelatie en Inspiratie* (Amsterdam: Buijten & Schipper-heijn, 1968), 108. The contemporary cited is the Reformed jurist A. Anema, who was a colleague of Bavinck at the Free University of Amsterdam. A similar assessment of Bavinck as a man between two poles is given by F. H. von Meyenfeldt, "Prof. Dr. Herman Bavinck: 1854–1954, 'Christus en de Cultuur,'" *Polemios* 9 (October 15, 1954); and G. W. Brillenburg-Wurth, "Bavincks Levenstrijd," *Gereformeerde Weekblad* 10/25 (December 17, 1954).

12. H. Bavinck, "De Theologie van Albrecht Ritschl," *Theologische Studiën* 6 (1888): 397. Cited by Jan Veenhof, *Revelatie en Inspiratie*, 346–47; emphasis added by Veenhof. Kenneth Kirk contends that this tension, which he characterizes as one between "rigor-ism" and "humanism," is a fundamental conflict in the history of Christian ethics from the outset. See K. Kirk, *The Vision of God* (London: Longmans, Green, 1931), 7–8.

13. See p. 161.

14. H. Bavinck, *Het Christendom*, in the series *Groote Godsdiensten*, vol. 2, no. 7 (Baarn: Hollandia, 1912), 60.

15. For a brief overview, see J. Bratt, *Dutch Calvinism in Modern America*, ch. 2, "Abra-ham Kuyper and Neo-Calvinism."

16. Kuyper chronicles these experiences in a revealing autobiographical work entitled *Confidentie* (Amsterdam: Höveker, 1873). See also the somewhat hagiographic biography of Kuyper by Frank Vandenberg (Grand Rapids: Eerdmans, 1960) and the more theolog-ically and historically substantive one by Louis Praamsma, *Let Christ Be King: Reflection on the Times and Life of Abraham Kuyper* (Jordan Station, Ont.: Paideia, 1985). Brief ac-counts can also be found in Benjamin B. Warfield's introduction to A. Kuyper, *Principles of Sacred Theology*, trans. J. H. De Vries (Grand Rapids: Charles Scribner's, 1898), and the translator's biographical note in A. Kuyper, *To Be Near to God*, trans. J. H. De Vries (Grand Rapids: Eerdmans, 1925).

17. See especially his famous address, *Het Modernisme, een Fata Morgana op Christel-ijke Gebied* (Amsterdam: De Hoogh, 1871). On page 52 of this work he acknowledges that he, too, once dreamed the dreams of modernism.

18. A. Kuyper, *Lectures on Calvinism* (Grand Rapids: Eerdmans, 1931), 10.

19. Ibid., 11–12.

20. Ibid., 79.

21. Kuyper's own position is developed in his *De Gemeene Gratie*, 3 vols. (Amsterdam and Pretoria: Höveker & Wormser, 1902). A thorough examination of Kuyper's views can be found in S. U. Zuidema, "Common Grace and Christian Action in Abraham Kuyper," in *Communication and Confrontation* (Toronto: Wedge, 1971), 52–105. Cf. J. Ridderbos, *De Theologische Cultuurbeschouwing van Abraham Kuyper* (Kampen: Kok, 1947). The doctrine of common grace has been much debated among conservative Dutch Reformed folk in the Netherlands and the United States, tragically leading to church divisions. For an overview of the doctrine in the Reformed tradition, see H. Kuiper, *Calvin on Common Grace* (Goes: Oosterbaan & Le Cointre, 1928).

22. "In this independent character a special *higher authority* is of necessity involved and this highest authority we intentionally call—*sovereignty in the individual social spheres*, in order that it may be sharply and decidedly expressed that these different de-velopments of social life have *nothing above themselves but God*, and that the state cannot intrude here, and has nothing to command in their domain" (*Lectures on Calvinism*, 91.)

23. On Kuyper's ecclesiology, see H. Zwaanstra, "Abraham Kuyper's Conception of the Church," *Calvin Theological Journal* 9 (1974): 149–81; on his attitude to the *volkskerk* tradition, see H. J. Langman, *Kuyper en de Volkskerk* (Kampen: Kok, 1950).

24. A. Kuyper, *Lectures on Calvinism*, 133; cf. *Principles*, 150–82. A helpful discussion of Kuyper's view of science is given by Del Ratzsch, "Abraham Kuyper's Philosophy of Science," *Calvin Theological Journal* 27 (1992): 277–303.

25. The relation between Bavinck and Kuyper, including differences as well as commonalities, is discussed in greater detail in John Bolt, "The Imitation of Christ Theme in the Cultural-Ethical Ideal of Herman Bavinck," unpublished Ph.D. diss., University of St. Michael's College, Toronto, Ont., 1982, especially ch. 3: "Herman Bavinck as a Neo-Calvinist Thinker."

26. H. Bavinck, *The Doctrine of God*, trans. W. Hendriksen (Grand Rapids: Eerdmans, 1951), 329.

27. H. Bavinck, *Gereformeerde Dogmatiek*, 4th ed. (Kampen: Kok, 1928), I, 89.

28. This is the conclusion of Jan Veenhof, *Revelatie en Inspiratie*, 346; and Eugene Heideman, *The Relation of Revelation and Reason in E. Brunner and H. Bavinck* (Assen: Van Gorcum, 1959), 191, 195. Cf. below, p. 200, n. 4.

29. H. Bavinck, "Common Grace," trans. Raymond Van Leeuwen, *Calvin Theological Journal* 24 (1989): 59–60, 61.

30. The four volumes of the first edition of *Gereformeerde Dogmatiek* were published in the years 1895 through 1901. The second revised and expanded edition appeared between 1906 and 1911; the third edition, unaltered from the second, in 1918; the fourth, unaltered except for different pagination, in 1928.

31. Chapter XI in all editions with the three sections: The Intermediate State, The Return of Christ, and The Consummation of the Age.

Chapter 1 The Question of Immortality

1. E. Haeckel, *The Riddle of the Universe at the Close of the Nineteenth Century*, trans. Joseph McCabe (New York: Harper & Brothers, 1900), 192; L. Büchner, *Kraft und Staff oder Grundzüge der natürlichen Weltordnung* (Leipzig: Thomas, 1902), 156–77. *Ed. note:* Bavinck's own citation is clearly to a different edition since his reference is vol. 1, p. 423. A multivolume edition of *Kraft und Stoff* was not traceable. The section in the edition cited in this note is titled "Gehirn und Seele." An English edition of Büchner's much-printed volume is available as *Force and Matter; or Principles of the Natural Order of the Universe*, 4th ed., translated from the 15th German ed. (New York: P. Eckler, 1891).

2. C. P. Tiele, *Elements of the Science of Religion* (Edinburgh and London: W. Blackwood and Sons, 1899), II, 113–14; O. Peschel, *Abhandlungen zur Erd und Völkerkunde* (Leipzig: Duncker & Humboldt, 1878), 257.

3. Ibid., 231f.

4. Tertullian, *A Treatise on the Soul*, 22; Origen, *On First Principles*, VI, 36; Irenaeus, *Against Heresies*, II, 34.

5. Justin Martyr, *Dialogue with Trypho*, 5; Theophilus, *To Autolycus*, II, 27.

6. A. von Harnack, *History of Dogma*, vol. 2, trans. N. Buchanan (London: Williams & Norgate, 1897), 213; W. Münscher, *Lehrbuch des christlichen Dogmengeschichte*, ed. Daniel von Coelln (Cassel: J. C. Krieger, 1832–38), I, 333; *Jonker, "De Leer der Conditioneele Onsterfelijkheid," *Theologische Studiën* 1 (1882): 167ff.; L. Atzberger, *Geschichte der Christliche Eschatologie* (Freiburg, i.B., and St. Louis, Mo.: Herder, 1896), 118f., 222f., 338f., 577f.

7. B. Spinoza, *Ethics*, V, 41.

8. See literature cited by K. G. Bretschneider, *Systematische Entwickelung aller in der Dogmatik* (Leipzig: J. A. Barth, 1841), 824.

9. F. Schleiermacher, *On Religion: Speeches to Its Cultured Despisers*, trans. John Oman (Louisville, Ky.: Westminster/John Knox, 1994 [1958]), 101. Cf. idem, *The Christian Faith*, ed. H. R. MacIntosh and J. S. Stewart (Edinburgh: T. & T. Clark, 1928), § 158, 1.

10. F. Richter, *Die Lehre von der letzten Dingen* (Breslau: J. Hebenstreit, 1833–44).

11. D. F. Strauss, *Die Christliche Glaube* (Tübingen: Osiander, 1840–41), II, 738; idem, *Der alte und der neue Glaube*, 2nd ed. (Leipzig: Friedrich, 1872), 123f.; *A. Schopenhauer, *Die Welt*, I, 330. [Bavinck is undoubtedly referring to Schopenhauer's *Die Welt als Wille*

und Vortstellung, found in vols. 2 and 3 of his *Sammtliche Werke* (Leipzig: F. M. Brodhaus, 1919) ed.]; Eduard von Hartman, *Religionsphilosophie* (Leipzig: Friedrich, 1885), II, 232.

12. S. Hoekstra, *De Hoop der Ontsterfelijkheid* (Amsterdam: P. N. van Kampen, 1867); L. Rauwenhoff, *Wijsbegeerte van de Godsdienst* (Leiden: Brill & van Doesburgh, 1887), 811.

13. F. H. R. Frank, *System der Christlichen Wahrheit,* 3rd ed. (Erlangen and Leipzig: Deichert, 1894), II, 427f.; A. F. C. Vilmar, *Handbuch der evangelischen Dogmatik* (Gütersloh: Bertelsman, 1895), 295.

14. I. A. Dorner, *A System of Christian Doctrine,* trans. A. Cave and J. S. Banks (Edinburgh: T. & T. Clark, 1882), IV, 373ff.; J. I. Doedes, *Inleiding tot de Leer van God* (Utrecht: Kemink, 1870), 248f.; J. J. van Oosterzee, *Christian Dogmatics,* trans. J. Watson and M. Evans (New York: Scribner, Armstrong, 1874), §68; Chr. H. Weisse, *Philosophische Dogmatik* (Leipzig: Hirzel, 1855–62), § 955–72; I. H. Fichte, *Die Idee der Persönlichkeit und der individuellen Fortdauer* (Leipzig: Dyk, 1855); *Göschel, *Von den Beweisen für die Unsterblichkeit der menschlichen Seele* (1835); F. A. Kahnis, *Die Luthersche Dogmatik* (Leipzig: Dorffling & Francke, 1861–68), II, 485f.

15. Cicero, *Tusculan disputations,* I, 3.

16. Runze, s.v. "Unsterblichkeit," in *Realencyklopädie für protestantische Theologie und Kirche (PRE),* 3rd ed., XX, 294f.

17. Willem Bilderdijk (1756–1831) was the great poet of Dutch nationalism who engaged in a titanic literary battle against the spirit of modernism (ed.).

18. B. Spinoza, *Ethics,*V, 41, 42.

19. J. Calvin, *Institutes,* III, ii, 26; xvi, 2.

20. Von Baer, cited by F. J. Splittgerber, *Tod, Fortleben und Auferstehung,* 3rd ed. (Halle: Fricke, 1879), 93. Further on immortality, see Steude, "Die Unsterblichkeitsbeweise," *Beweis des Glaubens* 39 (1903); 40 (1904): 73–82, 145–59, 172–83, 210–15; P. Knieb, *Die Beweis für die Unsterblichkeit der Seele als allgemein psychologischen Tatsachen* (Freiburg: Herder, 1903); *Riemann, *Was wissen wir über die Unsterblichkeit der Seele* (Magdeburg, 1900); H. Keyserling, *Unsterblichkeit, eine Kritik der Beziehungen zwischen Naturgeschehen und menschlichen Vorstellungswelt* (München, 1907); Th. Steinmann, *Der Religiose Unsterblichkeitsglaube* (Göttingen: Vandenhoeck & Ruprecht, 1912); G. Heinzelmann, *Der Begriff der Seele und die Idee der Unsterblichkeit bei Wilhelm Wundt,* Ph.D. diss., University of Göttingen, 1907; Robert J. Thompson, *The Proof of Life after Death* (Boston: Small, Maynard & Co., 1906); H. Frank, *Modern Light on Immortality* (Boston: Sherman, French & Co., 1909); D. S. MacKay, "Personal Immortality in the Light of Recent Science," *The North American Review* 185 (1907): 387–93; Josiah Royce, "Immortality," *The Hibbert Journal* 5 (1907): 724–44; Oliver Lodge, "The Immortality of the Soul," *The Hibbert Journal* 6 (1908): 826–51; *Jankelvitch, "La Mort et l'immortalite de'apres les donnees de la biologie," *Revue Philosophique* (1910), no. 4; A. Bruining, *Het Voortbestaan der Menschelijke Persoonlijkheid na den Dood* (Assen, 1904). Spiritualist proofs for immortality are advanced by Fred W. H. Meyers in his *Human Personality and Its Survival of Bodily Death,* 2nd ed. (London: Longmans, Green, 1903); see G. F. Stout, "Mr. F. W. Meyers on 'Human Personality and Its Survival of Bodily Death,'" *The Hibbert Journal* 2 (1903): 44–64; Oliver Lodge, *The Survival of Man* (Methuen, 1909) reviewed by Frank Padmore in *The Hibbert Journal* 8 (1910): 669–72; *Hesselink, *Wetenschap en Onsterfelijkheid* (Middelburg, 1904); H. N. de Fremery, *Wat Gebeurt er met Ons als Wij Sterven* (Bussum: Van Dishoeck, 1910).

21. B. Stade, *Geschichte des Volkes Israel* (Berlin: Baumgartel, 1887), I, 387–427; idem, *Uber die alttestamentische Vorstellungen vom Zustande nach dem Tode* (1877); F. Schwally, *Das Leben nach dem Tode nach dem Vorstellungen des alten Israel* (Giessen: J. Ricker, 1892); *Oort, "De Doodenvereering bij de Israelieten," *Theol. Tijdschrift* 15 (1881): 358–63; *Matthes, "Rouw en Dood en vereering bij Israel," *T.T.T.* (1905): 1–30; idem, *"Twee Israelitische Rouwbedrijven," *T.T.T.* (1910): 145–69.

22. J. Frey, *Tod, Seelenglaube und Seelenkult im alten Israel* (Leipzig: A. Deichert, 1898); C. Grüneissen, *Der Ahnenkultus und die Urreligon Israels* (Halle: Niemeyer, 1900); *Meusel, "War die vorjahwistische Religion Israels Ahnenkultus?" *Neue Kirchl. Zeits.* (1905): 484ff. Sidney Zandstra, "The Theory of Ancestor Worship Among the Hebrews," *Princeton Theological Review* 5 (1907): 281–87. [This bibliographic essay is very useful for its summary of works cited by Bavinck in notes 20, 21 (above) ed.].

23. Fr. Schwally, *Das Leben nach den Tode*, 75.

24. G. Wildeboer, *Jahvedienst en Volksreligie in Israel* (Groningen: Wolters, 1898).

25. F. Delitzsch, *A New Commentary on Genesis*, trans. Sophia Taylor (Edinburgh: T. & T. Clark, 1899), II, 264; L. Atzberger, *Die Christliche Eschatologie* (Freiburg i.B.: Herder, 1890), 24.

26. For Bavinck, the Dutch *Statenvertaling* (ed.).

27. O. Pfleiderer, *Religionsphilosophie auf geschichtlicher Grundlage* (Berlin: G. Reimer, 1896), 616.

28. Fl. Josephus, *Jewish Wars*, III, 8, 5.

29. Fl. Josephus, *Jewish Wars*, II 8, 14; *Antiquity of the Jews*, XVIII, 1, 4.

30. Fl. Josephus, *Jewish Wars*, II, 8, 11. On the eschatology of Judaism, see further also Fr. Schwally, *Das Leben nach dem Tode*, 131–92; P. Gröbler, "Die Ansichten über Unsterblichkeit und Auferstehung in der jüdischen Literatur der beiden letzten Jahrhunderte v. Chr.," *Theologische Studien und Kritiken* 52 (1879): 651–700; *Wünsche, "Die Vorstellung von Zustande nach dem Tode nach Apokrypha, Talmud, und Kirchenvätern," *Jahrbuch für Protestantische Theologie* (1880): 355–83, 435–523; L. Atzberger, *Christliche Eschatologie*, 96–156.

31. S. Episcopius, *Op. Theol.*, II, 2, 455; F. Schleiermacher, *The Christian Faith*, § 159, 2; P. van Limborch, *Theol. Christ.*, VI, 10, 4; *Oertel, *Hades*, 4–6; J. C. von Hofmann, *Der Schriftbeweis* (Nördlingen: Beck, 1857–60), III, 462.

32. Th. Kliefoth, *Christliche Eschatologie* (Leipzig: Dorffling & Franke, 1886), 37.

33. F. W. Weber, *System der altsynagogelen Palastinischen Theologie* (Leipzig: Dorffling & Franke, 1880), 330; S. D. F. Salmond, s.v. "Paradise," in *Hastings Dictionary of the Bible*, III, 668–772.

Chapter 2 After Death, Then What?

1. See L. Atzberger, *Geschichte der Christliche Eschatologie* (Freiburg i.B., and St. Louis, Mo.: Herder, 1890), 75–99.

2. Ibid., 275ff., 301ff.; J. Niederhuber, *Die Eschatologie des heiligen Ambrosius* (Paderhorn: Schöningh, 1907), 58f.; J. Schwane, *Dogmengeschichte* (Freiburg i.B.: Herder, 1882–95), II, 585.

3. Origen, *Against Celsus*, III, 75; VI, 25, 26; VI, 12, 13, 21, 64; V, 15, 16. Cf. G. Anrich, "Clemens und Origenes als Begründer der Lehre vom Fegfeur," in W. Nowack et al., *Theologische Abhandlung: Eine Festgabe für H. J. Holtzmann* (Tübingen, 1902), 97–120; R. Hofman, s.v. "Fegfeur," in *Realencyklopädie für protestantische Kirche und Theologie* (*PRE*), 3rd ed., V, 788–92.

4. "The Orthodox Confession of the Eastern Church," art. 64–68; in Philip Schaff, *Creeds of Christendom* (New York: Harper & Brothers, 1877), II, 342–48.

5. W. Münscher, *Lehrbuch des christlichen Dogmengeschichte*, ed. Daniel von Coelln, 3rd ed. (Cassel: J. C. Krieger, 1832–38), II, 313; J. Schwane, *Dogmengeschichte*, II, 587; III, 486; F. Kattenbusch, *Lehrbuch der Vergleichenden Confessionskunde* (Freiburg i.B.: J. C. B. Mohr [Paul Siebeck], 1892), I, 327.

6. Augustine, *The City of God*, XX, 25; XXI, 24.

7. Augustine, *The Enchiridion*, 69.

8. Tertullian, *On Monogamy*, 10, 11; *On Exhortation to Chastity*, 11.

9. P. Lombard, IV *Sent.*, 21; T. Aquinas, *Summa Theol.*, suppl., qu. 69, 74; Bonaventure, *The Breviloquium*, VII, 2, 3; Bellarmine, "de purgatorio," *Controversiis*, II, 228–69.

10. *Canons and Decrees of the Council of Trent*, VI, canon 30; XXII, c. 2, canon 3; XXV.

11. Denzinger, *Enchiridion*, no. 870, 875.

12. P. Lombard, II *Sent.*, dist. 33; T. Aquinas, *Summa Theol.*, suppl., qu. 69, art. 4.

13. Bavinck here in parentheses notes that the Dutch term for purgatory, *vagevuur*, is etymologically derived from *vagen*, *vegen*, which means to purify or cleanse (ed.).

14. *Roman Catechism*, I, c. 6, qu. 3. In addition to the works already cited, also see J. A. Möhler, *Symbolik* (Regensburg: G. J. Manz, 1871), §23; H. Faure, *De Troostingen des Vagevuurs*, trans. Br. Modestus (Amsterdam: Bekker, 1901); *F. Schmid, *Der Fegfeur nach katholischen Lehre* (Brixen, 1904); M. Landau, *Hölle und Fegfeur in Volksglaube, Dichtung und Kirchenlehre* (Heidelberg: Winter, 1910).

15. J. Köstlin, *The Theology of Luther*, trans. Charles E. Hay (Philadelphia: Lutheran Publication Society, 1897), II, 577.

16. J. Gerhard, *Loci Theol.*, XXVI, 160, 191; J. Quenstedt, *Theologia*, IV, 540, 567; H. Schmid, *Doctrinal Theology of the Evangelical Lutheran Church*, trans. Charles A. Hay and Henry E. Jacobs (Philadelphia: United Lutheran Publication House, 1899), § 63.

17. *Heidelberg Catechism*, qu. 57, 58; *Belgic Confession*, art. 37, *Helvetic Confession*, 11, 26; *Westminster Confession*, 32; F. Junius, *Theses Theologicae*, 55, 56; G. Voetius, *Select. Disp.*, V, 533–39.

18. J. Calvin, *Institutes*, III, xxv. 6: The fact that the blessed gathering of saintly spirits is called "Abraham's bosom" [Luke 16:22] is enough to assure us of being received after this pilgrimage by the common Father of the faithful, that he may share the fruit of his faith with us. Meanwhile, since Scripture everywhere bids us wait in expectation for Christ's coming, and defers until then the crown of glory, let us be content with the limits divinely set for us: namely, that the souls of the pious, having ended the toil of their warfare, enter into blessed rest, where in glad expectation they await the enjoyment of promised glory, and so all things are held in suspense until Christ the Redeemer appear. Cf. Calvin, *Psychopannychia*; A. Walaeus, *Synopsis Purioris Theologiae*, 40, 17; H. Witsius, *Oeconomy of the Covenants*, III, 14, 33; J. H. Heidegger, *Corpus Theologiae*, 28, 38.

19. See C. Vitringa, *Doctrina Christianae Religionis*, IV, 63–69. Hereafter cited as *Doctr. Christ. Ed. note*: Bavinck consistently cites Vitringa as M. Vitringa.

20. Ibid., 81, 82; G. W. von Leibnitz, *System der Theologie* (Mainz: Müller, 1820), 345; G. E. Lessing, *Erziehung des Menschengeschlechts*, ed. Louis Ferdinand Helbig (Bern and Las Vegas: Peter Lang, 1980); *J. F. von Meyer, *Blätter für höhere Wahrheit*, VI, 233; J. H. Jung-Stillung, *Theorie der Geisterkunde* (Leipzig: Dieter, ca. 1800), § 211; *Lange, *Dogmatik*, II, 1250f.; R. Rothe, *Theologische Ethik*, 2nd ed. (Wittenberg: Zimmerman, 1867–71), § 793–95; H. Martensen, *Christian Dogmatics*, trans. W. Urwick (Edinburgh: T. & T. Clark, 1871), § 276, 277; I. A. Dorner, *A System of Christian Doctrine*, trans. A. Cave and J. S. Banks (Edinburgh: T. & T. Clark, 1882), IV, § 153; J. J. van Oosterzee, *Christian Dogmatics*, trans. J. Watson and M. Evans (New York: Scribner, Armstrong, 1874), § 142. Especially Anglican theologians had much sympathy for the doctrine of purgatory; cf. Walter Wash, *The Secret History of the Oxford Movement*, 6th ed. (London: Church Association, 1899), 281ff.

21. Otto Fock, *Der Socianismus* (Kiel: C. Schröder, 1847), 714ff.

22. Cf. K. G. Bretschneider, *Handbuch der Dogmatike der evangelischlutherischen Kirche* (Leipzig: n.p., 1838), II, 395.

23. S. Episcopus, *Op. Theol.*, II, 455; P. van Limborch, *Theol. Christ.*, VI, 10, 8; J. Müller, *Die Christliche Lehre von der Sunde* (Bremen: C. Ed. Muller, 1889), II, 402–8; H. Martensen, *Christian Dogmatics*, §276; J. H. A. Ebrard, *Christliche Dogmatik*, 2nd ed. (Konigsberg: A. W. Unser, 1862–63), §570; I. A. Dorner, *Christian Doctrine*, IV, §153; F. H. R. Frank, *System der Christlichen Wahrheit*, 3rd rev. ed. (Erlangen and Leipzig: Deichert, 1847), II, 460.

24. Including Paracelsus, Helmont, Böhme, Oetinger, Ph. M. Hahn, Swedenborg, Priestly, Schott, and Jean Paul. Bretschneider, *Dogmatik*, II, 396; Rothe, *Theologische Ethik*, §111f., 793f.; F. Delitzsch, *A System of Biblical Psychology*, trans. Robert E. Wallis, 2nd ed. (Edinburgh: T. & T. Clark, 1875), 499ff.; F. J. Splittgerber, *Tod, Fortleben, und Auferstehung*, 3rd ed. (Halle: Fricke, 1879), 45.

25. The doctrine of the transmigration of souls, reincarnation, or metempsychosis was traditionally one of the most fundamental tenets of Hinduism (J. S. Speyer, *De Indische Theosophie en Hare Beteekenis voor Ons* [Leiden: S. C. van Doesburgh, 1910], 86f.) and, according to Herodotus, was embraced also by the Egyptians and found acceptance later in the case of Pythagoras, Empedocles, Plato, the Stoics, Neo-Platonists, Pharisees, Cabbalists, Gnostics, and Manicheees; in later years again in Nolanus, Helmont, Dippel, Edelmann (on these, see C. Vitringa, *Doctr. Christ.*, IV, 86–89); Lessing, Schlosser, Ungern-Sternberg, Schopenhauer (on these, see Otto Flink, *Schopenhauers Seelenwanderungslehre und ihre Quellen*, Ph.D. diss., University of Bern, 1906; cf. *Burger, *De Platonische Leer der Zielsverhuizing* [Amersfoort, 1877]; C. Andresen, *Die Lehre von der Widergeburt auf theistische Grundlage*, 2nd ed. [Hamburg: Grafe, 1899]; A. Bertholet, *Seelenwanderung* [Tübingen: J. C. B. Mohr (Paul Siebeck), 1906]; J. Baumann, *Unsterblichkeit und Seelenwanderung: Ein Vereinigungspunkt morgenlandischen und abendlandischen Weltansicht* [Leipzig: S. Hirzel, 1909].

26. H. Martensen, *Christian Dogmatics*, §277; F. Delitzsch, *A System of Biblical Psychology*, 477ff.; A. F. C. Vilmar, *Handbuch der evangelischen Dogmatik für studierende die Theologie* (Gütersloh: Bertelsmann, 1895), II, 290; F. J. Splittgerber, *Tod, Fortleben und Auferstehung*, 3rd ed. (Halle: Fricke, 1879), 110f.; H. Cremer, *Ueber den Zustand nach dem Tode* (Gütersloh: Bertelsmann, 1883), 9f.

27. *Lange, *Dogmatik*, II, 1250f.; Rothe, *Theologische Ethik*, §786, 787; Delitzsch, *Biblical Psychology*, 483; Th. Kliefoth, *Christliche Eschatologie* (Leipzig: Dorffling & Franke, 1886), 97–113; J. I. Doedes, *De Nederlandsche Geloofsbelijdenis* (Utrecht: Kemink, 1880–81), 521; J. J. van Oosterzee, *Christian Dogmatics*, §142.

28. See part 3 of this volume, *The Consummation*, for further discussion.

29. Henry Drummond, *Natural Law in the Spiritual World* (New York: J. Pott, 1887), 149ff.

30. For opposition to the idea of soul sleep, see Tertullian, *A Treatise on the Soul*, 58; J. Calvin, *Psychopannychia*; *Bullinger, *Huisboek*, Dec. 4, serm. 10; J. Cloppenburg, *Op. Theol.*, II, 413–17; G. Voetius, *Select. Disp.*, I, 832–34; H. Witsius, *Oeconomy of the Covenants*, III, 14, 18–22; B. De Moor, *Comm. Theol.*, VI, 594–602; C. Vitringa, *Doctr. Christ.*, IV, 82–86; J. Gerhard, *Loci Theol.*, XXVI, 293; F. Delitzsch, *Biblical Psychology*, 490; Splittgerber, *Tod, Fortleben und Auferstehung*, 102; H. W. Rinck, *Vom Zustande nach dem Tode*, 2nd ed. (Ludwigsburg and Basel: Balmer & Rieh, 1866), 19; Kliefoth, *Christliche Eschatologie*, 66; L. Altzberger, *Die Christliche Eschatologie* (Freiburg i.B.: Herder, 1890), 212.

31. The reading (v. 3) *ei ge kai ekdysamenoi* deserves preference, in my opinion, over *ei ge kai endysamenoi*.

32. H. J. Holtzmann, *Lehrbuch der neutestamentlicher Theologie* (Freiburg i.B. and Leipzig: Mohr, 1897), II, 199.

33. Cf. Fr. Delitzsch, *A System of Biblical Psychology*, esp. 503ff. (ed.).

34. F. W. Weber, *System der altsynagogalen palastinischen Theologie* (Leipzig: Dorffling & Franke, 1880), 324.

35. P. D. Chantepie de la Saussaye, *Lehrbuch der Religionsphilosophie* (Freiburg i.B.: Mohr [Siebeck], 1887–89), I, 79–87.

36. J. Schwane, *Dogmengeschichte*, I, 389ff.; II, 620ff.

37. See further Herman Bavinck, *Gereformeerde Dogmatiek*, II, 429ff.; III, 262, 263.

38. See *Canons and Decrees of the Council of Trent*, XXV; *Roman Catechism*, III, 2, qu. 4–14; P. Lombard, IV *Sent.*, dist. 45; T. Aquinas, *Summa Theol.*, II, 2, qu. 83, art. 11,

suppl., qu. 71, 72; Bellarmine, "de ecclesia triumphante," *Controversiis*, II, 269–368. For the history of saint veneration, see Ernst Lucius, *Die Anfänge des Heiligenkults in der Christliche Kirche* (Tübingen: Mohr, 1904); Charles R. Morey, "The Beginnings of Saint Worship," *Princeton Theological Review* 6 (April 1908): 278–90; F. Pfister, *Der Reliquien- kult im Altertum*, vol. 1, *Das Objekt des Reliquienkultus* (Giessen: A. Topelman, 1909); M. von Wulf, *Ueber Heilige und Heiligenverehrung in den ersten Christlichen Jahrhun- derten* (Leipzig: Eckhardt, 1910); G. Bonwetsch, s.v. "Heiligenverehrung," *PRE*, VII, 554– 59; A. Hauck, s.v. "Reliquien," *PRE*, XVI, 630–34.

39. *Apol. Conf.*, 21; *Art. Smalc.*, II, 2.

40. G. W. von Leibnitz, *System der Theologie*, 116–95.

41. J. C. Ryle, *Knots Untied* (London: Chas. J. Thynne, 1896), 491f.

42. *Beck, *Seelenlehre*, 40f.; F. Delitzsch, *Biblical Psychology*, 444f.; F. Splittberger, *Tod, Fortleben und Auferstehung*, 157ff.

43. See especially *J. C. Wötzel, *Meiner Gattin Wirkliche Erscheinung nach ihrem Tode* (Chemniz, 1804).

44. O. Zöckler, s.v. "Spiritismus," *PRE*, XVIII, 654–66.

45. B. Stade, *Geschichte des Volkes Israel* (Berlin: G. Grote, 1887–88), I, 443f.; F. Schwally, *Das Leben nach dem Tode nach dem Vorstellungen des Alten Israels* (Giessen: J. Ricker, 1892), 69f.

46. See Zöckler, "Spiritismus"; *PRE*, XVIII, 654–66; Kirchner, *Der Spiritismus, die Narrheit unseres Zeitalters* (Berlin: Habel, 1883); Ed. von Hartmann, *Der Spiritismus* (Leipzig: Friedrich, 1885); idem, *Die Geisterhypothese des Spiritismus und seine Phan- tome* (Leipzig: Friedrich, 1891).

47. H. Bavinck, *Gereformeerde Dogmatiek*, II, 429ff.

48. For example, J. H. Oswald, *Eschatologie* (Paderborn: F. Schöningh, 1869), 132.

49. *Canons and Decrees of the Council of Trent*, Session XXV (trans. J. Waterworth).

50. T. Aquinas, *Summa Theol.*, II, qu. 83, art. 4; suppl., qu. 72, art. 1; J. H. Oswald, *Es- chatologie*, 139.

51. J. H. Oswald, *Eschatologie*, 132, 167.

52. G. Bonwetsch, s.v. "Kanonization," *PRE*, X, 17–18.

53. J. H. Oswald, *Eschatologie*, 148, 174.

54. G. Voetius, *Sect. Disp.*, III, 880, 896.

55. J. H. Oswald, *Eschatologie*, 157.

Chapter 3 Between Death and Resurrection

1. H. Bavinck, *Gereformeerde Dogmatiek*, III, 408, 479ff.

2. Cf. Richard Muller, *Dictionary of Latin and Greek Theological Terms* (Grand Rapids: Baker, 1985), s.v. *vocatio*, 329: "General or universal calling is sometimes termed *vocatio realis*, or real calling, because it occurs in and through the things *(res)* of the world, whereas special, or evangelical, calling is sometimes termed a *vocatio verbalis*, since it comes only through the Word *(Verbum)*" (ed.).

3. Cf., e.g., J. H. A. Ebrard, *Christliche Dogmatik*, 2nd ed. (Konigsberg: A. W. Unser, 1862–63), §576.

4. B. De Moor, *Comm. Theol.*, II, 1081; C. Vitringa, *Doctr. Christ.*, IV, 87–97; K. G. Bretschneider, *Systematische Entwickelung aller in der Dogmatik* (Leipzig: J. A. Barth, 1841), 846; E. Spiess, *Entwicklungsgeschichte der Vorstellungen vom Zustande nach dem Tode* (Jena: Herman Costenoble, 1877), 31, 558; Paul Gennrich, *Die Lehre von der Wied- ergeburt* (Leipzig: Deichert, 1907), 275–355; *J. F. von Meyer, *Blätter für höhere Wahrheit* 1 (1830): 244–99; R. Falke, *Gibt es eine Seelenwanderung?* (Halle: S. E. Strein, 1904); Th. Traub, "Seelenwanderung," *Der Geisteskampf der Gegenwart* 45 (1909): 285–303.

5. P. D. Chantepie de la Saussaye, *Lehrbuch der Religionsgeschichte* (Freiburg i.B.: Mohr [Siebeck], 1887–89), II, 51.

6. F. W. Weber, *System der altsynagogalen Palastinischen Theologie* (Leipzig: Dorrflung & Franke, 1880), 327.

7. Cf. Richard Muller, *Dictionary of Latin and Greek Theological Terms*, s.v. *meritum de condigno* and *meritum de congruo*, 191f. (ed.).

8. *Westminster Catechism*, qu. 85.

9. J. H. Oswald, *Eschatologie* (Paderborn: F. Schöningh, 1869), 116.

10. F. Schwally, *Das Leben nach dem Tode nach dem Vorstellungen des alten Israels* (Giessen: J. C. Ricker, 1892), 188–90.

11. *Canons and Decrees of the Council of Trent*, XXII, 2, 3; XXV; Bellarmine, "de purgat.," *Controversiis*, II, 15–18; G. Perrone, *Praelectiones Theologicae* (Louvain: Vanlinthout & Vandezande, 1838–43), VI, 289; VIII, 29; H. Th. Simar, *Lehrbuch der Dogmatik* (Freiburg i.B.: Herder, 1879–80), 900.

12. C. Vitringa, *Doctr. Christ.*, IV, 79, 80; VIII, 509, 515; *Franz, *Das Gebet für die Todten* (Nordhausen, 1857); K. M. Leibbrand, *Das Gebet für die Todten in der evangelischen Kirche* (Stuttgart: Schweizerbart, 1864).

13. J. C. Suicerus, s.v. ταφη in *Thesaurus ecclesiasticus* (Amsterdam: H. H. Wetsten, 1682); B. De Moor, *Comm. Theol.*, V, 30–32.

14. Tertullian, *The Chaplet, or De Corona*, ch. 4. (translation from A. Roberts and J. Donaldson, eds., *The Ante-Nicene Fathers* [New York: Christian Literature Co., 1885], III, 95 [ed.]). Cf. Bellarmine, "de missa," *Controversiis*, II, c. 7; J. H. Oswald, *Eschatologie*, 95.

15. For the repudiation of the doctrine of purgatory, see J. Calvin, *Institutes*, III., v; A. Polanus, *Syn. Theol.*, VII, 25; D. Chamier, *Panstr. Cath.*, III, 26; W. Ames, *Bellarminus enervatus*, II, 5; G. Voetius, *Select. Disp.*, II, 1240; *Forbesius a Corse, *Instruct. hist. theol.*, XIII; J. Gerhard, *Loci. Theol.* XXVI, 181f.; J. Quenstedt, *Theol.*, IV, 555; Th. Kliefoth, *Christliche Eschatologie* (Leipzig: Dorrflung & Franke, 1886), 82f.; Charles H. H. Wright, *The Intermediate State and Prayers for the Dead Examined in the Light of Scripture and Ancient Jewish and Christian Literature* (London: Nisbet, 1900).

16. Th. Kliefoth, *Christliche Eschatologie*, 61–66.

17. B. B. Warfield, "The Development of the Doctrine of Infant Salvation," in his *Two Studies in the History of Doctrine* (New York: Christian Literature Co., 1897).

Chapter 4 Visions of the End

1. The law of entropy, according to which work can be completely converted into heat but heat can never be totally converted back to work, and which, applied to the universe by Clausius, leads to a state in which the temperature difference necessary for the conversion of heat into work has disappeared, has been used repeatedly as an argument for the end, hence also for the beginning of the world; and, further, even as proof for the existence of God. *L. Dressel, "Der Gottesbeweis auf Grund des Entropiesatzes," *Stimmen aus Maria Laach* (1909): 15–60; K. Isenkrahe, *Energie, Entropie, Weltanfgang, Weltende* (Trier: Lintz, 1910). But B. Bavinck, "Das Entropiegesetz und die Endlichkeit der Welt," *Der Geisteskampf der Gegenwart* 45 (1909): 260–67, questions the validity of that argument. Cf. also art. "Entropie" in *Meyers Konversationslexikon*.

2. Allard Pierson, *Eene Levensbeschouwing* (Haarlem: Kruseman, 1875), 269.

3. Bavinck may be referring to Friedrich von Hellwald (1842–92), *Die Erde und Ihre Volker: Ein Geographisches Hausbuch* (Stuttgart: Spemann, 1877–78) (ed.).

4. Th. Ziegler, in his *Sittliche Sein und sittliche Werden* (Strassbourg: K. I. Trübner, 1890), states: "What the final end, the goal of history itself, is I do not know and none of us knows" (141).

5. Cf. Ernst Haeckel, *The Riddle of the Universe*, trans. Joseph McCabe (New York: Harper & Brothers, 1900), 372; and esp. Nietzsche.

6. W. Windelband, *Geschichte und Wissenschaft*, 3rd ed. (Strassbourg: Heitz, 1904), 22. For the end of the world, see further Friedrich Albert Lange, *Geschichte des Materialismus und Kritik seiner Bedeutung in der Gegenwart*, 8th ed. (Leipzig: Baedeker, 1908), 552; Tilman Pesch, *Die Grosen Welträthsel*, 2nd ed. (Freiburg: Herder, 1892), II, 352ff.; *Mühlhäusser, *Die Zukunft der Menschheit* (Heilbron, 1881); *Reiff, *Die Zukunft der Welt*, 2nd ed. (Basel, 1875); *Fürer, *Weltende und Endgericht* (Gütersloh, 1896); H. Siebeck, *Der Religionsphilosophie* (Tübingen: J. C. B. Mohr, 1893), 399–427. See also H. Bavinck, *Philosophy of Revelation* (New York: Longmans, Green, 1909), 242–315.

7. See H. Bavinck, *Gereformeerde Dogmatiek*, III, 215ff.; and further T. Pfanner, *Systema theologiae gentilis purioris*, c. 18–20; *R. Schneider, *Christl. Klänge*, 250ff., 292f.; H. Lüken, *Die Traditionen der Menschengeschlechts*, 2nd ed. (Münster: Aschendorff, 1869), 407ff.; A. Kuyper, *Van de Voleinding* (Kampen: Kok, 1929–31), I, 64–127.

8. E. Lehmann, in P. D. Chantepie de la Saussaye, *Lehrbuch der Religionsgeschichte* (Freiburg i.B.: J. C. B. Mohr [Paul Siebeck], 1887–89), II, 225.

9. *C. Snouck Hurgronje, *Der Mahdi* (Separatabdruck von der Revue Coloniale Internationale, 1885).

10. For a correct understanding of this vision, see A. B. Davidson, *The Theology of the Old Testament* (New York: Charles Scribner's Sons, 1914), 343ff.

11. Cf. the literature cited above and, further, the history of chiliasm by Semisch-Bratke, s.v. "Chiliasmus," in *Realencyklopädie für Protestantische Theologie und Kirche (PRE)*, 3rd ed., III, 805–17; and G. E. Post, s.v. "Millennium," in *Hastings Dictionary of the Bible*, III, 370–73, and the literature cited there.

12. Cf. H. Brink, *Toetssteen der Waarheid en der Dwalingen* (Amsterdam: G. Borstius, 1685), 656f.; G. Voetius, *Select. Disp.*, II, 1266–72; S. Maresius, *Syst. Theol.*, VIII, 38; B. De Moor, *Comm.*, VI, 155.

13. E.g., R. Rothe, *Theologische Ethik*, 2nd ed. (Wittenberg: Zimmerman, 1867–71), §586f.; *Hofmann, *Weiss u. Erf.*, II, 372f.; *Lange, *Dogm.*, II, 1271f.; H. Martensen, *Christian Dogmatics*, trans. W. Urwick (Edinburgh: T. & T. Clark, 1871), §280; J. J. Van Oosterzee, *Christian Dogmatics*, trans. J. Watson and M. Evans (New York: Scribner, Armstrong, 1874), §146.

Of the many existing works on chiliasm, we will only mention here D. Bogue, *Discourses on the Millennium* (London: T. Hamilton, 1818); E. Guers, *Israel in the Last Days of the Present Economy* (London: Wertheim, MacIntosh, & Hunt, 1862); John Cumming, *De Groote Verdrukking* (Amsterdam, 1861); idem, *De Verlossing Nabij* (1862); idem, *De Duizendjarige Rust*, trans. G. Japerus (Amsterdam: H. de Hoogh, 1863); idem, *Beschouwingen over het Duizendjarige Rijk* (1866); J. A. Seiss, *The Apocalypse* (New York: Charles C. Cook, 1909). Published in recent years are, among others, *F. von Beuningen, *Dein Reich komme* (Riga, 1901) (the author fixes the date of Christ's coming in 1933) and Charles T. Russell in America, *The Millennial Dawn* (Allegheny, Pa.: Watchtower Bible and Tract Society, 1898–1901). According to Russell, the history of mankind is divided into three ages: in the first, before the flood, it was subject to the rule of angels. In the second, from the flood to the millennium, it is under the rule of Satan, so that only a few people are saved. In the third period, which started in 1914, it will be ruled by Christ for a thousand years. Then follows the renewal of the earth.

14. Cf. H. Bavinck, *Gereformeerde Dogmatiek*, III, 205.

15. Against chiliasm, cf. also Augustine, *The City of God*, XX, chs. 6–9; Luther in Julius Köstlin, *The Theology of Luther*, trans. Charles E. Hay (Philadelphia: Lutheran Publication Society, 1897), II, 575; J. Gerhard, *Loci Theol.*, XXIX, ch. 7; J. Quenstedt, *Theologia*, IV, 649; J. Calvin, *Institutes*, III, 25, 5; A. Walaeus, *Opera omnia*, I, 537–54; G. Voetius, *Select. Disp.*, II, 1248–72; F. Turretin, *Institutes of Elenctic Theology*, XX, q. 3; B. De Moor, *Comm. Theol.*, VI, 149–62; E. W. Hengstenberg, *Openbaring van Johannes* ('s Hertogenbosch: Muller, 1852); C. F. Keil, *Biblical Commentary on the Prophecies of Ezekiel*, trans. James Martin (Grand Rapids: Eerdmans, 1970, reprint), II, 382–434; Th. Kliefoth, *Chris-*

tliche Eschatologie (Leipzig: Dörfflung und Franke, 1886), 147ff.; F. A. Philippi, *Kirchliche Glaubenslehre*, 3rd ed. (Gütersloh: Bertelsmann, 1882–1902), VI, 214ff.; C. Hodge, *Systematic Theology* (New York: Charles Scribner's Sons: 1892), III, 805; B. Warfield, "The Millennium and the Apocalypse," *Princeton Theological Review* 2 (October 1904): 599–617; G. Vos, "The Pauline Eschatology and Chiliasm," *Princeton Theological Review* 9 (January 1911): 26–60; H. Hoekstra, *Het Chiliasme* (Kampen: Kok, 1903); A. Kuyper, *Van De Voleinding* (Kampen: Kok, 1931), IV, 254–62, 318–48.

Chapter 5 Israel, the Millennium, and Christ's Return

1. According to A. Kuenen, *The Prophets and Prophecy in Israel*, trans. Adam Milroy (Amsterdam: Philo, 1969 [reprint, London, 1877]).

2. E. Guers, *Israel in the Last Days*, trans. Aubrey Price (London: Wertheim, MacIntosh and Hunt, 1862), 155–57.

3. Cf. A. Harnack, *The Mission and Expansion of Christianity*, trans. James Moffatt (New York: Harper, 1908), 53ff.

4. On the conversion of the Jews, in addition to commentaries on Romans 11, compare also G. Voetius, *Select. Disp.*, II, 124ff.; H. Witsius, *The Oeconomy of the Covenants between God and Man*, IV, 15, 20–32; B. De Moor, *Comm. Theol.*, VI, 127–30; C. Hodge, *Systematic Theology* (New York: Charles Scribner's Sons, 1888), III, 805; Th. Kliefoth, *Christliche Eschatologie* (Leipzig: Dorfflung & Franke, 1886), 147ff. For the rest, one must not underestimate the number of Jews converted to Christianity over the centuries and also in the nineteenth century. In terms of percentages it is greater than the number of the Gentiles. Pastor Le Roy (*Der Geisteskampf der Gegenwart*, 47 [1911]: 112) calculated the number of Jews who became Christians in the nineteenth century at more than 220,000.

5. Emil Schürer, *The History of the Jewish People in the Age of Jesus Christ* (Edinburgh: T. & T. Clark, 1979 [1885]), II, 525–26.

6. Cf. Seiffert, s.v. "Antichrist," *Realencyklopädie für protestantische Theologie und Kirche*, 3rd ed., I, 577–84; M. R. James, s.v. "Man of Sin and Antichrist," *Hastings Dictionary of the Bible*, III, 226–28, and the literature cited here.

7. In English-speaking biblical scholarship this view is usually referred to as "preterist" (ed.).

8. "*Die Nähe der Parusie ist gewissermassen nur ein anderer Ausdruck für die absolute Gewissheit derselben.*" Baldensperger in H. J. Holtzmann, *Lehrbuch der neutestamentlichen Theologie* (Freiburg i.B. and Leipzig: Mohr, 1897), I, 312.

9. J. Gerhard, *Loci. Theol.*, XXVIII, de extr. jud., n. 35; J. Quenstedt, *Theologia*, IV, 614; D. Hollaz, *Examen Theologicum Acroamaticum*, 1249.

10. On the return of Christ, aside from the works cited above, cf. also T. Aquinas, *Summa Theol.*, III, qu. 59, art. 2., suppl., qu. 90, art. 1, 2; J. H. Oswald, *Eschatologie* (Paderborn: F. Schöningh, 1869), 234f.; *Jansen, *Prael.*, III, 1038; L. Atzberger, *Christliche Eschatologie* (Freiburg i.B.: Herder, 1890), 300f.; H. Simar, *Lehrbuch der Dogmatik* (Freiburg i.B.: Herder, 1879–80), §166; J. Gerhard, *Loci Theol.*, XVIII, de extr. jud. c. 3; J. Quenstedt, *Theologia*, 649; A. Polanus, *Syn. Theol.*, VI, c. 65; G. Voetius, *Select. Disp.*, II, 51, v; J. Marckius, *Exspectatio gloriae futurae Jesu Christi*, c. 1–24; C. Vitringa, *Doct. Christ.*, IV, 160; Kliefoth, *Christliche Eschatologie*, 228f.; F. W. Grosheide, *De Verwachting der Toekomst van Jezus Christus* (Amsterdam: Bottenburg, 1907).

Chapter 6 The Day of the Lord

1. F. W. Weber, *System der altsynagogalen palastinischen Theologie* (Leipzig: Dorffling & Franke, 1880), 354.

2. A. Kuyper, *Ons Program*, 4th rev. ed. (Amsterdam and Pretoria: Höveker & Wormser, 1880), 274–75; K. Sartorius, *Die Leichenverbrennung innerhalb der Christlichen*

Kirche (Basel: C. Detloff, 1886); P. Groenen, *Lijkverbranding* ('s Hertogenbosch: Teulings, 1909).

3. Irenaeus, *Against Heresies*, V, 12, 13; Augustine, *Enchiridion*, 26; *The City of God*, XX, 4, 13f.; T. Aquinas, *Summa Theol.*, III, qu. 75–86.

4. *Ed. note:* Bavinck draws a distinction here between *restauratie* (translated "rehabilitation") and *reformatie*. This distinction, for which he more frequently uses the contrast between *restauratie* and *herstel* (re-creation), is used repeatedly by Bavinck to make the important point that the fullness of redemption in Christ is more than a mere repristination of the original created and prefallen status of Adam. Though grace restores rather than abolishes nature, the *status gloriae* is more excellent than the *status integratis*. Cf. H. Bavinck, *Our Reasonable Faith*, trans. H. Zylstra (Grand Rapids: Eerdmans, 1956), 218–20. For a helpful discussion of Bavinck's understanding of grace's relation to nature, see Jan Veenhof, *Revelatie en Inspiratie* (Amsterdam: Buijten & Schipperheijn, 1968), 345–65. This section of Veenhof's work has been translated into English by Albert Wolters and published by the Institute for Christian Studies, Toronto, Ontario, Canada.

5. Tertullian, *On the Resurrection of the Flesh;* Augustine, *The City of God*, XXII, ch. 12–20; *Enchiridion*, 84–93; P. Lombard, IV *Sent.*, dist. 43; T. Aquinas, *Summa Theol.*, suppl., qu. 82–97; J. H. Oswald, *Eschatologie* (Paderborn: F. Schöningh, 1869), 262f.; J. Gerhard, *Loci Theol.*, XXVI, tract 2; J. Quenstedt, *Theologia*, IV, 576–605; A. Polanus, *Syn. Theol.*, VI, c. 66; *Synopsis Purioris Theologiae*, disp. 51; P. van Mastricht, *Theologia*, VIII, 4, 6; F. Turretin, *Institutes of Elenctic Theology*, XX, qu. 1–3; J. Marckius, *Exspectatio gloriae futurae Jesu Christi*, II, c. 1–18; C. Vitringa, *Doct. Christ.*, IV, 109–56; Th. Kliefoth, *Christliche Eschatologie* (Leipzig: Dorffling & Franke, 1886), 248f.; F. J. Splittgerber, *Tod, Fortleben und Auferstehung*, 3rd ed. (Halle: Fricke, 1879); C. E. Nitzsch, *Lehrbuch der evangelischen Dogmatik*, 3rd ed. prepared by Horst Stephan (Tübingen: J. C. B. Mohr, 1912), 614f.; [cf. idem, *System der Christlichen Lehre*, 5th rev. ed. (Bonn: Adolph Marcus, 1844), 319–40 (ed.)]. Schaeder, s.v. "Auferstehung," in *Realencyklopädie für Protestantische Theologie und Kirche (PRE)*, 3rd ed., I, 219–24.

6. On the final judgment, cf. P. Lombard, IV *Sent.*, dist. 43f.; T. Aquinas, *Summa Theol.*, suppl., qu. 88–90; J. H. Oswald, *Eschatologie*, 334f.; L. Atzberger, *Die Christliche Eschatologie* (Freiburg i.B.: Herder, 1890), 356–70; J. Gerhard, *Loci. Theol.*, XXVIII; J. Quenstedt, *Theologia*, IV, 605–34; A. Polanus, *Syn. Theol.*, VI, c. 69; *Synopsis Purioris Theologiae*, disp. 51; P. van Mastricht, *Theologia*, VIII, 4, 7; F. Turretin, *Institutes of Elenctic Theology*, XX, qu. 6; J. Marckius, *Exspectatio*, III, c. 1–18; B. De Moor, *Comm. Theol.*, VI, 706–18; Th. Kliefoth, *Eschatologie*, 236f., 275f.; Benzinger, s.v. "Gericht, göttliches," in *PRE*, VI, 568–85.

7. Cf. above, pp. 39f.

8. J. Wegschneider, *Institutiones theologiae christianae dogmaticae* (Halle: Gebauer, 1819), § 200; K. G. Bretschneider, *Handbuch der Dogmatik der evangelischlutherischen Kirche* (Leipzig: n.p., 1838), II, 468f., 581f.; F. Reinhard, *Grundriss der Dogmatik* (Munich: Seidel, 1802), 706f.; *Lange, *Posit. Dogm.*, §131; I. A. Dorner, *A System of Christian Doctrine*, trans. A. Cave and J. S. Banks (Edinburgh: T. & T. Clark, 1882), IV, 415–34; C. Nitzsch, *Dogmatik*, 624 [cf. *System der christlichen Lehre*, 319–40 (ed.)]; W. Schmidt, *Christliche Dogmatik* (Bonn: E. Weber, 1895–98), II, 517; H. Bavinck, *De Theologie van Daniel Chantepie de la Saussaye* (Leiden: Donner, 1884), 71–75; *H. Ernst, *Geloof en Vrijheid* (1886): 407–44; *J. A. Cramer, "Het Evangelie en de Eeuwige Straf," *Theologische Studiën* 20 (1902): 359–80. Cf. in England the advocates of the so-called future (or second) probation or of the wider hope, such as Robertson and F. D. Maurice ("The Word 'Eternal' and the Punishment of the Wicked," in *Theological Essays* [London: James Clarke, 1957 (1853)], 302–25); Thomas de Quincey, "On the supposed scriptural expression for eternity," 1852; Tennyson, *In Memoriam;* F. W. Farrar, *Eternal Hope* (London: Macmillan, 1883); and *Mercy and Judgment* (New York: E. P. Dutton, 1881), along with the literature produced in response to these two works, *The Wider Hope: Essays and Stric-*

tures of the *Doctrine and Literature of Future Punishment* by Numerous Writers, Lay and Clerical (London: Unwin, 1890). For America we need to mention the defenders of the Andover position adopted by five professors of Andover College: Churchhill, Harris, Hincks, Tucker, and Egb. C. Smith, who deviated from several articles of the creed, also that concerning eternal punishment; cf. *Andover Review* (April 1890): 434ff. We may also add here the opinion of those who find the scriptural data too uncertain to warrant a firm conclusion and therefore abstain from making clear pronouncements in one direction or another: James Orr, *The Christian View of God and the World*, 7th ed. (New York: Charles Scribner's Sons, 1904), 397; K. Girgensohn, *Zwölf Reden über die christliche Religion*, 4th ed. (München: C. H. Beck, 1921), 319–37.

9. L. Atzberger, *Geschichte der christlichen Eschatologie* (Freiburg i.B. and St. Louis, Mo.: Herder, 1896), 366–456.

10. Petavius, "de angelis," *Op. Theol.*, III, 7, 8.

11. Friedrich Schleiermacher, *The Christian Faith*, ed. H. R. MacIntosh and J. S. Stewart (Edinburgh: T. & T. Clark, 1928), §117–20, 163, Appendix on Eternal Damnation, 720–22; A. Schweizer, *Die Glaubenslehre der Evangelisch-Reformirten Kirche* (Zurich: Orell, Füssli, 1844–47), II, 577f., 591, 604; *Schoeberlein, *Prinzip u. System d. Dogm.*, 679; *Riemann, *Die Lehre von der Apokatastasis* (Magdeburg, 1897); O. Schrader, *Die Lehre von der Apokatastasis* (Berlin: R. Boll, 1901); W. Hastie, *The Theology of the Reformed Churches in Its Fundamental Principles* (Edinburgh: T. & T. Clark, 1904), 277ff.; J. Scholten, *Dogmatices christianae intitia*, 268f.; W. Francken, *Geloof en Vrijheid*, 1886; *J. C. Eyckman, "Algemeene of Conditioneele Onsterfelijkheid," *Theologische Studiën* 26 (1909): 359–80. Cf. J. Köstlin, s.v. "Apokatastasis," in *PRE*, I, 616–22.

12. O. Fock, *Der Socianismus* (Kiel: C. Schröder, 1847), 714f.

13. R. Rothe, *Theologische Ethik*, 2nd ed. (Wittenberg: Zimmerman, 1867–71), §470–72; Chr. Weisse, "Ueber die philosophische Bedeutung der Christliche Lehre von den Letzten Dinge," *Theologische Studien und Kritiken* 9/2 (1836): 271–340; idem, *Philosophische Dogmatik oder Philosophie des Christentums* (Leipzig: Hirzel, 1855–62), § 970.

14. Full title: *Life in Christ, a Study of the Scripture Doctrine on the Nature of Man, the Object of the Divine Incarnation and the Conditions of Human Immortality*, 3rd revised and enlarged edition (London: Elliot Stock, 1878).

15. See, e.g., C. A. Row, *Future Retribution* (New York: Whittaker, 1887); *Stokes, *Conditional Immortality;* S. D. McConnell, *The Evolution of Immortality* (New York: Macmillan, 1901); *Schultz, *Voraussetzungen der Christl. Lehre v.d. Unsterblichkeit*, 1861; H. Plitt, *Evangelische Glaubenslehre* (Gotha: n.p., 1863), II, 413; L. Lemme, *Endlosigkeit der Verdammnis und allgemeine Wiederbringung* (Berlin: Runge, 1898); P. Paulsen, *Das Leben nach dem Tode*, 2nd ed. (Stuttgart: Chr. Belser, 1905); Chr. Wobbermin, *Theologie und Metaphysik, das Verhaltnis der Theologie zur moderne Erkenntnistheorie und Psychologie* (Berlin: Alexander Duncker, 1901), 159, 201, 205; *Charles Byse, *L'immortalité conditionelle ou la vie en Christ*, Paris, 1880 (translation of E. White's *Life of Christ* [1878]); E. Pétavel-Ollif, *Le problème de l'immortalité* (Paris: Fischbacher, 1891); A. Decoppet, *Les grands problèmes de l'au-delà*, 8th ed. (Paris: Fischbacher, 1906); P. Vallatton, *La Vie après la Mort* (Laussane: Rouge & Co., 1906); P. Stapfer, *Questions esthétiques et religieuses* (Paris: F. Alcan, 1906), 178, 205; *Jonker, "De Leer der Conditioneele Onsterfelijkheid," *Theologische Studiën* 1 (1882); *M. v. E., "De Conditioneele Onsterfelijkheid," *St. v. Waarheid en Vrede* (July, 1907); *G. Posthumus Meyjes, Lecture before Excelsior, March 9, 1911.

16. See H. Bavinck, *Gereformeerde Dogmatiek*, III, 143ff.

17. E. White, *Life in Christ*, 358–90.

18. Augustine, *The City of God*, XXI, 11: "Not the *diuturnitas peccandi* but the *voluntas peccantis, quae huiusmodi est ut seper vellet peccare si posset.*"

19. Cf. August Strindberg, *The Dance of Death*, trans. Arvid Paulsen (New York: W. W. Norton, 1976), 41 (Act One, Scene One): "Don't you [believe in hell]—you who are living in one?" (German: "Glaubst du nicht daran [an die Hölle], wo du mitten in ihr bist?").

20. Cf. H. Bavinck, *Gereformeerde Dogmatiek*, II, 348, 351.

21. Augustine says: "The penalties of the damned are to some extent mitigated at certain intervals" *(poenas damnatorum certis temporum inter vallis aliquatenus mitigari, Enchiridion*, 110). Cf. Lombard, Thomas, Bonaventure on IV *Sent.*, 46. Remarkable, further, is that Ambrose and Jerome make a distinction between the impious (unbelievers, non-Christians) and sinners (Christians who lived and died as sinners), and restrict eternal punishment in hell to the former. So, at least, says J. Niederhuber, *Die Eschatologie des heiligen Ambrosius* (Paderborn: Schöningh, 1907), 120, 248.

22. See further Augustine, *Enchiridion*, 110–13; *The City of God*, XXI; P. Lombard, IV *Sent.*, dist. 46–50; T. Aquinas, *Summa Theol.*, suppl., qu. 97–99; Dante, *The Inferno;* Petavius, "de angelis," III, c. 4–8, *Op. Theol.*, IV; *Sachs, *Die ewige Dauer der Höllenstrafen* (Paderborn, 1882); J. Bautz, *Die Hölle in Anschluss an die Scholastiek dargestellt* (Mainz: Kircheim, 1905); *Stufler, *(Die Heiligkeit Gottes und der ewige Tod)* opposes Schell, who assumes the possibility of an *apokatastasis*. Kiefl undertook to defend him in *Herman Schell und die Ewigkeit der Höllenstrafen* (Mainz: Kircheim, 1907); and received a reply from Stufler, *Die Verteidigung Schells durch Prof. Kiefl* (Innsbruck: Rauch, 1905); A. M. Weiss, *Die religiose Gefahr* (Freiburg i.B.: Herder, 1904), 277, 353. Protestantism was consistent in its view of eternal punishment; see, briefly, B. De Moor, *Comm. Theol.*, III, 354–58; C. Vitringa, *Doct. Christ.*, IV, 175; II, 305, 320. In modern times the idea that the hereafter does not bring a state of bliss for everyone sometimes encounters greater appreciation on the basis of the absolute character of the moral law or on the basis of the law of retribution (karma) that makes the consequences of sin inevitable; cf. my *Philosophy of Revelation* (New York: Longmans, Green, 1909), 295, 314. On the ideas of pagans relative to reward and punishment on the other side of the grave, cf. F. Hettinger, *Apologie du Christianisme* (Barle-duc: L. Guerin, 1869–70), IV, 320.

Chapter 7 The Renewal of Creation

1. T. Aquinas, *Summa Theol.*, suppl., qu. 74, art. 7.

2. C. Vitringa, *Doctr. Christ.*, IV, 194–200.

3. Cf. T. Aquinas, *Summa Theol.*, suppl., qu. 74, art. 1, and qu. 91; L. Atzberger, *Die Christliche Eschatologie* (Freiburg i.B.: Herder, 1890), 372f.; F. Gomarus, *Opera*, I, 131–33, 416; F. Spanheim, *Dubia Evang.*, III, 670–712; Francis Turretin, *Institutes of Elenctic Theology*, XX, qu. 5; B. De Moor, *Comm. Theol.*, VI, 733–36; C. Vitringa, *Doctr. Christ.*, IV, 186–215; Th. Kliefoth, *Christliche Eschatologie* (Leipzig: Dorfflung & Franke, 1886), 297f.

4. Franz Delitzsch, *Biblical Commentary on the Prophecies of Isaiah*, trans. James Martin (Grand Rapids: Eerdmans, 1954 [1887]), II, 517. *Ed. note:* Bavinck only cites part of this passage from the German: *Das ist ja eben der Unterschied des A. und N. T., dass das A. T. das Jenseits verdiesseitigt, das N. T. das Diesseits verjenseitigt; dass das A. T. das Jenseits in den Gesichtskreis des Diesseits herabzieht, das N. T. das Diesseits in das Jenseits emporhebt.*

5. As H. Bois thinks ("La terre et le ciel," *Foi et Vie* [15 Aout–1 Oct. 1906]) because "the term 'heaven' runs less danger of materializing the future life" (585) ("le terme ciel fait moins courir le danger de matérialiser la vie future").

6. See note 4 in previous chapter (ed.).

7. O. Pfleiderer, *Grundriss der Christlichen Glaubens und Sittenlehre*, 4th ed. (Berlin: G. Reimer, 1888), §177; A. E. Biedermann, *Christliche Dogmatik* (Zurich: Orell, Füssli, 1869), §974f.; J. Scholten, *Dogmatices christianae initia*, c. 7.

8. A. Ritschl, *The Christian Doctrine of Justification and Reconciliation*, trans. H. R. MacIntosh and A. B. Macaulay (Edinburgh: T. & T. Clark, 1900), § 51, 53, 58, 65.

9. T. Aquinas, *Summa Theol.*, I, 2, qu. 3, art. 4.

10. Duns Scotus, IV *Sent.*, dist. 49, qu. 4.

11. Bonaventure, IV *Sent.*, dist. 49, p. 1, art. unic. qu. 4, 5. Cf. G. Voetius, *Select. Disp.*, II, 1217–39.

12. Cf. pp. 144f.

13. Cf. H. Bavinck, *Gereformeerde Dogmatiek*, I, 290ff.

14. Augustine, *Letters*, 102; *The City of God*, XVIII, 47, and other places. Cf. H. Reuter, *Augustinische Studien* (Gotha: F. A. Perles, 1887), 90ff.

15. In W. Münscher, *Lehrbuch des christlichen Dogmengeschichte*, ed. Daniel von Coelln (Cassel: J. C. Krieger, 1832–38), II, 147.

16. D. Strauss, *Die Christliche Glaubenslehre* (Tübingen: Osiander, 1840–41), I, 271.

17. U. Zwingli, *Exposition of the Christian Faith*, ch. x, "Everlasting Life," in *On Providence and Other Essays*, ed. for Samual Macauley Jackson by William J. Hinkle (Durham, N.C.: Labyrinth, 1983 [1922]), 272. In the eighteenth century the doctrine that also pagans could be saved had many advocates: e.g., Leibniz, in A. Pichler, *Die Theologie des Leibnitz* (München: J. G. Cotta, 1869–70), I, 360ff.; J. Eberhard, *Neue Apologie des Sokrates oder Untersuchung der Lehre von der Seligheit der Heiden* (Berlin: F. Nicolai, 1772); cf. K. G. Bretschneider, *Systematische Entwicklung aller in der Dogmatik* (Leipzig: J. A. Barth, 1841), 679. In the Netherlands the philosophical novel *Belisaire* by Jean Francois Marmontel, published in 1766, occasioned a vehement dispute on whether the virtue practiced by Socrates, Titus, Antoninus, and so on, could bring them to blessedness in heaven. The Rev. P. Hofstede denied it but the Remonstrant minister Nozeman defended the idea; cf. A. Ypey, *Geschiedenis van de Christelijke Kerk in de Achttiende Eeuw* (Utrecht: Van Ijzergorst, 1797–1811), III, 166f.; A. Ypey and I. J. Dermout, *Geschiedenis der Nederlandsche Hervormde Kerk* (Breda: F. B. Hollingerus Pijpers, 1824), III, 539; J. P. de Bie, *Het Leven en Werken van Petrus Hofstede* (Rotterdam: Daamen, 1899).

18. So, for example, à Lasco, in Kuyper, *Heraut*, 1047; Zanchius, in W. T. Shedd, *Dogmatic Theology* (New York: Charles Scribner's Sons, 1888), I, 436; II, 704; W. Bilderdijk, *Brieven* (Amsterdam: W. Messchert, 1836–37), V, 81; Kuyper, *Heraut*, 594, 1047; A. Ebrard, *Das Dogma vom heiligen Abendmahl und seine Geschichte* (Frankfurt a.M.: Heinrich Zimmer, 1845–46), II, 77. For Roman Catholic views, see J. Pohle, *Lehrbuch der Dogmatik*, 4th ed. (Paderborn: F. Schöningh, 1908–10), II, 414–33.

19. Cf. the literature in C. Vitringa, *Doctr. Christ.*, I, 29.

20. P. Lombard, II *Sent.*, dist. 33.

21. J. Gerhard, *Loci Theol.*, XVI, §169; J. F. Buddeus, *Inst. Theol.*, V, 1, 6.

22. *Canons of Dordt*, I, 7; G. Voetius, *Select. Disp.*, II, 417.

23. P. Vermigli, *Loci Comm.*, 76, 436; and similarly Beza, Pareus, Zanchius, Perkins, and others.

24. F. Junius, *Op. Theol. Select.*, II, 333.

25. G. Voetius, *Select. Disp.*, II, 413; further: C. Vitringa, *Doctr. Christ.*, II, 51, 52. Cf. esp. B. B. Warfield, "The Development of the Doctrine of Infant Baptism," in *Two Studies in the History of Doctrine* (New York: Christian Literature Co., 1897), 143–299.

26. G. Voetius, *Select. Disp.*, II, 537, 538, 781; F. Spanheim, *Dubia Evang.*, III, 1291; Witsius, *Apost. Geloof*, II, 2, 15; *ed. note*: Bavinck is likely referring to Witsius's *Exercitationes sacra in symbolum quod Apostolorum dicitur* or the Dutch translation, *Oeffeningen over de grondstukken van het Algemeyne Christelijke Gelloove*.

27. Calvin, *Institutes*, IV, xvi, 19.

28. "In der That es lässt sich das Paradoxon rechtfertigen, gerade die partikularistische Prädestinationslehre habe jene universalistisch klingenden Phrasen ermöglicht" (H. Reuter, *Augustinische Studien*, 92).

29. Examples: P. Vermigli, *Loci Comm.*, III, 17, 8; similarly Camero, Tilenus, Spanheim, and others.

30. T. Aquinas, *Summa Theol.*, III, qu. 96; Bonaventure, *The Breviloquium*, VII, 7.

31. Cf. H. Bavinck, *Gereformeerde Dogmatiek*, II, 531, and p. —— above.

32. On the topic of heavenly blessedness, cf. Augustine, *The City of God*, XXII, ch. 29, 30; P. Lombard, IV *Sent.*, dist. 49; T. Aquinas, *Summa Theol.*, suppl., qu. 92–96; Bonaventure, *The Breviloquiam*, VII, c. 7; J. H. Oswald, *Eschatologie* (Paderborn: F. Schöningh, 1869), 38–57; L. Atzberger, *Christliche Eschatologie* (Freiburg i.B: Herder, 1890), 238f.; *O. Ritschl, "Luthers Seligkeitsvorstellung in ihrer Entstehung und Bedeutung," *Christ. Welt* (1889): 874–80; J. Gerhard, *Loci Theol.*, XXXI; J. Quenstedt, *Theologia*, I, 550–60; A. Polanus, *Syn. Theol.*, VI, c. 72–75; A. Walaeus, *Synopsis Purioris Theologiae*, disp. 52; P. van Mastricht, *Theologia*, VIII, 4, 10; F. Turretin, *Institutes of Elenctic Theology*, XX, qu. 8–13; J. Marckius, *Exspectatio gloriae futurae Jesu Christi*, III, c. 8, 10, 11; B. De Moor, *Comm. Theol.*, VI, 718–33; C. Vitringa, *Doctr. Christ.*, IV, 179; Th. Kliefoth, *Eschatologie*, 311f.; M. Kahler, s.v. "Ewiges Leben," *Realencyklopädie für protestantische Kirche und Theologie*, 3rd ed., XI, 330–34; idem, s.v. "Seligkeit," ibid., XVIII, 179–84.

Bibliography

1. The improvement of this bibliography over Bavinck's original in the *Gereformeerde Dogmatiek* is largely thanks to a valuable tool he did not have available to him—the Internet—and its diligent perusal by Calvin Theological Seminary graduate students Raymond Blacketer and Claudette Grinnell, whose help is gratefully acknowledged here.

Select Scripture Index

Old Testament

1 Samuel
28 54f.

Ezekiel
16:53–63 61f.
40–48 86, 95f.

New Testament

Matthew
12:32 65
16:28 123
23:37–39 102
24 108f., 124
24:14 114
24:34 124

Mark
9:1 123
13 108f.

Luke
9:27 123
13:33–35 102
21 108f.
21:24 102f.

Acts
3:19–21 103f.

Romans
11:11–32 104f.

1 Corinthians
3:12–15 65
15 137f.
15:20–28 116
15:29 70

2 Corinthians
5:1–4 50

1 Thessalonians
4:13–18 116

2 Thessalonians
2 113

Hebrews
12:1 56
12:22–24 71

1 Peter
3:18–22 60f.
4:6 61f.

Revelation
20 112, 114f., 117f.
21–22 159f.

Note: This index only includes Scripture references discussed by Bavinck in some significant detail (ed.).

Herman Bavinck (1854–1921) taught theology at the Theological School in Kampen, The Netherlands, and at the Free University of Amsterdam for almost forty years. At the Free University he succeeded the famous theologian and politician Abraham Kuyper. Among Bavinck's most influential publications were *Reformed Dogmatics* and *Our Reasonable Faith*.

John Bolt is professor of theology at Calvin Theological Seminary (Grand Rapids, Michigan), an editor of *Calvin Theological Journal*, and executive editor of the Dutch Reformed Translation Society.

John Vriend has been a full-time translator since 1982. Among the authors he has translated are G. C. Berkouwer and Hendrikus Berkhof. Vriend was born in the Netherlands, moved to North America at the age of fourteen, then spent four years in Amsterdam studying at the Free University.